DEVOTIONAL THOUGHTS ON THE BIBLE
Charles Haddon Spurgeon

DEVOTIONAL THOUGHTS ON THE BIBLE

Charles Haddon Spurgeon

THE PENTATEUCH

Prepared by Larry Brown

 EVANGELICAL PRESS

EVANGELICAL PRESS

Evangelical Press
Faverdale North, Darlington, DL3 0PH England

Evangelical Press USA
P. O. Box 825, Webster NY 14580 USA

email: sales@evangelicalpress.org
www.evangelicalpress.org

© Larry Brown, 2007. All rights reserved. No part of this publication may be reproduced, stored in a retrieval system or transmitted, in any form, or by any means, electronic, mechanical, photocopying, recording or otherwise, without the prior permission of the publishers.

All Scripture quotations are from the Holy Bible, King James Version (KJV). Public domain.

British Library Cataloguing in Publication Data available
ISBN-13 978 0 85234 605 1   ISBN 0 85234 605 1

PRINTED AND BOUND IN THE USA

To Dad, who bought me Spurgeon for Christmas

DEVOTIONAL THOUGHTS ON THE BIBLE
Charles Haddon Spurgeon

FOREWORD

It was C. H. Spurgeon's custom to read a lengthy portion of Scripture before he preached to his congregation. There is nothing unusual about that; many pastors do so. But it was also Spurgeon's custom to give an exposition of the portion as he read it. These 'pastoral expositions', as I call them, were given in anticipation of the message he was about to deliver.

My friend, brother Larry Brown, has done a great service for the kingdom of God by compiling these expositions into these volumes. They are heart-warming, practical applications of Holy Scripture, filled with the sweet savour of 'Jesus Christ and him crucified'. They will greatly benefit the reader as a daily devotional.

Additionally, I am sure that many pastors and teachers will use these brief expositions as a commentary. I have done so for many years, searching through the sixty-three volumes of Spurgeon's sermons for the exposition of a passage. Now, for the first time, these pastoral expositions have been extracted and made available for use as devotional reading.

Pastor Don Fortner
Grace Baptist Church of Danville, Kentucky, USA

DEVOTIONAL THOUGHTS ON THE BIBLE

Charles Haddon Spurgeon

PREFACE

Perhaps the most widely read and often quoted preacher in history is Charles Haddon Spurgeon. His published sermons, totaling sixty-three volumes, demonstrate his remarkable gifts, his understanding of the Scriptures, his theological acumen, his mastery of the English language, his ability to illustrate the profound truths of the gospel with simplicity, and his tremendous intellect.

Spurgeon preached Christ and preached Christ passionately. Without question, he was used of God for the furtherance of the gospel around the world in a remarkable way and continues to be, through his written works. Spurgeon's deep, yet simple trust and understanding of our Lord Jesus Christ, his great mercy, grace, and love is evident in his writings. His great longing was to have others come to know, trust, love, and worship our Lord. To that end he laboured tirelessly in publishing the gospel.

In addition to his volumes of sermons, Spurgeon edited *The Sword and the Trowel* magazine, wrote and published *The Golden Alphabet* (an exposition of Psalm 119), *Around the Wicket Gate*, *The Salt Cellars*, *Till He Come* (a series of communion sermons), *Words of Wisdom for Daily Life*, *Words of Cheer for Daily Life*, *All of Grace* (a four-volume autobiography),

PREFACE   *Charles Haddon Spurgeon*

Faith's Checkbook, Morning and Evening Devotional, Spurgeon's Devotional Bible (morning and evening expositions), *The Treasury of David* (a seven-volume exposition of the Psalms), *John Ploughman's Talks, A Catechism for Children, My Sermon Notes,* and *A Commentary on the Gospel of Matthew.* He also compiled *Our Own Hymn Book* for his congregation at the Metropolitan Tabernacle in London. All of these volumes have been reproduced many times and are still available today.

But there is another aspect of Spurgeon's preaching and writing that is hardly known: when he preached before thousands each Sunday at the Metropolitan Tabernacle, he read and gave a brief exposition of a passage of Scripture before his morning sermon. These were transcribed and possess a literary characteristic found in none of his other writings. The subject matter almost always grips you in the initial verses and comments, the language is simple, and their flow is staccato. In making spontaneous remarks on the passages, he often interrupts his readings mid-verse, mid-sentence, and in many instances, mid-phrase! It is this unique trait that makes them so easily read. When compiled and sequenced as a body of readings, the expositions are extensive enough to cover virtually the entire Bible, giving a remarkable overview of its contents. These expositions are now being published in volumes, each giving general coverage to a particular section of the Bible.

Without question, these devotionals could be the most popular published in a generation, and their value as family devotionals is beyond measure. May they be blessed of God to the good of many, for the glory of Christ.

Perhaps Charles Spurgeon expressed it best when, commenting on Psalm 90:17, he said:

> *Let not what we do for thee fall to the ground like a badly built wall! Let not our work be consumed in the great testing fire, but the work of our hands establish thou it!*

DEVOTIONAL THOUGHTS ON THE BIBLE

Charles Haddon Spurgeon

ACKNOWLEDGEMENTS

The draft manuscript from which these devotionals were arranged and compiled contained over 1,755,000 words, 2,700 single-spaced pages, and comments on over 1,400 expositions. The final publications would have been impossible without the generous assistance in proofing and editing from these people:

Al and Rebecca Smith, Bill and Michelle Augustine, Bill and Vicci Rolley, Bob and Carol Pruitt, Bob and Mary Lou Duff, Bob and Sally Poncer, Carter and Joyce Brown, Chris Kendziora, Daniel and Sandy Parks, David and Betty Burge, David and Celeste Peterson, Don and Shelby Fortner, Don Williams, Don and Mary Bell, Evelyn M. Wang, Gene and Judy Harmon, Geoff and Valerie Thomas, Jim and Nancy Byrd, Bobbie and Judy Estes, Tim and Debbie James, and, most of all, Carol.

DEVOTIONAL THOUGHTS ON THE BIBLE

Charles Haddon Spurgeon

GENESIS

GENESIS 1

Gen. 1:1 In the beginning God created the heaven and the earth.

When that 'beginning' was, we cannot tell. It may have been long ages before God fitted up this world for the abode of man, but it was not self-existent; it was created by God, it sprang from the will and the word of the all-wise Creator.

2 And the earth was without form, and void; and darkness was upon the face of the deep. —

When God began to arrange this world in order, it was shrouded in darkness, and it had been reduced to what we call, for want of a better name, 'chaos'. This is just the condition of every soul of man when God begins to deal with him in his grace; it is formless and empty of all good things. 'There is none righteous, no, not one: There is none that understandeth, there is none that seeketh after God. They are all gone out of the way' [Romans 3:10-12].

2 And the Spirit of God moved upon the face of the waters.

This was the first act of God in preparing this planet to be the abode of man, and the first act of grace in the soul is for the Spirit of God to move within it. How that Spirit of God comes there, we know not;

we cannot tell how he acts, even as we cannot tell how the wind bloweth where it listeth, but until the Spirit of God moves upon the soul nothing is done towards its new creation in Christ Jesus.

3-4 And God said, Let there be light: and there was light. And God saw the light, that it was good: and God divided the light from the darkness.

'Light be.' 'Light was.' God had but to speak the word, and the great wonder was accomplished. How there was light before there was any sun — for the sun was not created until the fourth day of the week — it is not for us to say. But God is not dependent upon his own creation. He can make light without a sun, he can spread the gospel without the aid of ministers, he can convert souls without any human or angelic agency, for he does as he wills in the heavens above and on the earth beneath.

5 And God called the light Day, and the darkness he called Night. And the evening and the morning were the first day.

It is a good thing to have the right names for things. An error is often half-killed when you know the real name of it; its power lies in its being indescribable; but as soon as you can call it 'darkness', you know how to act towards it. It is a good thing also to know the names of truths, and the names of other things that are right. God is very particular in the Scripture about giving people their right names. The Holy Spirit says, 'Judas, not Iscariot', so that there should be no mistake about the person intended. Let us also always call persons and things by their right names: 'God called the light Day, and the darkness he called Night.' 'And the evening and the morning were the first day.' Darkness first and light afterwards. It is so with us spiritually: first darkness, then light. I suppose that, until we get to heaven, there will be both darkness and light in us; and as to God's providential dealings, we must expect darkness as well as light. They will make up our first day and our last day, till we get where there are no days but the Ancient of Days.

6-8 And God said, Let there be a firmament in the midst of the waters, and let it divide the waters from the waters. And God made the firmament, and divided the waters which were under the firmament from the waters which were above the firmament: and it was so. And God called the firmament Heaven. And the evening and the morning were the second day.

'The firmament' — an expanse of air in which floated the waters which afterwards condensed, and fell upon the earth in refreshing showers. These waters above were divided from the waters below. Perhaps they were all one steamy conglomeration before, but now they are separated. Note those four words, 'and it was so'. Whatever God ordains always comes. You will find that it is true of all his promises that whatever he has said shall be fulfilled to you, and you shall one day say of it all, 'and it was so'. It is equally certain concerning all his threatenings that what he has spoken shall certainly be fulfilled, and the ungodly will have to say 'and it was so'. These words are often repeated in this chapter. They convey to us the great lesson that the word of God is sure to be followed by the deed of God. He speaks, and it is done.

9-13 And God said, Let the waters under the heaven be gathered together unto one place, and let the dry land appear: and it was so. And God called the dry land Earth; and the gathering together of the waters called he Seas: and God saw that it was good. And God said, Let the earth bring forth grass, the herb yielding seed, and the fruit tree yielding fruit after his kind, whose seed is in itself, upon the earth: and it was so. And the earth brought forth grass, and herb yielding seed after his kind, and the tree yielding fruit, whose seed was in itself, after his kind: and God saw that it was good. And the evening and the morning were the third day.

Having attended to the air, God further exercised his power by setting the earth in order. Observe the remarkable fact that no sooner had God made the dry land appear than it seemed as if he could not bear the sight of it in its nakedness. What a strange place this world must have looked, with its plains and hills and rooks and vales without one single blade of grass or a tree or a shrub; so at once, before that day was over, God threw the mantle of verdure over the earth and clad its mountains and valleys with forests and plants and flowers, as if to show us that the fruitless is uncomely in God's sight, that the man who bears no fruit unto God is unendurable to him. There would be no beauty whatever in a Christian without any good works and with no graces. As soon as ever the earth appeared, then came the herb and the tree and the grass. So, dear brethren, in like manner, let us bring forth fruit unto God, and bring it forth abundantly, for herein is our heavenly Father glorified, that we bear much fruit.

14-19 And God said, Let there be lights in the firmament of the heaven to divide the day from the night; and let them be for signs, and for seasons, and for days, and years: And let them be for lights in the firmament of the heaven to give light upon the earth: and it was so. And God made two great lights; the greater light to rule the day, and the lesser light to rule the night: he made the stars also. And God set them in the firmament of the heaven to give light upon the earth, And to rule over the day and over the night, and to divide the light from the darkness: and God saw that it was good. And the evening and the morning were the fourth day.

Whether the sun and moon are here said to be absolutely created, or whether they were only created so far as our planet was concerned by the dense vapours being cleared away so that the sun and moon and stars could be seen, is a matter of no consequence at all to us. Let us rather learn a lesson from them. These lights are to rule, but they are to rule by giving light. And, brethren, this is the true rule in the church of God. He who gives most light is the truest ruler, and the man who aspires to leadership in the church of God, if he knows what he is at, aspires to be the servant of all by laying himself out for the good of all, even as our Saviour said to his disciples, 'Whosoever of you will be the chiefest, shall be servant of all.' The sun and moon are the servants of all mankind, and therefore do they rule by day and by night. Stoop, my brothers, if you wish to lead others. The way up is downward. To be great, you must be little. He is the greatest who is nothing at all unto himself, but all for others.

20-23 And God said, Let the waters bring forth abundantly the moving creature that hath life, and fowl that may fly above the earth in the open firmament of heaven. And God created great whales, and every living creature that moveth, which the waters brought forth abundantly, after their kind, and every winged fowl after his kind: and God saw that it was good. And God blessed them, saying, Be fruitful, and multiply, and fill the waters in the seas, and let fowl multiply in the earth. And the evening and the morning were the fifth day.

There was no life in the sea or on the land until all was ready for it. God would not make a creature to be unhappy. There must be suitable food to feed upon and the sun and moon to cheer and comfort ere a single bird shall chirp in the thicket or a solitary trout shall leap in the stream. So, after God has given men light and blessed them in various ways, their spiritual life begins to develop, to the glory of God. We have thoughts that soar like fowl in the open firmament of heaven, and other thoughts that dive into the mysteries of God, as the fish dive in the sea, and these are after-developments, after-growths of that same power which at the first said, 'Let there be light.'

24-25 And God said, Let the earth bring forth the living creature after his kind, cattle, and creeping thing, and beast of the earth after his kind: and it was so. And God made the beast of the earth after his kind, and cattle after their kind, and every thing that creepeth upon the earth after his kind: and God saw that it was good.

There is as much wisdom and care displayed in the creation of the tiniest creeping insect as in the creation of leviathan himself. Those who use the microscope are as much amazed at the greatness and the goodness of God as those are who use the telescope. He is as great in the little as he is in the great. After each day's work, God looks upon it, and it is well for us every night to review our day's work. Some men's work will not bear looking at, and tomorrow becomes all the worse to them because today was not considered and its sin repented of by them. But if the errors of today are marked by us, a repetition of them may be avoided on the morrow. It is only God who can look upon any one day's work and say of it, as a whole, and in every part, that it is 'good'. As for us, our best things need sprinkling with the blood of Christ, which we need not only on the lintels and side posts of our house but even on the altar and the mercy-seat at which we worship God.

26-28 And God said, Let us make man in our image, after our likeness: and let them have dominion over the fish of the sea, and over the fowl of the air, and over the cattle, and over all the earth, and over every creeping thing that creepeth upon the earth. So God created man in his own image, in the image of God created he him; male and female created he them. And God blessed them, and God said unto them, Be fruitful, and multiply, and replenish the earth, and subdue it: and have dominion over the fish of the sea, and over the fowl of the air, and over every living thing that moveth upon the earth.

God evidently meant the two persons, male and female, to complete the man, and the entireness of the manhood lies in them both. The earth is completed now that man has come upon it, and man is completed when the image of God is upon him, when Christ is formed in him the hope of glory, but not till then. When we have received the power of God, and have dominion over ourselves and over all earthly things, in the power of God's eternal Spirit, then are we where and what God intends us to be.

29-30 And God said, Behold, I have given you every herb bearing seed, which is upon the face of all the earth, and every tree, in the which is the fruit of a tree yielding seed; to you it shall be for meat. And to every beast of the earth, and to every fowl of the air, and to every thing that creepeth upon the earth, wherein there is life, I have given every green herb for meat: and it was so.

Now you see God's commissariat. He has not made all these creatures in order to starve them, but he has supplied them with great variety and abundance of food, that their wants may be satisfied. Does God care for the cattle, and will he not feed his own children? Does he provide for ravens and sparrows, and will he suffer you to lack anything, O ye of little faith? Observe that God did not create man until he had provided for him neither will he ever put one work of his providence or of his grace out of its proper place, but that which goes before shall be preparatory to that which follows after.

31 And God saw every thing that he had made, and, behold, it was very good. And the evening and the morning were the sixth day.

Taken in its completeness, and all put together, God saw that it was very good. We must never judge anything before it is complete.

GENESIS 2:1-17; REVELATION 22

Gen. 2:1-8 Thus the heavens and the earth were finished, and all the host of them. And on the seventh day God ended his work which he had made; and he rested on the seventh day from all his work which he had made. And God blessed the seventh day, and sanctified it: because that in it he had rested from all his work which God created and made. These are the generations of the heavens and of the earth when they were created, in the day that the LORD God made the earth and the heavens, And every plant of the field before it was in the earth, and every herb of the field before it grew: for the LORD God had not caused it to rain upon the earth, and there was not a man to till the ground. But there went up a mist from the earth, and watered the whole face of the ground. And the LORD God formed man of the dust of the ground, and breathed into his nostrils the breath of life; and man became a living soul. And the LORD God planted a garden eastward in Eden; and there he put the man whom he had formed.

Everything was ready for man's use, every fruit-bearing tree for his nourishment, every creature to do his bidding, for it was the will of God that he should 'have dominion over the fish of the sea, and over the fowl of the air, and over the cattle, and over all the earth, and over every creeping thing that creepeth upon the earth'. God did not place the man formed in his image, after his likeness, in an unfurnished house or an empty world and leave him to provide for himself all that he required, but he prepared everything that man could possibly need, and completed the whole plan by planting 'a garden eastward in Eden; and there he put the man whom he had formed'.

9 And out of the ground made the LORD God to grow every tree that is pleasant to the sight, and good for food; the tree of life also in the midst of the garden, and the tree of knowledge of good and evil.

That tree of life in the midst of the earthly paradise was to be symbolic of another tree of life in the paradise above, from which the children of God shall never be driven as Adam and Eve were driven out of Eden.

10-14 And a river went out of Eden to water the garden; and from thence it was parted, and became into four heads. The name of the first is Pison: that is it which compasseth the whole land of Havilah, where there is gold; and the gold of that land is good: there is bdellium and the onyx stone. And the name of the second river is Gihon: the same is it that compasseth the whole land of Ethiopia. And the name of the third river is Hiddekel: that is it which goeth toward the east of Assyria. And the fourth river is Euphrates.

That river in Eden also reminds us of the 'pure river of water of life clear as crystal, proceeding out of the throne of God and of the Lamb', of which we read almost at the end of the revelation that was given to John in Patmos. Thus the beginning and the end of the Bible call our attention to the tree of life and the river of life in the paradise below and the better paradise above.

15 And the LORD God took the man, and put him into the garden of Eden to dress it and to keep it.

There was to be occupation for man even in paradise, just as they who are before the throne of God in glory 'serve him day and night in his temple'. Idleness gives no joy, but holy employment will add to the bliss of heaven.

16-17 And the LORD God commanded the man, saying, Of every tree of the garden thou mayest freely eat: But of the tree of the knowledge of good and evil, thou shalt not eat of it: for in the day that thou eatest thereof thou shalt surely die.

Apparently, Adam was not forbidden to eat of the fruit of the tree of life, though, after his fall, he was cast out of Eden, as God said, 'lest he put forth his hand, and take also of the tree of life, and eat, and live for ever'. He might freely eat the fruit of every tree in the garden except one: 'of the tree of the knowledge of good and evil, thou shalt not eat of it'. It was a slight prohibition, yet the test was more than man, even in a state of innocence, was able to endure. And, alas, his failure involved all his descendants, for he was the federal head of the human race, and 'by one man sin entered into the world, and death by sin; and so death passed upon all men'. Happily, there is another federal Head, and therefore we read, 'For if through the offence of one many be dead, much more the grace of God, and the gift by grace, which is by one man, Jesus Christ, hath abounded unto many' [Romans 5:15].

Rev. 22:1 And he shewed me a pure river of water of life, clear as crystal, proceeding out of the throne of God and of the Lamb.

Rivers partake of the character of the source from which they come; that which proceeds 'out of the throne of God and of the Lamb' may well be 'a pure river of water of life, clear as crystal'. What but good and perfect gifts can come down from the throne of God? What but pure streams of mercy can flow from the throne of the Lamb?

2 In the midst of the street of it, —

For heaven is a place of sacred intercourse and hallowed communion: 'in the midst of the street of it,' —

2 and on either side of the river, was there the tree of life, which bare twelve manner of fruits, —

Every variety of joy and blessedness, —

2 and yielded her fruit every month: —

For the felicities of heaven are ever fresh and ever new; we shall never be satiated or wearied with that heavenly fruit.

2 and the leaves of the tree were for the healing of the nations.

Everything in heaven is the very best of the best. The leaves of the trees in earthly gardens are blown about by the blast, and we take but little note of them; but the leaves of the tree of life are 'for the healing of the nations'. O happy place, where even the leaves on the tree have such virtue in them!

3 And there shall be no more curse: —

No more thorns or thistles, no more pangs of child-bearing, no more sickness, or sorrow, or death.

3 but the throne of God and of the Lamb shall be in it; and his servants shall serve him:

They shall have nothing else to do, and it shall be their supreme delight to serve him perfectly and unceasingly.

4 And they shall see his face; —

Not through a glass darkly, but face to face shall they behold their

God. Surely that will be the very heaven of heaven.

4 *and his name shall be in their foreheads.*

Aaron was to wear upon his forehead a plate of pure gold, with 'HOLINESS TO THE LORD' engraved upon it, that the children of Israel might be accepted before the Lord, but the saints in glory are to have the name of their God 'in their foreheads'. In the very forefront of their glorified personalities there shall be the marks to betoken that they are the children of God.

5 *And there shall be no night there; —*

The saints in glory will have no need of sleep, so 'there shall be no night there', but one perpetual day of holy, unwearying service. There shall be no night of ignorance, of sorrow, of sin, of death; there shall be no powers of darkness there, and no darkness in which they might work their evil deeds.

5 *and they need no candle, neither light of the sun; for the Lord God giveth them light: —*

Directly and distinctly, without using any means, by his own immediate presence, 'the Lord God giveth them light.'

5 *and they shall reign for ever and ever.*

Earthly kings die, or their empires on earth are taken from them; but as for us whom God hath chosen by his grace, our kingdom is like that of our Lord and Saviour; it is an everlasting kingdom.

'They shall reign for ever and ever.' I wonder that some wise man does not try to prove that this means that the saints shall reign only for a short time. They have whittled 'everlasting punishment' down to next to nothing, why do they not try to reduce the duration of heaven, bliss, in the same way? The same words are used concerning the one as concerning the other, so we shall always hold to the eternity both of the one and of the other — the bliss and the woe are equally 'for ever and ever'.

6-7 And he said unto me, These sayings are faithful and true: and the Lord God of the holy prophets sent his angel to shew unto his servants the things which must shortly be done. Behold, I come quickly: blessed is he that keepeth the sayings of the prophecy of this book.

You have the witness of God, you have the witness of the angel of God, you have the witness of Christ, you have the witness of John, and all of them agree that 'these sayings are faithful and true', and that they relate to facts that shall in due course be established.

8 And I John saw these things, and heard them. And when I had heard and seen, I fell down to worship before the feet of the angel which shewed me these things.

And, according to the Church of Rome, he was quite right; but, according to the Word of God, he was quite wrong.

9 Then saith he unto me, See thou do it not: for I am thy fellowservant, and of thy brethren the prophets, and of them which keep the sayings of this book: worship God.

Worship none but God; take care not to break the first two of the ten commandments either by worshipping another God or by worshipping the true God under any form of similitude whatsoever.

10 And he saith unto me, Seal not the sayings of the prophecy of this book: for the time is at hand.

There is no need to roll it up, and set a seal to it; as it is so soon to be fulfilled, leave it open.

11 He that is unjust, let him be unjust still: and he which is filthy, let him be filthy still: and he that is righteous, let him be righteous still: and he that is holy, let him be holy still.

The Lord's messenger speaks as if 'the time' were so nearly come that there was no opportunity left for any charge to be made, and this is what will happen, sooner or later, to all men. When they die, their characters will be fixed for ever. The wax will cool, and the impress that it bears will be retained eternally.

12-13 And, behold, I come quickly; and my reward is with me, to give every man according as his work shall be. I am Alpha and Omega, the beginning and the end, the first and the last.

These must be the words of the Lord Jesus Christ himself; no mere messenger, however high his rank, would have dared to say, 'I am Alpha and Omega, the beginning and the end, the first and the last.'

14-15 Blessed are they that do his commandments, that they may have right to the tree of life, and may enter in through the gates into the city. For without are dogs, and sorcerers, and whoremongers, and murderers, and idolaters, and whosoever loveth and maketh a lie.

We thank God that they are shut out of heaven, for, albeit that we wish all men could be there, yet we would wish none to be there whose characters are of such a kind as this, unless they were washed and cleansed. Heaven would be no heaven if such men could be admitted there. They shall not be; they must, by infallible justice, be excluded from the realms of bliss.

16 I Jesus have sent mine angel to testify unto you these things in the churches. I am the root and the offspring of David, and the bright and morning star.

So glory is dawning, for Christ the bright and morning star has risen.

17 And the Spirit and the bride say, Come. And let him that heareth say, Come. And let him that is athirst come. And whosoever will, let him take the water of life freely.

Here we have the last invitations in the Word of God; may all who have not yet accepted them do so now, lest they should never again be uttered in their hearing.

18-21 For I testify unto every man that heareth the words of the prophecy of this book, If any man shall add unto these things, God shall add unto him the plagues that are written in this book: And if any man shall take away from the words of the book of this prophecy, God shall take away his part out of the book of life, and out of the holy city, and from the things which are written in this book. He which testifieth these things saith, Surely I come quickly. Amen. Even so, come, Lord Jesus. The grace of our Lord Jesus Christ be with you all. Amen.

So the blessed Book closes appropriately with grace, for 'tis grace that —

> *[Grace] all the work shall crown*
> *Through everlasting days;*
> *It lays in heaven the topmost stone,*
> *And well deserves the praise.*

GENESIS 3

Gen. 3:1 Now the serpent was more subtil than any beast of the field which the LORD God had made. And he said unto the woman, Yea, hath God said, Ye shall not eat of every tree of the garden?

He began with a question. How much of evil begins with questioning! The serpent does not dare to state a lie, but he suggests one: 'Has God refused you all the fruit of these many trees that grow in the garden?'

2-3 And the woman said unto the serpent, We may eat of the fruit of the trees of the garden: But of the fruit of the tree which is in the midst of the garden, God hath said, Ye shall not eat of it, neither shall ye touch it, lest ye die.

Eve had begun to feel the fascination of the evil one, for she softened down the word of God. The Lord had said concerning the tree of the knowledge of good and evil, 'In the day that thou eatest thereof thou shalt surely die.' A little of the spirit of doubt had crept into Eve's mind, so she answered, 'God hath said, "Ye shall not eat of it, neither shall ye touch it, lest ye die."'

4-5 And the serpent said unto the woman, Ye shall not surely die: For God doth know that in the day ye eat thereof, then your eyes shall be opened, and ye shall be as gods, knowing good and evil.

The serpent insinuated that God selfishly kept them back from the tree, lest they should grow too wise, and become like God himself. The evil one suggested ambition to the woman's mind, and imputed wicked designs to the ever-blessed and holy God. He did not say any more; the devil is too wise to use many words. I am afraid that the servants of God sometimes weaken the force of the truth by their verbosity, but not so did the serpent when he craftily suggested falsehoods to Mother Eve; he said enough to accomplish his evil purpose, but no more.

6 And when the woman saw —

Sin came into the human race by the eye; and that is the way that Christ comes in, by the eye of faith, the spiritual eye. 'Look unto me, and be ye saved', is the counterpart of this word, 'when the woman saw'.

6 that the tree was good for food, and that it was pleasant to the eyes, and a tree to be desired to make one wise, she took of the fruit thereof, and did eat, and gave also unto her husband with her; and he did eat.

This was a distinct act of rebellion on the part of both of them. It may seem a small thing; but it meant a great deal. They had cast off their allegiance to God; they had set up on their own account; they thought they knew better than God, and they imagined they were going to be gods themselves.

7 And the eyes of them both were opened, and they knew that they were naked; and they sewed fig leaves together, and made themselves aprons.

All they had gained by their sin was a discovery of their nakedness. Poor creatures, how the serpent laughed as his words were fulfilled, 'your eyes shall be opened'! They were opened, indeed; and Adam and Eve did know good and evil. Little could they have dreamed in what a terrible sense the serpent's words would come true.

8 And they heard the voice of the LORD God walking in the garden in the cool of the day: —

No doubt, when they had heard the voice of the Lord before, they had run to meet him, as children do to a father when he comes home 'in the cool of the day'. But now, how different is their action!

8 and Adam and his wife hid themselves from the presence of the LORD God amongst the trees of the garden.

What fools they were to think that they could hide themselves from God! The fig leaves were to hide their nakedness, and now the trees themselves were to hide them from God.

9-11 And the LORD God called unto Adam, and said unto him, Where art thou? And he said, I heard thy voice in the garden, and I was afraid, because I was naked; and I hid myself. And he said, Who told thee that thou wast naked? Hast thou eaten of the tree, whereof I commanded thee that thou shouldest not eat?

God comes to judge his fallen creature, yet he deals kindly with him. The Lord will have it from his own lips that he has offended; he summons no other witness.

12 And the man said, The woman whom thou gavest to be with me, she gave me of the tree, and I did eat.

This is a clear proof of his guilt, first, that he throws the blame on her whom he was bound to love and shield, and, next, that he throws the blame on God himself: 'The woman whom thou gavest to be with me, she gave me of the tree.' Ah me, what mean creatures men are when sin comes in and shame follows at its heels!

13 And the LORD God said unto the woman, What is this that thou hast done? And the woman said, The serpent beguiled me, and I did eat.

How often we throw the blame of our sin on the devil, who certainly has enough to bear without the added guilt of our iniquity! What Eve said was true; but it was not a sufficient reason for her sin. She should not have been beguiled by the serpent.

14-15 And the LORD God said unto the serpent, Because thou hast done this, thou art cursed above all cattle, and above every beast of the field; upon thy belly shalt thou go, and dust shalt thou eat all the days of thy life: And I will put enmity between thee and the woman, and between thy seed and her seed; it shall bruise thy head, and thou shalt bruise his heel.

Here was the first proclamation of the gospel. Strange to say, while God pronounces a curse upon the enemy of mankind, he is uttering a blessing upon the whole of those who belong to Christ, for *he* is that seed of the woman, and all that belong to him are a simple-minded, child-like people, children of the woman. Their opponents are the seed of the serpent, crafty, cunning, wise, full of deceit; and there is enmity between these two seeds. Christ is the Head of the one seed, and Satan is the head of the other; and our Lord Jesus Christ has had his heel bruised, and he suffered in that bruising of his heel; but he has broken the head of the dragon, he has crushed the power of evil, he has put his potent foot upon the old serpent's head.

16-18 Unto the woman he said, I will greatly multiply thy sorrow and thy conception; in sorrow thou shalt bring forth children; and thy desire shall be to thy husband, and he shall rule over thee. And unto Adam he said, Because thou hast hearkened unto the voice of thy wife, and hast eaten of the tree, of which I commanded thee, saying, Thou shalt not eat of it: cursed is the ground for thy sake; in sorrow shalt thou eat of it all the days of thy life; Thorns also and thistles shall it bring forth to thee; and thou shalt eat the herb of the field;

He had been accustomed to eat of the fruit of the many trees of paradise; now he must come down and eat 'the herb of the field'. He is lowered from royal dainties to commoner fare.

19 In the sweat of thy face shalt thou eat bread, till thou return unto the ground; —

Thou shalt get thy life out of the ground till thou thyself shalt go into the ground.

19-21 for out of it wast thou taken: for dust thou art, and unto dust shalt thou return. And Adam called his wife's name Eve; because she was the mother of all living. Unto Adam also and to his wife did the LORD God make coats of skins, and clothed them.

This was a very significant gospel action. The Lord took away from Adam and Eve the withered fig-leaves but put on them the skins of animals, to show, in symbol, that we are covered with the sacrifice of Christ. The giving up of a life yielded a better covering than the growth of nature; and so today, the death of Christ yields us a better covering than we could ever find in anything that grew of our poor fallen nature. Blessed be God for thus thinking of us when providing raiment for our first parents!

22 And the LORD God said, Behold, the man is become as one of us, to know good and evil: and now, lest he put forth his hand, and take also of the tree of life, and eat, and live for ever:

That would have been a horrible thing, for man to be incapable of death, and so to continue for ever in a sinful world. It is by passing through death that we come out into the realm of perfection.

23-24 Therefore the LORD God sent him forth from the garden of Eden, to till the ground from whence he was taken. So he drove out the man; and he placed at the east of the garden of Eden Cherubims, and a flaming sword which turned every way, to keep the way of the tree of life.

'O, what a fall was there, my countrymen! Then I, and you, and all of us fell down', while sin triumphed over us; yet even the Fall by Adam's sin was not without the promise of a gracious recovery through the last Adam, the Lord from heaven. Well does Dr Watts set forth the contrast between the fall of the angels and the Fall of man:

> *Down headlong from their native skies*
>   *The rebel angels fell,*
> *And thunderbolts of flaming wrath*
>   *Pursued them deep to hell.*
>
> *Down from the top of earthly bliss*
>   *Rebellious man was hurl'd;*
> *And Jesus stoop'd beneath the grave*
>   *To reach a sinking world.*

He took not on him the nature of angels; but he took *our* nature and died in *our* stead. May we trust his death to bring us life and thereby be saved from the consequences of the Fall!

GENESIS 3

Gen. 3:1-9 Now the serpent was more subtil than any beast of the field which the LORD God had made. And he said unto the woman, Yea, hath God said, Ye shall not eat of every tree of the garden? And the woman said unto the serpent, We may eat of the fruit of the trees of the garden: But of the fruit of the tree which is in the midst of the garden, God hath said, Ye shall not eat of it, neither shall ye touch it, lest ye die. And the serpent said unto the woman, Ye shall not surely die: For God doth know that in the day ye eat thereof, then your eyes shall be opened, and ye shall be as gods, knowing good and evil. And when the woman saw that the tree was good for food, and that it was pleasant to the eyes, and a tree to be desired to make one wise, she took of the fruit thereof, and did eat, and gave also unto her husband with her; and he did eat. And the eyes of them both were opened, and they knew that they were naked; and they sewed fig leaves together, and made themselves aprons. And they heard the voice of the LORD God walking in the garden in the cool of the day: and Adam and his wife hid themselves from the presence of the LORD God amongst the trees of the garden. And the LORD God called unto Adam, and said unto him, Where art thou?

In tones of mingled pity and rebuke he asked, 'Where art thou?'

10-11 And he said, I heard thy voice in the garden, and I was afraid, because I was naked; and I hid myself. And he said, —

Note the calm majesty of every word. Here is no human passion, but divine dignity: 'And he said.'

11-12 Who told thee that thou wast naked? Hast thou eaten of the tree, whereof I commanded thee that thou shouldest not eat? And the man said, The woman whom thou gavest to be with me, she gave me of the tree, and I did eat.

There is no sign of true confession here. Adam had been an unfallen creature a few hours before, but now, he had broken the commandment of the Lord, and you can see how completely death was brought into his moral nature; for if it had not been so, he would have said 'My God, I have sinned, canst thou and wilt thou forgive me?' But instead of doing so, he laid the blame for his sin upon his wife, which was an utterly mean action: 'The woman whom thou gavest to be with me, she gave me of the tree, and I did eat.' He almost seemed to lay the blame upon God because he had given him the woman to be with him. He was guilty of unkindness to his wife and of blasphemy against his Maker, in seeking to escape from confessing the sin which he had committed. It is an ill sign with men when they cannot be brought frankly to acknowledge their wrong-doing.

13 And the LORD God said unto the woman, What is this that thou hast done? —

Oh, that question! How far reaching it is! By her action, and her husband's, the floodgates had been pulled up, and the flood of sin had been let loose upon the world. They had struck a match and set the world on fire with sin. Every one of our sins is essentially of the same nature and has in it, substantially, the same mischief. Oh, that at any time when we have sinned, God would ask each one of us the question, 'What is it that thou hast done?'

13 And the woman said, The serpent beguiled me, and I did eat.

Still, you see, there is no confession of guilt, but only the attempt to push the blame off upon somebody else. The Lord God did not ask the serpent anything, for he knew that he was a liar, but he at once pronounced sentence upon him.

14-15 And the LORD God said unto the serpent, Because thou hast done this, thou art cursed above all cattle, and above every beast of the field; upon thy belly shalt thou go, and dust shalt thou eat all the days of thy life: And I will put enmity between thee and the woman, and between thy seed and her seed; it shall bruise thy head, and thou shalt bruise his heel.

And, now, there is no creature so degraded as that once bright angel, who is now the devil. He is always going about with serpentine wriggling, seeking to do more mischief. On his belly does he go, and still is dust his meat. That which is foul, material, carnal, he delights in. And his head is bruised, blessed be the name of the woman's promised seed! The old serpent's head is bruised with a fatal bruising, while the wounded heel of our Saviour is the joy and delight of our hearts.

16-17 Unto the woman he said, I will greatly multiply thy sorrow and thy conception; in sorrow thou shalt bring forth children; and thy desire shall be to thy husband, and he shall rule over thee. And unto Adam he said, Because thou hast hearkened unto the voice of thy wife, and hast eaten of the tree, of which I commanded thee, saying, Thou shalt not eat of it: cursed is the ground for thy sake; in sorrow shalt thou eat of it all the days of thy life;

How obliquely fell the curse! Not, 'Cursed art thou', as the Lord said to the serpent; but, 'Cursed is the ground for thy sake.'

18-21 Thorns also and thistles shall it bring forth to thee; and thou shalt eat the herb of the field; In the sweat of thy face shalt thou eat bread, till thou return unto the ground; for out of it wast thou taken: for dust thou art, and unto dust shalt thou return. And Adam called his wife's name Eve; because she was the mother of all living. Unto Adam also and to his wife did the LORD God make coats of skins, and clothed them.

Some creature had to die in order to provide them with garments, and you know who it is that died in order that we might be robed in his spotless righteousness. The Lamb of God has made for us a garment which covers our nakedness so that we are not afraid to stand even before the bar of God.

22-24 And the LORD God said, Behold, the man is become as one of us, to know good and evil: and now, lest he put forth his hand, and take also of the tree of life, and eat, and live for ever: Therefore the LORD God sent him forth from the garden of Eden, to till the ground from whence he was taken. So he drove out the man; and he placed at the east of the garden of Eden Cherubims, and a flaming sword which turned every way, to keep the way of the tree of life.

GENESIS 7

Gen. 7:1 And the LORD said unto Noah, Come thou and all thy house into the ark; —

Notice that the Lord did not say to Noah, 'Go into the ark', but 'Come', plainly implying that God was himself in the ark, waiting to receive Noah and his family into the big ship that was to be their place of refuge while all the other people on the face of the earth were drowned. The distinctive word of the gospel is a drawing word: 'Come.' Jesus says, 'Come unto me, all ye that labour and are heavy laden, and I will give you rest'; and he will say to his people at the last, 'Come, ye blessed of my Father inherit the kingdom prepared for you from the foundation of the world.' 'Depart' is the word of justice and judgement, but 'Come' is the word of mercy and grace. 'The Lord said unto Noah, Come thou and all thy house into the ark.'

1 for thee have I seen righteous before me in this generation.

Therefore God drew a distinction between him and the unrighteous, for he always hath a special regard for godly people.

2-3 Of every clean beast thou shalt take to thee by sevens, the male and his female: and of beasts that are not clean by two, the male and his female. Of fowls also of the air by sevens, the male and the female; to keep seed alive upon the face of all the earth.

Of the clean creatures which might be offered in sacrifice to God you see that there was a larger proportion than there was of the unclean, that there might be sufficient for sacrifice without the destruction of any species. The unclean beasts were mostly killers and devourers of others, and therefore their number was to be less than that of the clean species. Oh, that the day might soon come when there would be more of clean men and women than of unclean, when there would be fewer sinners than godly people in the world, though even then there would be the ungodly 'by two' like the unclean beasts.

4 For yet seven days, and I will cause it to rain upon the earth forty days and forty nights; and every living substance that I have made will I destroy from off the face of the earth.

It is the prerogative of the king to have the power of life and death, and it is the sole prerogative of the King of kings that — 'He can create, and he can destroy.' But what destructive power is brought into operation because of human sin! Sin must be a very heinous thing, since God, who despiseth not the work of his own hands, will sooner break up the human race and destroy every thing that liveth rather than that sin should continue to defile the earth. He has destroyed the earth once by water because of sin, and he will the second time destroy it by fire for the selfsame reason. Wherever sin is, God will hunt it; with barbed arrows will he shoot at it; he will cut it in pieces with his sharp two-edged sword, for he cannot endure sin. Oh, how foolish are they who harbour it in their own bosoms, for it will bring destruction to them if they keep it there!

5 And Noah did according unto all that the LORD commanded him.

Here was positive proof of his righteousness, in that he was obedient to the word of the Lord. A man who does not obey God's commands may talk about righteousness, even the righteousness which is of faith, but it is clear that he does not possess it, for faith works by love, and the righteousness which is by faith is proved by obedience to God. 'Noah did according unto all that the Lord commanded him', and so proved that he was righteous before God.

6 And Noah was six hundred years old when the flood of waters was upon the earth.

He was nearly 500 years old when he began to preach about the flood — a good old age to take up such a subject. For 120 years he pursued his theme — three times as long as most men are ever able to preach — and now at last God's time of long-suffering is over, and he proves the truthfulness of the testimony of his servant by sending the flood that Noah had foretold.

7-8 And Noah went in, and his sons, and his wife, and his sons' wives with him, into the ark, because of the waters of the flood. Of clean beasts, and of beasts that are not clean, and of fowls, and of every thing that creepeth upon the earth,

This largest and most complete menagerie that was ever gathered together was not collected by human skill; divine power alone could have accomplished such a task as that.

9 There went in two and two unto Noah into the ark, the male and the female, as God had commanded Noah.

They 'went in'. Noah had not to hunt or search for them, but they came according to God's plan and purpose, even as, concerning the salvation which is by Christ Jesus, his people shall be willing to come to him in the day of his power; with joyfulness shall they come into the ark of their salvation.

10-11 And it came to pass after seven days, that the waters of the flood were upon the earth. In the six hundredth year of Noah's life, in the second month, the seventeenth day of the month, the same day were all the fountains of the great deep broken up, and the windows of heaven were opened.

Perhaps the world was in its prime, when the trees were in bloom, and the birds were singing in their branches, and the flowers were blooming on the earth, 'the same day were all the fountains of the great deep broken up, and the windows of heaven were opened'.

12-13 And the rain was upon the earth forty days and forty nights. In the selfsame day entered Noah, and Shem, and Ham, and Japheth, the sons of Noah, and Noah's wife, and the three wives of his sons with them, into the ark;

These eight persons are very carefully mentioned. 'The Lord knoweth them that are his', 'and they shall be mine, saith the Lord of hosts, in that day when I make up' — or, shut up — 'my jewels', as he was about to do in this case. In similar fashion, God makes a very careful enumeration of all those who believe in him, precious are they in his sight, and they shall be preserved when all others are destroyed.

14 They, and every beast after his kind, and all the cattle after their kind, and every creeping thing that creepeth upon the earth after his kind, and every fowl after his kind, every bird of every sort.

'Every bird of every sort', that is, every kind of bird; they are all mentioned over again. God makes much of salvation; oh, that we also did! We may recount and rehearse the story of our rescue from universal destruction, and we need not be afraid or ashamed of repeating it. As the Holy Ghost repeats the words we have here, you and I may often tell out the story of our salvation and dwell upon the minute particulars of it, for every item of it is full of instruction.

15-16 And they went in unto Noah into the ark, two and two of all flesh, wherein is the breath of life. And they that went in, went in male and female of all flesh, as God had commanded him: and the LORD shut him in.

Now the jewels are all in, and therefore, the casket is closed.

17 And the flood was forty days upon the earth; —

Just as it had been foretold, for God's providence always tallies with his promises or with his threats: 'Hath he said, and shall he not do it?'

17 and the waters increased, and bare up the ark, and it was lift up above the earth.

You can see it begin to move until it is afloat. The same effect is often produced on us; when the flood of affliction is deep, then we begin to rise. Oh, how often have we been lifted up above the earth by the very force that threatened to drench and drown us! David said, 'It is good for me that I have been afflicted', and many another saint can say that he never was floated until the floods were out, but then he left the worldliness with which he had been satisfied before, and he began to rise to a higher level than he had previously attained.

18-19 And the waters prevailed, and were increased greatly upon the earth; and the ark went upon the face of the waters. And the waters prevailed exceedingly upon the earth; and all the high hills, that were under the whole heaven, were covered.

If Moses had meant to describe a partial deluge upon only a small part of the earth, he used very misleading language; but, if he meant to teach that the deluge was universal, he used the very word which we might have expected that he would use. I should think that no person, merely by reading this chapter, would arrive at the conclusion that has been reached by some of our very learned men — too learned to hold the simple truth. It looks as if the deluge must have been universal when we read not only that 'the waters prevailed exceedingly upon the earth' but also that 'all the high hills, that were under the whole heaven' that is, all beneath the canopy of the sky, 'were covered'. What could be more plain and clear than that?

20-24 Fifteen cubits upward did the waters prevail; and the mountains were covered. And all flesh died that moved upon the earth, both of fowl, and of cattle, and of beast, and of every creeping thing that creepeth upon the earth, and every man: All in whose nostrils was the breath of life, of all that was in the dry land, died. And every living substance was destroyed which was upon the face of the ground, both man, and cattle, and the creeping things, and the fowl of the heaven; and they were destroyed from the earth: and Noah only remained alive, and they that were with him in the ark. And the waters prevailed upon the earth an hundred and fifty days.

This is the counterpart of what will follow the preaching of the gospel. Those who are in Christ shall live, shall rise, and shall reign with him for ever, but none of those who are outside of Christ shall so live. 'Noah only remained alive, and they that were with him in the ark.'

GENESIS 8

Gen. 8:1 And God remembered Noah, —

Noah had been shut up in the ark for many a day, and at the right time God thought of him, practically thought of him, and came to visit him. Dear heart, you have been shut out from the world now for many days, but God has not forgotten you. God remembered Noah, and he remembers you.

1 and every living thing, and all the cattle that was with him in the ark: —

Does God remember cattle? Then he will certainly remember men made in his own image. He will remember you, though you think yourself the most worthless one on the face of the earth: 'God remembered

Noah, and every living thing, and all the cattle that was with him in the ark.'

1 and God made a wind to pass over the earth, and the waters assuaged;

Winds and waves are wholly under God's control. I suppose that this was a very drying wind, so the waters began to turn to vapour, and gradually to disappear. It is God who sends the winds; they seem most volatile and irregular, but God sends them to do his bidding. Blow it east, or blow it west, the wind comes from God; and whether the waters increase or are assuaged, it is God's doing. Are the waters very deep with you, dear friend? God can dry them up, and singularly enough, he can stop one trouble with another; he can dry up the water with the wind. I have known him very strangely with his people, and when they thought they were quite forgotten, he has proved that he remembered them, and both the winds of heaven and the waters of the sea have had to work their good. There is not an angel in heaven but God will make him to be a servant to you if you need him; there is not a wind in any quarter of the globe but God will guide it to you if it is necessary; and there are no waves of the sea but shall obey the Lord's will concerning you.

2 The fountains also of the deep and the windows of heaven were stopped, and the rain from heaven was restrained;

God works upwards and stops the windows of heaven; he works downwards and stays the breaking up of the fountains of the deep:

He everywhere hath sway,
And all things serve his might.

Be not afraid; he can open the windows of heaven and pour down abundant blessings for you, and he can let down the cellar-flaps of the great deep and stop its flowing fountains:

When he makes bare his arm,
Who shall his work withstand?

3-5 And the waters returned from off the earth continually: and after the end of the hundred and fifty days the waters were abated. And the ark rested in the seventh month, on the seventeenth day of the month, upon the mountains of Ararat. And the waters decreased continually until the tenth month: in the tenth month, on the first day of the month, were the tops of the mountains seen.

God told Noah when to go into the ark, but he did not tell him when he should come out again. The Lord told Noah when to go in, for it was necessary for him to know that; but, he did not tell him when he should come out, for it was unnecessary that he should know that. God always lets his people know what is practically for their good. There are many curious points on which we should *like* to have information, but God has not revealed it, and when he has not revealed anything, we had better not try to unravel the mystery. No good comes of prying into unrevealed truth. Noah knew that he would come out of the ark one day, for was he not preserved for there to be a seed to keep the race alive? Noah was not told when he should be released, and the Lord does not tell you when your trouble will come to an end. It will come to an end; therefore wait, and be patient, and do not want to know the time of your deliverance. We should know too much if we knew all that will happen in the future. It is quite enough for us if we do our duty in the present and trust God for the rest. Still, I think that Noah must have been very pleased when he felt the ark grating at last on the mountains of Ararat. He could not build a dock for his big ship; but God had prepared a berth for it on the mountainside. Now, as he looked out, he could see, here and there, a mountaintop rising like an island out of the great expanse of water.

6-7 And it came to pass at the end of forty days, that Noah opened the window of the ark which he had made: And he sent forth a raven, which went forth to and fro, —

Sometimes alighting on the ark; then flying away again.

7-10 until the waters were dried up from off the earth. Also he sent forth a dove from him, to see if the waters were abated from off the face of the ground; But the dove found no rest for the sole of her foot, and she returned unto him into the ark, for the waters were on the face of the whole earth: then he put forth his hand, and took her, and pulled her in unto him into the ark. And he stayed yet other seven days; —

I wonder whether Noah sent out these creatures on the Sabbath mornings. The mention of seven days, and the resting in between seems to look like it. Oh, dear friends, sometimes people send out a raven on the Lord's Day morning, and it never brings them anything. Send out a dove rather than a raven; come to the house of God with quiet, gentle, holy expectation, and your dove will come back to you. It may be that it will bring you something worth bringing one of these days, as Noah's dove brought to him.

10-11 and again he sent forth the dove out of the ark; And the dove came in to him in the evening; and, lo, in her mouth was an olive leaf pluckt off: so Noah knew that the waters were abated from off the earth.

The waters were abated as far as the fruit trees; not only the tallest forest trees, but some of the fruit trees were uncovered from the water. The dove had plucked off 'an olive leaf'. Perhaps you have seen a picture of the dove carrying an olive branch in its mouth, which, in the first place, a dove could not pluck out of the tree, and in the second place, a dove could not carry an olive branch even if she could pluck it off. It was an olive leaf, that is all. Why cannot people keep to the words of Scripture? If the Bible mentions a leaf, they make it a bough; and if the Bible says it is a bough, they make it a leaf.

12 And he stayed yet other seven days; and sent forth the dove; which returned not again unto him any more.

Noah could read something from that leaf that the dove brought to him, but he learned more when she did not return to him. He knew that she had found a proper resting-place, and that the earth was clear of the flood.

13 And it came to pass in the six hundredth and first year, in the first month, the first day of the month, the waters were dried up from off the earth: —

That was a happy New Year's day for Noah. He was glad to find himself

13 and Noah removed the covering of the ark, and looked, and, behold, the face of the ground was dry.

at rest once more, though not yet at liberty.

13 and Noah removed the covering of the ark, and looked, and, behold, the face of the ground was dry.

Why did not Noah come out? Well, you see, he had gone in by the door, and he meant to come out by the door, and he that opened the door for him and shut him in, must now open the door for him and let him out. He waits God's time, and we are always wise in doing that. You lose a great deal of time by being in a hurry. Many people think they have done a great deal when they have really done nothing. Better take time in order to save time. Slow is sometimes faster than fast. So Noah removed the covering of the ark, and looked out, but he did not go out till God commanded him to do so.

14 And in the second month, —

Nearly two months Noah waited for the complete drying of the earth.

14 on the seven and twentieth day of the month, was the earth dried.

'The face of the ground was dry' in the first month; 'the earth was dried', the second month. Noah might have thought it was dry enough before; but God did not think so, there was enough mud to breed a pestilence, so Noah must wait until God had made the earth ready for him.

15-16 And God spake unto Noah, saying, Go forth of the ark, —

Noah must wait till God speaks to him. Oh, that some people would wait for God's command, but they will not! He shall bless thy going out and thy coming in if thou wilt go forth and come in when he bids thee. 'Go forth', says the Lord, 'Go forth of the ark.'

16-19 thou, and thy wife, and thy sons, and thy sons' wives with thee. Bring forth with thee every living thing that is with thee, of all flesh, both of fowl, and of cattle, and of every creeping thing that creepeth upon the earth; that they may breed abundantly in the earth, and be fruitful, and multiply upon the earth. And Noah went forth, and his sons, and his wife, and his sons' wives with him: Every beast, every creeping thing, and every fowl, and whatsoever creepeth upon the earth, after their kinds, went forth out of the ark.

That was a very wonderful procession, it was the new beginning of everything upon the earth. Whatever evolution, or any other folly or evil of man, may have done, everything had to begin again over. Everybody was drowned save these great fathers of the new age, and all must begin from this stock.

20 And Noah builded an altar unto the LORD; and took of every clean beast, and of every clean fowl, and offered burnt offerings on the altar.

Common sense would have said, 'Spare them, for you will want every one of them.' But grace said, 'Slay them, for they belong to God. Give Jehovah his due.' I have often admired that widow of Sarepta. When she had but a handful of meal, she made a little cake for God's prophet first, but then God multiplied her meal and her oil. Oh, if we would but seek first the kingdom of God and his righteousness, all things should be added unto us! Out of the small stock he had, Noah took of the clean beasts, and of the clean fowls, and offered burnt offerings on the altar.

21 And the LORD smelled a sweet savour; —

Noah's faith was pleasing to God. It was Noah's confidence in a bleeding sacrifice that gave him acceptance with the Lord. God thought upon his Son, and that great sacrifice to be offered long afterwards on the cross, and he 'smelled a sweet savour'.

21 and the LORD said in his heart, I will not again curse the ground any more for man's sake; for the imagination of man's heart is evil from his youth; neither will I again smite any more every thing living, as I have done.

God always speaks comfortable words to those who bring an acceptable sacrifice. If you would hear the voice of a divine promise, go to the atoning blood of Jesus. If you would know what perfect reconciliation means, go to the altar where the great sacrifice was presented.

22 While the earth remaineth, seedtime and harvest, and cold and heat, and summer and winter, and day and night shall not cease.

They never have ceased. We have this year had a long and dreary winter; it looked as if spring would never come. Only a few days ago, the chestnuts were just beginning to turn green, and then there came the little spikes, and now you can see them in full flower. How faithfully God fulfils his covenant with the earth! How truly will he keep his covenant with every believing sinner! Oh, trust ye in him, for his promise will stand fast for ever!

GENESIS 8:15-22; JEREMIAH 33:15-26

Gen. 8:15-21 And God spake unto Noah, saying, Go forth of the ark, thou, and thy wife, and thy sons, and thy sons' wives with thee. Bring forth with thee every living thing that is with thee, of all flesh, both of fowl, and of cattle, and of every creeping thing that creepeth upon the earth; that they may breed abundantly in the earth, and be fruitful, and multiply upon the earth. And Noah went forth, and his sons, and his wife, and his sons' wives with him: Every beast, every creeping thing, and every fowl, and whatsoever creepeth upon the earth, after their kinds, went forth out of the ark. And Noah built an altar unto the LORD; and took of every clean beast, and of every clean fowl, and offered burnt offerings on the altar. And the LORD smelled a sweet savour; —

Until then, the earth had been obnoxious to Jehovah. He had put it away from him as a foul thing, drowned beneath the flood; but after the offering of Noah's sacrifice, the Lord smelled 'a savour of rest'.

21-22 and the LORD said in his heart, I will not again curse the ground any more for man's sake; for the imagination of man's heart is evil from his youth; neither will I again smite any more every thing living, as I have done. While the earth remaineth, seedtime and harvest, and cold and heat, and summer and winter, and day and night shall not cease.

Thus we see what we may expect so long as the earth remains, for the mouth of the Lord hath spoken it. Now let us read a few verses from Jeremiah's prophecy.

Jer. 33:15 In those days, and at that time, will I cause the Branch of righteousness to grow up unto David; and he shall execute judgment and righteousness in the land.

In the latter days, at the glorious appointed time, Jesus Christ will grow up like a Branch out of the stem of Jesse. The dynasty of David now seems like a tree cut down, whose stock is buried under the ground, but 'the Branch of righteousness' shall appear in due time, and Jesus, the Son of David, 'shall execute judgement and righteousness in the land'.

16 In those days shall Judah be saved, and Jerusalem shall dwell safely: and this is the name wherewith she shall be called, The LORD our righteousness.

What a wonderful unity there is between Christ and his church! She actually takes his name: 'The Lord our righteousness'.

17-18 For thus saith the LORD; David shall never want a man to sit upon the throne of the house of Israel; Neither shall the priests the Levites want a man before me to offer burnt offerings, and to kindle meat offerings, and to do sacrifice continually.

This shows that the covenant was not a literal and fleshly one, made with David and his seed according to the flesh, or with the priests and their seed according to the flesh. There is a kingdom that can never be moved, and our Lord sits on that throne; there is a priesthood which is everlasting, it is held by that great High Priest who hath offered one sacrifice for sins for ever, and who abides a Priest for ever after the order of Melchizedek.

19-22 And the word of the LORD came unto Jeremiah, saying, Thus saith the LORD; If ye can break my covenant of the day, and my covenant of the night, and that there should not be day and night in their season; Then may also my covenant be broken with David my servant, that he should not have a son to reign upon his throne; and with the Levites the priests, my ministers. As the host of heaven cannot be numbered, neither the sand of the sea measured: so will I multiply the seed of David my servant, and the Levites that minister unto me.

So that they are at this day the seed of Jesus, the Son of David, who shall count them? And the company of those whom he hath made to be kings and priests unto God, who but he can number them?

23-26 Moreover the word of the LORD came to Jeremiah, saying, Considerest thou not what this people have spoken, saying, The two families which the LORD hath chosen, he hath even cast them off? thus they have despised my people, that they should be no more a nation before them. Thus saith the LORD; If my covenant be not with day and night, and if I have not appointed the ordinances of heaven and earth; Then will I cast away the seed of Jacob and David my servant, so that I will not take any of his seed to be rulers over the seed of Abraham, Isaac, and Jacob: for I will cause their captivity to return, and have mercy on them.

This shall be literally fulfilled in the latter days, I doubt not, but it is even now being fulfilled to the spiritual seed of Jacob and David. The covenant of grace is made sure to all the seed, even to as many as have believed on Christ's name.

GENESIS 8:20-22; 9:8-17; ISAIAH 54:1-10

Gen. 8:20-21 And Noah builded an altar unto the LORD; and took of every clean beast, and of every clean fowl, and offered burnt offerings on the altar. And the LORD smelled a sweet savour; —

A savour of rest, —

21-22 and the LORD said in his heart, I will not again curse the ground any more for man's sake; for the imagination of man's heart is evil from his youth; neither will I again smite any more every thing living, as I have done. While the earth remaineth, seedtime and harvest, and cold and heat, and summer and winter, and day and night shall not cease.

So that you all live under a covenant — a gracious covenant, and by virtue of it, the day succeeds the night, the summer follows the winter, and the harvest in due course rewards the labour of the seedtime. All this ought to make us long to be under the yet fuller and higher covenant of grace, by which spiritual blessings would be hastened to us — an eternal day to follow this earthly night, and a glorious harvest to follow this time of seed-sowing.

Gen. 9:8-10 And God spake unto Noah, and to his sons with him, saying, And I, behold, I establish my covenant with you, and with your seed after you; And with every living creature that is with you, of the fowl, of the cattle, and of every beast of the earth with you; from all that go out of the ark, to every beast of the earth.

Happy fowls and happy cattle and happy beasts of the earth to be connected with Noah and to go out of the ark to come under a covenant of preservation; and we — though only worthy to be typified by these creatures which God had preserved in the ark — are thrice happy to be in the same covenant with him who is our Noah, our rest, our sweet savour unto God.

11-16 And I will establish my covenant with you, neither shall all flesh be cut off any more by the waters of a flood; neither shall there any more be a flood to destroy the earth. And God said, This is the token of the covenant which I make between me and you and every living creature that is with you, for perpetual generations: I do set my bow in the cloud, and it shall be for a token of a covenant between me and the earth. And it shall come to pass, when I bring a cloud over the earth, that the bow shall be seen in the cloud: And I will remember my covenant, which is between me and you and every living creature of all flesh; and the waters shall no more become a flood to destroy all flesh. And the bow shall be in the cloud; and I will look upon it, —

What a wonderful expression that is! It is similar to that remarkable declaration of Jehovah, recorded in Exodus 12:13. 'When I see the blood, I will pass over you.' The blood was not to be sprinkled inside the house where the Israelites might be comforted by a sight of it, but outside the house, where only God could see it. It is for our sake that the rainbow is set in the cloud, and we can see it there; yet infinite mercy represents it as being there as a refreshment to the memory of God: 'The bow shall be in the cloud; and I will look upon it.'

16 that I may remember the everlasting covenant between God and every living creature of all flesh that is upon the earth.

So, when my eye of faith is dim, and I cannot see the covenant sign, I will remember that there is an eye which never can be dim, which always sees the covenant token; and so I shall still be secure notwithstanding the dimness of my spiritual vision. For our comfort, we must see it; but for our safety, blessed be God, it is only needful that he should see it.

17 And God said unto Noah, This is the token of the covenant, which I have established between me and all flesh that is upon the earth.

Now let us read what the Lord says, through the prophet Isaiah, concerning this covenant.

Isa. 54:1 Sing, O barren, thou that didst not bear; break forth into singing, and cry aloud, thou that didst not travail with child: for more are the children of the desolate than the children of the married wife, saith the LORD.

This promise is made to the long-barren and desolate Gentile church that may well sing, for God has visited her in mercy, and at this day, her children are more numerous than those of the Jewish church. We have waited, but we have been well repaid for our waiting, for we have a larger and richer blessing than God's ancient people ever enjoyed.

2-4 Enlarge the place of thy tent, and let them stretch forth the curtains of thine habitations: spare not, lengthen thy cords, and strengthen thy stakes; For thou shalt break forth on the right hand and on the left; and thy seed shall inherit the Gentiles, and make the desolate cities to be inhabited. Fear not; for thou shalt not be ashamed: neither be thou confounded; for thou shalt not be put to shame: for thou shalt forget the shame of thy youth, and shalt not remember the reproach of thy widowhood any more.

O child of God, have you passed through a time of great sorrow, in which the Lord seemed to desert you quite? Have all your hopes been blighted, and have all your joys fallen, like untimely figs from the trees? Yet the days of your rejoicing shall be many, you shall soon put aside your sackcloth and ashes, and dancing and holy gladness shall be your portion.

5 For thy Maker is thine husband; —

Rejoice, O church of God, that thou hast such a husband! Rejoice, every member of the church of God, that thou hast such a husband to help thee! 'Thy Maker is thine husband.'

5 the LORD of hosts is his name; and thy Redeemer the Holy One of Israel; The God of the whole earth shall he be called.

Well might Paul write, in the Epistle to the Romans, 'Is he the God of the Jews only? Is he not also of the Gentiles? Yes, of the Gentiles also'; and Isaiah here says, inspired by the same Spirit who taught Paul what to write, 'The God of the whole earth shall he be called.'

6-7 For the LORD hath called thee as a woman forsaken and grieved in spirit, and a wife of youth, when thou wast refused, saith thy God. For a small moment have I forsaken thee; —

A moment is a small period of time, but it is made to appear still smaller by that little word 'small'.

7-8 but with great mercies will I gather thee. In a little wrath I hid my face from thee for a moment; but with everlasting kindness will I have mercy on thee, saith the LORD thy Redeemer.

Oh, what a blessed mouthful this text is! I might rather say, 'What a heart full! What a soul full!' It fills, and overfills my soul, and gives me sweet content: 'With everlasting kindness will I have mercy on thee, saith the Lord thy Redeemer.'

9 For this is as the waters of Noah unto me: for as I have sworn that the waters of Noah should no more go over the earth; so have I sworn that I would not be wroth with thee, nor rebuke thee.

See how our faithful and unchanging God lays the foundation for our hopes:

In oaths, and promises, and blood.

10 For the mountains shall depart, and the hills be removed; but my kindness shall not depart from thee, neither shall the covenant of my peace be removed, saith the LORD that hath mercy on thee.

Or, as the Hebrew has it, 'saith the Lord, the Pitier'. Was there ever a sweeter title to comfort our hearts than this, 'the Lord, the Pitier'?

GENESIS 12:1-7; 14:17-24; 22:15-18

We will read two or three passages in the Book of Genesis concerning God blessing his servant Abraham. Turn first to the twelfth chapter.

Gen. 12:1 Now the LORD had said unto Abram, Get thee out of thy country, and from thy kindred, and from thy father's house, unto a land that I will shew thee:

It was God's intention to keep his truth and his pure worship alive in the world by committing it to the charge of one man, and the nation that should spring from him. In the infinite sovereignty of his grace, he chose Abraham — passing by all the rest of mankind — and elected him to be the depository of the heavenly light, that through him it might be preserved in the world until the days when it should be more widely scattered. It seemed essential to this end that Abraham should come right out from his fellow-countrymen, and be separate unto Jehovah; so the Lord said to him, 'Get thee out of thy country, and from thy kindred, and from thy father's house, unto a land that I will shew thee.'

2-3 And I will make of thee a great nation, and I will bless thee, and make thy name great; and thou shalt be a blessing: And I will bless them that bless thee, and curse him that curseth thee: and in thee shall all families of the earth be blessed.

There, you see, was the missionary character of the seed of Abraham, if they had but recognized it. God did not bless them for themselves alone, but for all nations: 'In thee shall all families of the earth be blessed.'

4 So Abram departed, as the LORD had spoken unto him; and Lot went with him: and Abram was seventy and five years old when he departed out of Haran.

He had already attained a fine old age, but he had another century of life before him, which he could not then foresee, or expect. If, at his age, he had said, 'Lord, I am too old to travel, too old to leave my country, and to begin to live a wandering life', we could not have wondered; but he did not talk in that fashion. He was commanded to go and we read, 'So Abram departed, as the Lord had spoken unto him.'

5-6 And Abram took Sarai his wife, and Lot his brother's son, and all their substance that they had gathered, and the souls that they had gotten in Haran; and they went forth to go into the land of Canaan; and into the land of Canaan they came. And Abram passed through the land unto the place of Sichem, unto the plain of Moreh. And the Canaanite was then in the land.

Fierce and powerful nations possessed the country; it did not seem a very likely place to be the heritage of a peace-loving man like Abraham. God does not always fulfill his promises to his people at once; else, where would be the room for faith? This life of ours is to be a life of faith, and it will be well rewarded in the end. Abraham had not a foot of land to call his own, except that cave of Machpelah which he bought of the sons of Heth for a burying-place for his beloved Sarah.

7 And the LORD appeared unto Abram, and said, Unto thy seed will I give this land: and there builded he an altar unto the LORD, who appeared unto him.

Thus, you see, Abraham began his separated life with a blessing from the Lord his God. Further on in his history he received a still larger blessing when he returned from his victory over the kings.

Gen. 14:17-19 And the king of Sodom went out to meet him after his return from the slaughter of Chedorlaomer, and of the kings that were with him, at the valley of Shaveh, which is the king's dale. And Melchizedek king of Salem brought forth bread and wine: and he was the priest of the most high God. And he blessed him, —

In the name of God, Melchizedek blessed Abraham. This mysterious personage, the highest type of our Lord Jesus Christ, blessed Abraham; 'And without all contradiction the less is blessed of the better' [Hebrews 7:7]. 'He blessed him.'

19-20 and said, Blessed be Abram of the most high God, possessor of heaven and earth: And blessed be the most high God, which hath delivered thine enemies into thy hand. And he gave him tithes of all.

Abraham recognized the priest of God as his spiritual superior, 'and he gave him tithes of all'.

21 And the king of Sodom said unto Abram, Give me the persons, and take the goods to thyself.

It was according to the rule of war that, if persons who had made an invasion were afterwards themselves captured, then if the new captor gave up the persons, he was fully entitled to take the goods to himself.

22-23 And Abram said to the king of Sodom, I have lift up mine hand unto the LORD, the most high God, the possessor of heaven and earth, That I will not take from a thread even to a shoelatchet, and that I will not take any thing that is thine, lest thou shouldest say, I have made Abram rich:

The patriarch is greater than the king. He has a right to all his spoil; but he will not touch it, lest the glory of his God should thereby be stained. Abraham will have nothing but what his God shall give him; he will not take anything from the king of Sodom. I like to see this glorious independence of the believing man. 'I have a right to this', says he, 'but I will not take it; what are mere earthly rights to me? My chief business is to honour the God through whom I am, and whom I serve; and if the taking of this spoil would dishonour him, I will not take even so much as a thread or a shoelatchet.'

24 Save only that which the young men have eaten, and the portion of the men which went with me, Aner, Eshcol, and Mamre; let them take their portion.

'Though I am willing to give up my share of the spoil, that is no reason why these men should do the same.' Christian men ought not to expect worldlings to do what they cheerfully and willingly do themselves; and indeed, it is not much use to expect it, for they are not likely to do it. Now let us read in the twenty-second chapter of this same Book of Genesis. Abraham had endured the supreme test of his faith and had, in full intent, offered up his son Isaac at the command of God, his hand being withheld from the actual sacrifice only by an angelic voice.

Gen. 22:15-17 And the angel of the LORD called unto Abraham out of heaven the second time, And said, By myself have I sworn, saith the LORD, for because thou hast done this thing, and hast not withheld thy son, thine only son: That in blessing I will bless thee, —

'Whenever I am engaged in blessing, I will bless thee. I win not pronounce a benediction in the which thou shalt not share: "In blessing I will bless thee."'

17-18 and in multiplying I will multiply thy seed as the stars of the heaven, and as the sand which is upon the sea shore; and thy seed shall possess the gate of his enemies; And in thy seed shall all the nations of the earth be blessed; because thou hast obeyed my voice.

See the result of one man's grand act of obedience, and note how God can make that man to be the channel of blessing to all coming ages. Oh, that you and I might possess the Abrahamic faith which thus practically obeys the Lord, and brings a blessing to all the nations of the earth!

GENESIS 14:17-24; 15

Gen. 14:17-18 And the king of Sodom went out to meet him after his return from the slaughter of Chedorlaomer, and of the kings that were with him, at the valley of Shaveh, which is the king's dale. And Melchizedek king of Salem brought forth bread and wine: and he was the priest of the most high God.

One who exercised both the kingship and the priesthood, the only person that we know of who did this, and who, therefore, is a wonderful type of that marvellous King-Priest of whom we read in Psalm 110, and in the Epistle to the Hebrews.

19-20 And he blessed him, and said, Blessed be Abram of the most high God, possessor of heaven and earth: And blessed be the most high God, which hath delivered thine enemies into thy hand. And he gave him tithes of all.

It must have been peculiarly refreshing to Abraham to be met by a man of kindred spirit, and one whom he recognized as his superior. No doubt he was weary, though triumphant; and so, just then, the Lord sent him special refreshment, and, beloved, how sweet it is to us when the greater Melchizedek meets us! Jesus Christ our great King-Priest, still meets us, and brings us bread and wine. Often, the very symbols on his table have been refreshing to us, but their inner meaning has been far more sustaining and comforting to our spirit. There is no food like the bread and wine that our blessed Melchizedek brings forth to us, even his own flesh and blood. Well may we give him tithes of all that we have. Nay, more, we may say to him, 'Take not tithes, O Lord, but take all!'

21 And the king of Sodom said unto Abram, Give me the persons, and take the goods to thyself.

They were all Abraham's by right as the spoils of war.

22-23 And Abram said to the king of Sodom, I have lift up mine hand unto the LORD, the most high God, the possessor of heaven and earth, That I will not take from a thread even to a shoelatchet, and that I will not take any thing that is thine, lest thou shouldest say, I have made Abram rich:

Sometimes, a child of God will find himself cast, through force of circumstances, into very curious companionship. For the sake of Lot, Abraham had to go and fight the enemies of the king of Sodom, and sometimes, in fighting for religious liberty, we have had to be associated with persons from whom we differ as much as Abraham differed from the king of Sodom; but, right must be fought for under all circumstances. Yet, sooner or later, there comes a crucial test in which our true character will be discovered. Shall we personally gain anything by this association? We loathe it even while we recognize that it is needful for the time being, but we have not entered it for the sake of personal gain.

24 Save only that which the young men have eaten, and the portion of the men which went with me, Aner, Eshcol, and Mamre; let them take their portion.

They had a right to it. What we do ourselves, we do not always expect others to do. There is a higher code of morals for the servant of God than for other men; and we may often think of what they do, and not condemn them, although we could not do the same ourselves, for we are lifted into a higher position as the servant of the Lord.

Gen. 15:1-3 After these things the word of the LORD came unto Abram in a vision, saying, Fear not, Abram: I am thy shield, and thy exceeding great reward. And Abram said, LORD God, what wilt thou give me, seeing I go childless, and the steward of my house is this Eliezer of Damascus? And Abram said, Behold, to me thou hast given no seed: and, lo, one born in my house is mine heir.

Perhaps he did not doubt the promise, but he wanted to have it explained to him. He may have wondered if it meant that one born in his house, though not his son, was to be his heir and that, through him, the blessing would come. He takes the opportunity of making an enquiry, that he may know how to act. At the same time, there does seem to be a clashing between Abraham's question, 'What wilt thou give me?' and the declaration of God, 'I am thy shield, and thy exceeding great reward.' There is a great descent from the language of the Lord to that of the most stable believer, and when you and I are even at our best, I have no doubt that, if all could be recorded that we think and say, some of our fellow-believers would feel that the best of men are but men at the best, and that God's language is after a nobler fashion than ours will ever be, till we have seen his face in glory.

4-5 And, behold, the word of the LORD came unto him, saying, This shall not be thine heir; but he that shall come forth out of thine own bowels shall be thine heir. And he brought him forth abroad, and said, Look now toward heaven, and tell the stars, if thou be able to number them: and he said unto him, So shall thy seed be.

Now was his faith tried indeed: he had no child, he was himself old, and his wife also was old; yet, the Lord's promise was, 'So shall thy seed be' as the stars of heaven. Could he believe it? He did.

6 And he believed in the LORD; and he counted it to him for righteousness.

Oh, what a blessing to learn the way of ample faith in God! This is the saving quality in many a life. Look through Paul's list of the heroes of faith: some of them are exceedingly imperfect characters; some we should hardly have thought of mentioning, but they had faith; and although men, in their faulty judgement, think faith to be an inferior virtue and often scarcely look upon it as a virtue at all, yet, in the judgement of God, faith is the supremest virtue. 'This', said Christ, 'is the work of God', the greatest of all works, 'that ye believe on him whom he hath sent'. To trust, to believe, this shall be counted to us for righteousness even as it was to Abraham.

7-8 And he said unto him, I am the LORD that brought thee out of Ur of the Chaldees, to give thee this land to inherit it. And he said, LORD God, whereby shall I know that I shall inherit it?

What? Abraham, is not God's promise sufficient for thee? O father of the faithful, though thou dost believe, and art counted as righteous through believing, dost thou still ask, 'Whereby shall I know?' Ah, beloved! Faith is often marred by a measure of unbelief; or, if not quite unbelief, yet there is a desire to have some token, some sign, beyond the bare promise of God.

9-11 And he said unto him, Take me an heifer of three years old, and a she goat of three years old, and a ram of three years old, and a turtledove, and a young pigeon. And he took unto him all these, and divided them in the midst, and laid each piece one against another: but the birds divided he not. And when the fowls came down upon the carcases, Abram drove them away.

Here is a lesson for us. Perhaps you have some of these unclean birds coming down upon your sacrifice just now. That raven that you did not lock up well at home, has come here after you. Eagles and vultures and all kinds of kites, in the form of carking cares and sad memories and fears and doubts, come hovering over the sacred feast. Drive them away! God give you grace to drive them away by the power of his gracious Spirit!

12 And when the sun was going down, a deep sleep fell upon Abram; and, lo, an horror of great darkness fell upon him.

He had asked for a manifestation, a sign, a token, and, lo, it comes in the 'horror of great darkness'. Do not be afraid, beloved, if your soul sometimes knows what horror is. Remember how the favoured three, on the Mount of Transfiguration, 'feared as they entered into the cloud'; yet, it was there that they were to see their Master in his glory. Remember what the Lord said to Jeremiah concerning Jerusalem and his people, 'They shall fear and tremble for all the goodness and for all the prosperity that I procure unto it.' That is the right spirit in which to receive prosperity, but as for adversity, rejoice in it, for God often sends the richest treasures to his children in wagons drawn by black horses. You may except that some great blessing is coming nigh to you when a 'horror of great darkness' falls upon you.

13 And he said unto Abram, Know of a surety that thy seed shall be a stranger in a land that is not theirs, and shall serve them; and they shall afflict them four hundred years;

It was to be a long while before the nation should enter upon its inheritance. Here is a promise that was to take 400 years to ripen! Some of you cannot believe the promise if its fulfillment is delayed for four days; you can hardly keep on praying, if it takes four years; what would you think of a 400-years promise? Yet it was to be so long in coming to maturity because it was so vast. If Abraham's seed was to be like the stars of heaven for multitude, there must be time for the increase to come.

14-17 And also that nation, whom they shall serve, will I judge: and afterward shall they come out with great substance. And thou shalt go to thy fathers in peace; thou shalt be buried in a good old age. But in the fourth generation they shall come hither again: for the iniquity of the Amorites is not yet full. And it came to pass, that, when the sun went down, and it was dark, behold a smoking furnace, and a burning lamp that passed between those pieces.

True emblems of the church of God with her smoke and her light, her trying affliction, yet the grace by which she still keeps burning and shining in the world.

18-21 In the same day the LORD made a covenant with Abram, saying, Unto thy seed have I given this land, from the river of Egypt unto the great river, the river Euphrates: The Kenites, and the Kenizzites, and the Kadmonites, and the Hittites, and the Perizzites, and the Rephaims, and the Amorites, and the Canaanites, and the Girgashites, and the Jebusites.

He mentions the adversaries to show how great would be the victories of the race that should come and dispossess them. Let us always look upon the list of our difficulties as only a catalogue of our triumphs. The greater our troubles, the louder our song at the last.

GENESIS 18:17-33; 19:12-28

Gen. 18:17-19   And the LORD said, Shall I hide from Abraham that thing which I do; Seeing that Abraham shall surely become a great and mighty nation, and all the nations of the earth shall be blessed in him? For I know him, that he will command his children and his household after him, and they shall keep the way of the LORD, to do justice and judgment; that the LORD may bring upon Abraham that which he hath spoken of him.

Abraham is called 'the friend of God'. It was not merely that God was his Friend; that was blessedly true, and it was a great wonder of grace; but he was honoured to be called 'the friend of God' — one with whom God could hold sweet converse, a man after his own heart, in whom he trusted, to whom he revealed his secrets.

I am afraid there are not many men of Abraham's sort in the world even now; but, wherever there is such a man, with whom God is familiar, he will be sure to be one who orders his household aright. If the Lord is my Friend, and if I am indeed his friend, I shall wish him to be respected by my children, and I shall endeavour to dedicate my children to his service. I fear that the decline of family godliness, which is so sadly remarkable in these days, is the source of a great many of the crying sins of the age; the church of God at large would have been more separate from the world if the little church in each man's house had been more carefully trained for God. If you want the Lord to confide in you and to trust you with his secrets, you must see that he is able to say of you what he said of Abraham, 'he will command his children and his household after him'.

20-22 And the LORD said, Because the cry of Sodom and Gomorrah is great, and because their sin is very grievous; I will go down now, and see whether they have done altogether according to the cry of it, which is come unto me; and if not, I will know. And the men turned their faces from thence, and went toward Sodom: but Abraham stood yet before the LORD.

He was in no hurry to close that blessed interview; when he had once come into the Lord's immediate presence, he lingered there. Those who are friends of God like to be much in their Lord's company.

23 And Abraham drew near, —

There is nothing like coming very close to God in prayer: 'Abraham drew near.' He was about to use his influence with his great Friend, not for himself but for these men of Sodom, who were going to be destroyed. Happy are those who, when they are near to God, use the opportunity in pleading for others, aye, even for the most wicked and abandoned of men.

23-25 and said, Wilt thou also destroy the righteous with the wicked? Peradventure there be fifty righteous within the city: wilt thou also destroy and not spare the place for the fifty righteous that are therein? That be far from thee to do after this manner, to slay the righteous with the wicked: and that the righteous should be as the wicked, that be far from thee: Shall not the Judge of all the earth do right?

Abraham bases his argument upon the justice of God; and when a man dares to do that, it is mighty pleading, for, depend upon it, God will never do an unjust thing. If thou darest to plead his righteousness, his infallible justice, thou pleadest most powerfully.

26-30 And the LORD said, If I find in Sodom fifty righteous within the city, then I will spare all the place for their sakes. And Abraham answered and said, Behold now, I have taken upon me to speak unto the LORD, which am but dust and ashes: Peradventure there shall lack five of the fifty righteous: wilt thou destroy all the city for lack of five? And he said, If I find there forty and five, I will not destroy it. And he spake unto him yet again, and said, Peradventure there shall be forty found there. And he said, I will not do it for forty's sake. And he said unto him, Oh let not the LORD be angry, and I will speak: Peradventure there shall thirty be found there. And he said, I will not do it, if I find thirty there.

This time the patriarch has advanced by ten; before, it was by fives. Pleading men grow bolder and braver in their requests. A man who is very familiar with God will, by and by, venture to say that which, at the first, he would not have dared to utter.

31-32 And he said, Behold now, I have taken upon me to speak unto the LORD: Peradventure there shall be twenty found there. And he said, I will not destroy it for twenty's sake. And he said, Oh let not the LORD be angry, and I will speak yet but this once: Peradventure ten shall be found there. And he said, I will not destroy it for ten's sake.

He went no farther than to plead that Sodom might be spared if ten righteous persons could be found in it. I have heard some say that it was a pity Abraham did not go on pleading with God; but I would not dare to say so. He knew better when to begin and when to leave off than you and I do; there are certain restraints in prayer which a man of God cannot explain to others, but which he, nevertheless, himself feels. God moves his servants to pray in a certain case, and they do pray with great liberty and manifest power. Another case may seem to be precisely like it: yet the mouth of the former suppliant is shut, and in his heart he does not feel that he can pray as he did before. Do I blame the men of God? Assuredly not; the Lord dealeth wisely with his servants, and he tells them, by gentle hints, which they quickly understand, when and where to stop in their supplications.

33 And the LORD went his way, as soon as he had left communing with Abraham: and Abraham returned unto his place.

We know that the angels went down to Sodom, where they were received by Lot, and despitefully used by the Sodomites. We will continue our reading at the twelfth verse of the next chapter.

Gen. 19:12 And the men said unto Lot, Hast thou here any besides? son in law, and thy sons, and thy daughters, and whatsoever thou hast in the city, bring them out of this place:

Let me bid every Christian man to look about him, among all his kith and kin, to see which of them yet remain unconverted. Let your prayers go up for them all: 'Son in law, and thy sons, and thy daughters.'

13-14 For we will destroy this place, because the cry of them is waxen great before the face of the LORD; and the LORD hath sent us to destroy it. And Lot went out, and spake unto his sons in law, which married his daughters, and said, Up, get you out of this place; for the LORD will destroy this city. But he seemed as one that mocked unto his sons in law.

'The old man is in his dotage', said they. 'He always was peculiar, he never acted like the rest of the citizens; he came in here as a stranger, and he has always been strange in his behaviour.'

15-16 And when the morning arose, then the angels hastened Lot, saying, Arise, take thy wife, and thy two daughters, which are here; lest thou be consumed in the iniquity of the city. And while he lingered, the men laid hold upon his hand, and upon the hand of his wife, and upon the hand of his two daughters; the LORD being merciful unto him: and they brought him forth, and set him without the city.

I have always felt pleased to think that there were just hands enough to lead out these four people, Lot, and his wife, and their two daughters. Had there been one more, there would have been no hand to lay hold of the fifth person; but these two angels, with their four hands, could just lead these four persons outside the doomed city. God will always have agents enough to save his elect; there shall be sufficient gospel preaching, even in the darkest and deadest times, to bring his redeemed out of the City of Destruction. God will miss none of his own.

17 And it came to pass, when they had brought them forth abroad, that he said, Escape for thy life; look not behind thee, neither stay thou in all the plain; escape to the mountain, lest thou be consumed.

Perhaps the old man's legs trembled under him; he felt that he could not run so far; and, beside, the mountain seemed so bleak and dreary, he could not quite quit the abodes of men.

18-21 And Lot said unto them, Oh, not so, my LORD: Behold now, thy servant hath found grace in thy sight, and thou hast magnified thy mercy, which thou hast shewed unto me in saving my life; and I cannot escape to the mountain, lest some evil take me, and I die: Behold now, this city is near to flee unto, and it is a little one: Oh, let me escape thither, (is it not a little one?) and my soul shall live. And he said unto him, See, I have accepted thee concerning this thing also, that I will not overthrow this city, for the which thou hast spoken.

I think that I have said to you before that this sparing of Zoar is an instance of the cumulative power of prayer. I may liken Abraham's mighty pleading to a ton weight of prayer, supplication that had a wonderful force and power. Lot's petition is only like an ounce of prayer. Poor little Lot, what a poor little prayer his was! Yet that ounce turned the scale. So, it may be that there is some mighty man of God who is near to prevailing with God, but he cannot quite obtain his request; but you, poor feeble pleader that you are, shall add your feather's weight to his great intercession, and then the scale will turn. This narrative always comforts me I think that Zoar was preserved, not so much by the prayer of Lot, as by the greater prayer of Abraham which had gone before; yet the mighty intercession of the friend of God did not prevail until it was supported by the feeble petition of poor Lot.

22 Haste thee, escape thither; —

The hand of justice was held back until God's servant was safe. There can be no destruction of the world, there can be no pouring out of the last plagues, there can be no total sweeping away of the ungodly till, first of all, the servants of God are sealed in their foreheads, and taken to a place of security. The Lord will preserve his own. He lets the scaffold stand until the building is finished; then, it will come down fast enough.

22-28 for I cannot do anything till thou be come thither. Therefore the name of the city was called Zoar. The sun was risen upon the earth when Lot entered into Zoar. Then the LORD rained upon Sodom and upon Gomorrah brimstone and fire from the LORD out of heaven; and he overthrew those cities, and all the plain, and all the inhabitants of the cities, and that which grew upon the ground. But his wife looked back from behind him, and she became a pillar of salt. And

Abraham gat up early in the morning to the place where he stood before the LORD: And he looked toward Sodom and Gomorrah, and toward all the land of the plain, and beheld, and, lo, the smoke of the country went up as the smoke of a furnace.

What must Abraham's meditations have been! What should be the meditations of every godly man as he looks towards Sodom, and sees the smoke of its destruction? It might do some men great good if they would not persistently shut their eyes to the doom of the wicked. Look, look, I pray you, upon that place of darkness and woe where every impenitent and unbelieving spirit must be banished for ever from the presence of the Lord! Look till the tears are in your eyes as you thank God that you are rescued from so terrible a doom! Look till your heart melts with pity for the many who are going the downward road, and who will eternally ruin themselves unless almighty grace prevent!

GENESIS 22:1-19

Gen. 22:1 And it came to pass after these things, that God did tempt —

That is, 'God did test or try.'

1-2 Abraham, and said unto him, Abraham: and he said, Behold, here I am. And he said, Take now thy son, —

'But, Lord, I have two sons, Ishmael and Isaac.'

2 thine only son —

'But, Lord, both Ishmael and Isaac are my sons, and each of them is the only son of his mother.'

2 Isaac, whom thou lovest, —

See how definitely God points out to Abraham the son who is to be the means of the great trial of his father's faith: 'Take now thy son, thine only son Isaac, whom thou lovest.'

2 and get thee into the land of Moriah; and offer him there for a burnt offering upon one of the mountains which I will tell thee of.

It was usually the way, in God's commands to Abraham, to make him sail under sealed orders. When he was first bidden to leave his country and his kindred, and his father's house, he had to go to a land that God would shew him. They have true faith who can go forth at God's command, not knowing whither they are going. So Abraham did, and now the Lord says to him, 'Take Isaac, and offer him for a burnt offering upon one of the mountains which I will tell thee of.'

3   And Abraham rose up early in the morning, —

Obedience should be prompt, we should show our willingness to obey the Lord's command by not delaying: 'Abraham rose up early in the morning.'

3   and saddled his ass, and took two of his young men with him, and Isaac his son, and clave the wood for the burnt offering, and rose up, and went unto the place of which God had told him.

All the details are mentioned, for true obedience is very careful of detail. They who would serve God aright must serve him faithfully in little things as well as in great ones. There must be a saddling of the ass, a calling of the two young men as well as Isaac, and a cleaving of the wood for the burnt offering. We must do everything that is included in the bounds of the divine command, and do it all with scrupulous exactness and care. Indifferent obedience to God's command is practically disobedience, careless obedience is dead obedience, the heart is gone out of it. Let us learn from Abraham how to obey.

4   Then on the third day Abraham lifted up his eyes, and saw the place afar off.

His was deliberate obedience; he could bear suspense, thinking over the whole matter for three days, and setting his face like a flint to obey his Lord's command.

5   And Abraham said unto his young men, Abide ye here with the ass; and I and the lad will go yonder and worship, and come again to you.

Abraham did not deceive the young men, he believed that he and Isaac would come to them again. He believed that though he might be compelled to say of his son, 'God was able to raise him up, even from the dead; from whence also he received him in a figure.' Abraham bade the young men stay where they were, they must not see all that he was to do before the Lord. Oftentimes, our highest obedience must be a solitary one; friends cannot help us in such emergencies, and it is better for them and better for us that they should not be with us.

6 And Abraham took the wood of the burnt offering, and laid it upon Isaac his son; and he took the fire in his hand, and a knife; —

That knife was cutting into his own heart all the while, yet he took it. Unbelief would have left the knife at home, but genuine faith takes it.

6-8 and they went both of them together. And Isaac spake unto Abraham his father, and said, My father: and he said, Here am I, my son. And he said, Behold the fire and the wood: but where is the lamb for a burnt offering? And Abraham said, My son, God will provide himself a lamb for a burnt offering: so they went both of them together.

Abraham here spoke like a prophet; in fact, throughout this whole incident, he never opened his mouth without a prophetic utterance; and I believe that, when men walk with God, and live near to God, they will possibly, even without being aware of it, speak very weighty words which will have much more in them than they themselves apprehend. Is it not written, concerning the man whose delight is in the law of the Lord, 'his leaf also shall not wither'? Not only shall his fruit be abundant, but his casual word, 'his leaf also shall not wither'. So was it with it Abraham. He spoke like a prophet of God when he was really speaking to his son in the anguish of his spirit, and in his prophetic utterance we find the sum and substance of the gospel: 'My son, God will provide himself a lamb for a burnt offering.' He is the great Provider, and he provides the offering, not only for us, but for himself, for the sacrifice was necessary to God as well as to man. And it is a burnt offering, not only a sin-offering but an offering of a sweet savour unto himself. 'So they went both of them together.' Twice we are told this, for this incident is a type of the Father going with the Son and the Son going with the Father up to the great sacrifice on Calvary. It was not Christ alone who willingly died, or the Father alone who gave his Son, but 'they went both of them together', even as Abraham and Isaac did here.

9 And they came to the place which God had told him of; and Abraham built an altar there, —

See him pulling out the large, rough, unhewn stones that lay round about the place and then fling them up into an altar.

9-10 and laid the wood in order, and bound Isaac his son, and laid him on the altar upon the wood. And Abraham stretched forth his hand, and took the knife to slay his son.

So that, in intent and purpose, he had consummated the sacrifice, and therefore we read in Hebrews 11:17, 'By faith Abraham, when he was tried, offered up Isaac: and he that had received the promises offered up his only begotten son.' He had virtually done so in the esteem of God, though no trace of a wound could be found upon Isaac. How often God takes the will for the deed with his people! When he finds them willing to make the sacrifice that he demands, he often does not require it at their hands. If you are willing to suffer for Christ's sake, it may be that you shall not be caused to suffer, and if you are willing to be a martyr for the truth, you may be permitted to wear the martyr's crown even though you are never called to stand at the stake, the scaffold or the block.

11 And the angel of the LORD called unto him out of heaven, and said, Abraham, Abraham: and he said, Here am I.

Abraham always gives the same answer to the Lord's call, 'Here am I.'

12 And he said, Lay not thine hand upon the lad, neither do thou any thing unto him: for now I know that thou fearest God, seeing thou hast not withheld thy son, thine only son from me.

The needful test had been applied, and Abraham's faith had endured the trial. God knows all things by his divine omniscience, but now he knew by this severe test and trial which he had applied, that Abraham really loved him best of all. Notice that the angel says, 'Now I know that thou fearest God.' I do not think that the gracious use of godly fear has ever been sufficiently estimated by the most of us; here, the stress is not laid upon the faith, but upon the filial fear of Abraham. That holy awe, that sacred reverence of God is the very essence of our acceptance with him. 'The fear of the Lord is the beginning of wisdom.' 'The Lord taketh pleasure in them that fear him.' This is a very different thing from slavish fear; it is a right sort of fear, the kind of fear that love does not cast out, but which love lives with in happy fellowship.

13 And Abraham lifted up his eyes, and looked, and behold behind him a ram caught in a thicket by his horns: and Abraham went and took the ram, and offered him up for a burnt offering in the stead of his son.

Here is another type of our Saviour's great sacrifice on Calvary: the ram offered in the place of Jesus. How often do you and I have our great Substitute very near to us, yet we do not see him because we do not lift up our eyes and look. 'Abraham lifted up his eyes, and looked, and behold behind him a ram caught in a thicket by his horns.' So, if you lift up your eyes and look the right, aye, you will see the great sacrifice close by you held fast for you, even as this ram was caught to die instead of Isaac. Oh, that you may have grace to turn your head in the right direction and look to Christ and live!

14 And Abraham called the name of that place Jehovah-jireh: as it is said to this day, In the mount of the LORD it shall be seen.

God will foresee; 'God will' — as we usually say — 'provide', which is being interpreted, foresee. He will have everything ready against the time when it will be needed. He who provided the ram for a burnt offering in the place of Isaac will provide everything else that is required. You may depend upon it that he who, in the greatest emergency that could ever happen, provided his only-begotten and well-beloved Son to die us the Substitute for sinners, will have foreseen every other emergency that can occur, and will have fore-provided all that is needful to meet it. Blessed be the name of Jehovah-jireh!

15-16 And the angel of the LORD called unto Abraham out of heaven the second time, and said, By myself have I sworn, saith the LORD, —

'Because he could swear by no greater, he sware by himself' [Hebrews 6:13].

16-18 for because thou hast done this thing, and hast not withheld thy son, thine only son: That in blessing I will bless thee, and in multiplying I will multiply thy seed as the stars of the heaven, and as the sand which is upon the sea shore; and thy seed shall possess the gate of his enemies; and in thy seed shall all the nations of the earth be blessed; because thou hast obeyed my voice.

There stands the old covenant, the covenant of grace made with Abraham concerning his seed. Paul writes to the Galatians, 'Now to Abraham and his seed were the promises made. He saith not, And to seeds, as of many; but as of one, And to thy seed, which is Christ.' It is in Christ that all the nations of the earth are to be blessed. If there is a nation that has not yet heard the gospel, it must hear it, for so the promise stands, 'In thy seed shall all the nations of the earth be blessed.' We may look for a glorious future from the preaching of Christ throughout every land, for so the covenant was made with Abraham, because he had obeyed God's voice.

God had been good to Abraham before that time, for he was his beloved friend, but now he lifts him up to a higher platform altogether and makes him a greater blessing than ever. It may be that God is about to test and try some of you in order that he may afterwards make you to be greater and more useful than you have ever been before.

19 So Abraham returned unto his young men, —

As he said that he would.

19 and they rose up and went together to Beersheba; and Abraham dwelt at Beersheba.

So the Lord bore his servant through this great trial and blessed him more than he had ever blessed him before.

GENESIS 24:1-16

Gen. 24:1 And Abraham was old, and well stricken in age: and the LORD had blessed Abraham in all things.

Happy man that can say that, who has a blessing everywhere! And yet Abraham had his 'but', for as yet Isaac was unmarried, and perhaps he little dreamed that for twenty years afterwards he who was to build the house of Abraham was to remain childless. Yet so it was. There was always a trial for Abraham's faith, but even his trials were blessed, for God 'blessed Abraham in all things'.

2 And Abraham said unto his eldest servant of his house, that ruled over all that he had, Put, I pray thee, thy hand under my thigh:

According to the Eastern manner of swearing.

3 And I will make thee swear by the LORD, the God of heaven, and the God of the earth, that thou shalt not take a wife unto my son of the daughters of the Canaanites, among whom I dwell:

This holy man was careful of the purity of his family; he knew what an ill-effect a Canaanitish wife might have upon his son, and also upon his offspring. He was, therefore, particularly careful here. I would that all parents were the same.

4-5 But thou shalt go unto my country, and to my kindred, and take a wife unto my son Isaac. And the servant said unto him, Peradventure the woman will not be willing to follow me unto this land: must I needs bring thy son again unto the land from whence thou camest?

The servant was very careful. Those that swear too readily they know not what, will ere long swear till they care not what. Better still is it for the Christian to remember the word of Christ to swear not at all, neither by heaven, nor by earth, nor by any other oath. Doubtless the doctrine of the Saviour is that all oaths of every sort are lawful to the Christian, but if they ever be taken, it should be with deep circumspection and with earnest prayerfulness, that there be no mistake about the matter.

6 And Abraham said unto him, Beware thou that thou bring not my son thither again.

He knew that God had called him and his kindred to inherit the land of Canaan, and, therefore, he was not willing that they should go back to their former dwelling-places.

7 The LORD God of heaven, which took me from my father's house, and from the land of my kindred, and which spake unto me, and that sware unto me, saying, Unto thy seed will I give this land; he shall send his angel before thee, and thou shalt take a wife unto my son from thence.

What simple faith! This was the very glory of Abraham's faith: it was so simple, so childlike. It might be many miles to Padanaram, but it does not matter to faith. 'My God will send his angel.' Oh! we are always making difficulties and suggesting hardships; but if our faith were in lively exercise, we should do God's will far more readily. 'Who art thou, O great mountain? before Zerubbabel thou shalt become a plain' [Zechariah 4:7]. Brethren, let us be of good heart and of good courage in all matters, for doubtless the angel of God will go before us.

8-11 And if the woman will not be willing to follow thee, then thou shalt be clear from this my oath: only bring not my son thither again. And the servant put his hand under the thigh of Abraham his master, and sware to him concerning that matter. And the servant took ten camels of the camels of his master, and departed; for all the goods of his master were in his hand: and he arose, and went to Mesopotamia, unto the city of Nahor. And he made his camels to kneel down without the city by a well of water at the time of the evening, even the time that women go out to draw water.

Now I think I may freely say that this looks something like what we call 'a wild-goose chase'. He was to go and find a wife for a young man left at home; he knew nothing of the people among whom he was to sojourn, but he believed that the angel of God would guide him aright. What ought he to do, now he had come near to the time when the decision must be made? He should seek counsel of God; observe that he did so.

12-14 And he said, O LORD God of my master Abraham, I pray thee, send me good speed this day, and shew kindness unto my master Abraham. Behold, I stand here by the well of water; and the daughters of the men of the city come out to draw water: And let it come to pass, that the damsel to whom I shall say, Let down thy pitcher, I pray thee, that I may drink; and she shall say, Drink, and I will give thy camels drink also: let the same be she that thou hast appointed for thy servant Isaac; and thereby shall I know that thou hast shewed kindness unto my master.

I do not know that he is to be imitated in setting a sign to God; perhaps not, but he did his best; he left the matter with God, and a thing is always in good hands when it is left with him. There is a deal of wisdom in this sign, however. Why did he not say, 'The damsel that shall first offer me to drink'? No; she might be a little too forward, and a forward woman was not a fit spouse for the good and meditative Isaac. He himself was to address her first, and then she must be ready, with all cheerfulness, to do far more than he asks. She was to offer him to drink and draw water for his camels. She would thus not be afraid of work, she would be courteous, and she would be kind; all these meeting in one might show him, and by this test he might very wisely discover, that she was a fitting woman for Isaac and might become his spouse.

15 And it came to pass, before he had done speaking, —

Aye, he did not know that promise, 'While they are yet speaking I will hear' [Isaiah 65:24], but God keeps his promises before he makes them; therefore, I am sure he will keep them after he has made them.

15-16 that, behold, Rebekah came out, who was born to Bethuel, son of Milcah, the wife of Nahor, Abraham's brother, with her pitcher upon her shoulder. And the damsel was very fair to look upon, a virgin, neither had any man known her: and she went down to the well, and filled her pitcher, and came up.

And so on; I need not read the rest of the story, because we now find that, through earnest prayer, the good servant has been rightly led.

GENESIS 27:1-29

Gen. 27:1-4 And it came to pass, that when Isaac was old, and his eyes were dim, so that he could not see, he called Esau his eldest son, and said unto him, My son: and he said unto him,

Behold, here am I. And he said, Behold now, I am old, I know not the day of my death: Now therefore take, I pray thee, thy weapons, thy quiver and thy bow, and go out to the field, and take me some venison; And make me savoury meat, such as I love, and bring it to me, that I may eat; that my soul may bless thee before I die.

A sad misfortune to lose the sight of the eyes! How greatly, how much more than we do, ought we to thank God for the prolongation of our sight, and it has been well remarked by one of our greatest men of science that 'we seldom hear Christian men thank God as they should for the use of spectacles in these modern times'. A philosopher has written a long paper concerning the blessings which he found in old age from this invention, and we, enabled still to read the Word when our sight decays, should be exceedingly grateful for it. After all, with all alleviations, it is a very great trial to be deprived of one's eyesight; but, those who are are in good company. Whilst that may include some of the greatest divines in modern history, they have here one of the best of men — one of the patriarchs, whose eyes were dim so that he could not see. He seems to have had some sort of mistiness of soul about this time, which was far worse, and so he desired to give the blessing to Esau, whom God had determined should never have it.

5-11 And Rebekah heard when Isaac spake to Esau his son. And Esau went to the field to hunt for venison, and to bring it. And Rebekah spake unto Jacob her son, saying, Behold, I heard thy father speak unto Esau thy brother, saying, Bring me venison, and make me savoury meat, that I may eat, and bless thee before the LORD before my death. Now therefore, my son, obey my voice according to that which I command thee. Go now to the flock, and fetch me from thence two good kids of the goats; and I will make them savoury meat for thy father, such as he loveth: And thou shalt bring it to thy father, that he may eat, and that he may bless thee before his death. And Jacob said to Rebekah his mother, Behold, Esau my brother is a hairy man, and I am a smooth man:

He does not appear to have raised any objection to what she proposed on moral grounds, but only on the ground of the difficulty of it and the likelihood of being discovered. It only shows how low the moral sense may be in some who, nevertheless, have a desire towards God and have a faith in him. In those darker days we can hardly expect to find so much of the excellences of the spirit as we ought to find nowadays in those who possess the spirit of God fully.

12-15 My father peradventure will feel me, and I shall seem to him as a deceiver; and I shall bring a curse upon me, and not a blessing. And his mother said unto him, Upon me be thy curse, my son: only obey my voice, and go fetch me them. And he went, and fetched, and brought them to his mother: and his mother made savoury meat, such as his father loved. And Rebekah took goodly raiment of her eldest son Esau, which were with her in the house, and put them upon Jacob her younger son:

And Esau, altogether a man of the world, one very like the sons of other families around about, took care to adorn himself in goodly raiment. It seems always more becoming to the worldling than the Christian. Jacob had a suit good enough for this occasion, but the worldly man had not. I would that those who fear God were less careful about the adornments of their persons. There are far better ornaments than gold can buy — ornaments neat, and raiment comely — may we all possess them.

16-19 And she put the skins of the kids of the goats upon his hands, and upon the smooth of his neck: And she gave the savoury meat and the bread, which she had prepared, into the hand of her son Jacob. And he came unto his father, and said, My father: and he said, Here am I; who art thou, my son? And Jacob said unto his father, I am Esau thy first born; I have done according as thou badest me: arise, I pray thee, sit and eat of my venison, that thy soul may bless me.

Which, whatever may be said about it, was a plain lie, and is not to be excused upon any theory whatever. It was as much a sin in Jacob as it would be in us, except that perhaps he had less light, and the general cunning of those who surrounded him may have made it more easy with him and a less tax on conscience for him to do this than it would be in our case. 'I am Esau', said he. Why is all this recorded in the Bible? It is not to the credit of these men. No! the Holy Spirit does not write for the credit of man. He writes for the glory of God's grace. He writes for the warning of believers now, and these things are examples unto us that we may avoid the blots and flaws in good men and may, thereby, ourselves become more what we should be.

20 And Isaac said unto his son, How is it that thou hast found it so quickly, my son? And he said, Because the LORD thy God brought it to me.

Here he draws God's name into this lie, and this is worse still.

21-29 And Isaac said unto Jacob, Come near, I pray thee, that I may feel thee, my son, whether thou be my very son Esau or not. And Jacob went near unto Isaac his father; and he felt him, and said, The voice is Jacob's voice, but the hands are the hands of Esau. And he discerned him not, because his hands were hairy, as his brother Esau's hands: so he blessed him. And he said, Art thou my very son Esau? And he said, I am. And he said, Bring it near to me, and I will eat of my son's venison, that my soul may bless thee. And he brought it near to him, and he did eat: and he brought him wine and he drank. And his father Isaac said unto him, Come near now, and kiss me, my son. And he came near, and kissed him: and he smelled the smell of his raiment, and blessed him, and said, See, the smell of my son is as the smell of a field which the LORD hath blessed: Therefore God give thee of the dew of heaven, and the fatness of the earth, and plenty of corn and wine: Let people serve thee, and nations bow down to thee: be lord over thy brethren, and let thy mother's sons bow down to thee: cursed be every one that curseth thee, and blessed be he that blesseth thee.

So he tied his own hands: he could not revoke his blessing, or, had he done so, he would have brought the curse upon himself.

GENESIS 32

Gen. 32:1 And Jacob went on his way, and the angels of God met him.

What an encouragement the visit of these angels must have been to Jacob after the strife which he had had with Laban! But, dear friends, angels often come to meet us, though we know it not. As in the old classic story, the poor man said, 'This is a plain hut, but God has been here', so we may say of every Christian's cottage, 'Though it be poor, an angel has come here', for David says, 'The angel of the Lord encampeth round about them that fear him, and delivereth them.' As the angels of God met Jacob, I trust that, if you have come here after some stern battle and trial and difficulty, you may find the angels of God meeting you here. They do come into the assemblies of the saints. Paul tells us that the woman ought to have her head covered in the assembly 'because of the angels', that is, because they are there to see that all things are done decently and in order.

2 And when Jacob saw them, he said, This is God's host: and he called the name of that place Mahanaim.

He gave it a name to commemorate God's having sent the angels and called it 'two camps' or 'two hosts'.

3 And Jacob sent messengers before him to Esau his brother unto the land of Seir, the country of Edom.

He is out of one trouble with Laban; now he is into another with Esau. Well did John Bunyan say,

> *A Christian man is seldom long at ease;*
> *When one trouble's gone, another doth him seize.*

4-5 And he commanded them, saying, Thus shall ye speak unto my lord Esau; Thy servant Jacob saith thus, I have sojourned with Laban, and stayed there until now: And I have oxen, and asses, flocks, and menservants, and womenservants: and I have sent to tell my lord, that I may find grace in thy sight.

This is very respectful language, and rather obsequious, too; but, when a man knows that he has done wrong to another, he ought to be prepared to humble himself to the injured individual. Though it happened long ago, yet Jacob really had injured his brother Esau; it was but right that, in meeting him again, he should put himself into a humble position before him. There are some proud people who, when they know that they have done wrong yet will not own it. It is very hard to end a quarrel when one will not yield and the other feels that he will not either. But there is good hope of things going right when Jacob, who is the better of the two brothers, is also the humbler of the two.

6-7 And the messengers returned to Jacob, saying, We came to thy brother Esau, and also he cometh to meet thee, and four hundred men with him. Then Jacob was greatly afraid and distressed: —

And well he might be, for an angry brother with 400 fierce followers must mean mischief.

7-8 and he divided the people that was with him, and the flocks, and herds, and the camels, into two bands; And said, If Esau come to the one company, and smite it, then the other company which is left shall escape.

This is characteristic of Jacob. He was a man of plans and arrangements, a man of considerable craftiness, which some people nowadays call 'prudence'. He used means, and he sometimes used them a little too much. Perhaps he did so in this case; but, at the same time, he was a man of faith, and therefore, he betook himself to prayer.

9-12 And Jacob said, O God of my father Abraham, and God of my father Isaac, the LORD which saidst unto me, Return unto thy country, and to thy kindred, and I will deal well with thee: I am not worthy of the least of all the mercies, and of all the truth, which thou hast shewed unto thy servant; for with my staff I passed over this Jordan; and now I am become two bands. Deliver me, I pray thee, from the hand of my brother, from the hand of Esau: for I fear him, lest he will come and smite me, and the mother with the children. And thou saidst, I will surely do thee good, and make thy seed as the sand of the sea, which cannot be numbered for multitude.

A prayer most humble, most direct in its petitions, and also full of faith. That was a grand argument for him to use: 'Thou saidst, I will surely do thee good.' This is one of the mightiest pleas that we can urge in praying to God: 'Do as thou hast said. Remember the word unto thy servant, upon which thou hast caused me to hope.' O brethren, if you can remind God of his own promise, you must win the day, for promised mercies are sure mercies:

> *As well might he his being quit,*
> *As break his promise, or forget.*

'Hath he said, and shall he not do it?' Only for this will he be enquired of by the house of Israel to do it for them, and we must take care that we call his promise to mind, and plead it at the mercy seat.

13-21 And he lodged there that same night; and took of that which came to his hand a present for Esau his brother; Two hundred she goats, and twenty he goats, two hundred ewes, and twenty rams, Thirty milch camels with their colts, forty kine, and ten bulls, twenty she asses, and ten foals. And he delivered them into the hand of his servants, every drove by themselves; and said unto his servants, Pass over before me, and put a space betwixt drove and drove. And he commanded the foremost, saying, When Esau my brother meeteth thee, and asketh thee, saying, Whose art thou? and whither goest thou? and whose are these before thee? Then thou shalt say, They be thy servant Jacob's; it is a present sent unto my lord Esau: and, behold, also he is behind us. And so commanded he the second, and the third, and all that followed the droves, saying, On this manner shall ye speak unto Esau, when ye find him. And say ye moreover, Behold, thy servant Jacob is behind us. For he said, I will appease him with the present that goeth before me, and afterward I will see his face; peradventure he will accept of me. So went the present over before him: and himself lodged that night in the company.

If Jacob had been true to his faith in God, he would have dispensed with these very prudent preparations; for, after all, the faithfulness of God was Jacob's best defense. It was from God that his safety came, and not from his own plotting, and planning, and scheming. There are some of you, dear brethren, who have minds that are naturally given to inventions and devices and plans and plots, and I believe that, where this is the case, you have more to battle against than those have who are of a simple mind, and who cast themselves more entirely upon the Lord. It is a blessed thing to be such a fool that you do not know anyone to trust in except your God. It is a sweet thing to be so weaned from your wisdom that you fall into the arms of God. Yet, if you do feel that it is right to make such plans as Jacob made, take care that you do what Jacob also did. Pray as well as plan, and if your plans be numerous, let your prayers be all the more fervent, lest the natural tendency of your constitution should degenerate into reliance upon the arm of flesh, and dependence upon your own wisdom, instead of absolute reliance upon God.

22-24 And he rose up that night, and took his two wives, and his two womenservants, and his eleven sons, and passed over the ford Jabbok. And he took them, and sent them over the brook, and sent over that he had. And Jacob was left alone; and there wrestled a man with him until the breaking of the day.

It was the man Christ Jesus putting on the form of manhood before the time when he would actually be incarnate, and the wrestling seems to have been more on his side than on Jacob's, for it is not said that Jacob wrestled, but that 'there wrestled a man with him'. There was something that needed to be taken out of Jacob — his strength and his craftiness; and this angel came to get it out of him. But, on the other hand, Jacob spied his opportunity, and finding the angel wrestling with him, he in his turn began to wrestle with the angel.

25 And when he saw that he prevailed not against him, he touched the hollow of his thigh; and the hollow of Jacob's thigh was out of joint, as he wrestled with him.

So that he was made painfully to realize his own weakness while he was putting forth all his strength.

26 And he said, Let me go, for the day breaketh. And he said, I will not let thee go, except thou bless me.

Bravely said, O Jacob! And ye sons of Jacob, learn to say the same. You may have what you will if you can speak thus to the covenant angel, 'I will not let thee go, except thou bless me.'

27-28 And he said unto him, What is thy name? And he said, Jacob. And he said, Thy name shall be called no more Jacob, —

A supplanter —

28 but Israel: —

A prince of God —

28-29 for as a prince hast thou power with God and with men, and hast prevailed. And Jacob asked him, and said, Tell me, I pray thee, thy name. —

That has often been the request of God's people: they have wanted to know God's wondrous name. The Jews superstitiously believe that we have lost the sound of the name of Jehovah — that the name is unpronounceable now altogether. We think not; but, certainly, no man knows the nature of God, and understands him, but he to whom the Son shall reveal him. Perhaps Jacob's request had somewhat of curiosity in it, so the angel would not grant it.

29 And he said, Wherefore is it that thou dost ask after my name? And he blessed him there.

He did not give him what he asked for, but he gave him something better, and, in like manner, if the Lord does not open up a dark doctrine to you, but gives you a bright privilege, that will be better for you.

30-32 And Jacob called the name of the place Peniel: for I have seen God face to face, and my life is preserved. And as he passed over Penuel the sun rose upon him, and he halted upon his thigh. Therefore the children of Israel eat not of the sinew which shrank, which is upon the hollow of the thigh, unto this day: because he touched the hollow of Jacob's thigh in the sinew that shrank.

GENESIS 32

Gen. 32:1 And Jacob went on his way, and the angels of God met him.

When he left the promised land, he had a vision of angels, ascending and descending upon the ladder, as if to bid him farewell. Now that he is going back, the angels are there again to speed him on his way home to the land of the covenant, the land which the Lord had promised to give to Abraham and his seed.

2 And when Jacob saw them, he said, This is God's host: and he called the name of that place Mahanaim.

The marginal reading is 'Two hosts, or, camps'. The angels of the Lord were encamping round about the man who feared him, though there had been much in his character and conduct which the Lord could not approve.

3 And Jacob sent messengers before him to Esau his brother unto the land of Seir, the country of Edom.

After a visit from angels, afflictions and trials often come. John Bunyan wrote, as I have often reminded you:

> *The Christian man is seldom long at ease;*
> *When one trouble's gone, another doth him seize.*

And, though the rhyme is rather rough, the statement is perfectly true. Full often, we are hardly out of one trial before we are into another.

4-5 And he commanded them, saying, Thus shall ye speak unto my lord Esau; Thy servant Jacob saith thus, I have sojourned with Laban, and stayed there until now: And I have oxen, and asses, flocks, and menservants, and womenservants: and I have sent to tell my lord, that I may find grace in thy sight.

It is very proper, when we have offended other people, and especially if we feel that we have done them wrong, as Jacob had done to Esau, that we should use the humblest terms concerning ourselves, and the best terms we can about those whom we have offended. Yet I must say that I do not like these terms that Jacob uses; they do not seem to me to be the right sort of language for a man of faith: 'My lord Esau, thy servant Jacob saith thus.' What business had God's favoured one to speak 'thus' to such a profane person as Esau, who for one morsel of meat sold his birthright? Surely, there was more of the Jacob policy than there was of the Israel faith in this form of speech.

6-7 And the messengers returned to Jacob, saying, We came to thy brother Esau, and also he cometh to meet thee, and four hundred men with him. Then Jacob was greatly afraid and distressed: —

'Four hundred men with him'! 'That must mean mischief to me, and my company. Surely, he is coming thus to avenge himself for the wrong I did him, long ago. My brother's heart is still hot with anger against me.' So, 'Jacob was greatly afraid and distressed.'

7-8 and he divided the people that was with him, and the flocks, and herds, and the camels, into two bands; And said, If Esau come to the one company, and smite it, then the other company which is left shall escape.

This man Jacob was always planning and scheming. See how he plots and arranges everything to the best advantage. I blame him not for this; yet, methinks he is to be blamed that he did not pray first. Surely, it would have been the proper order of things if the prayer had preceded the planning, but Jacob planned first and prayed afterwards. Well, even that was better than planning and not praying at all; so, there is something commendable in his action, though not without considerable qualification.

9 And Jacob said, O God of my father Abraham, and God of my father Isaac, the LORD —

Jacob uses that august name 'Jehovah' — 'the LORD'.

9-10 which saidst unto me, Return unto thy country, and to thy kindred, and I will deal well with thee: I am not worthy of the least of all the mercies, and of all the truth, which thou hast shewed unto thy servant; for with my staff I passed over this Jordan; and now I am become two bands.

Not even one servant had he with him when he fled away across the river; he was alone and unattended. Now he was coming back at the head of a great family, with troops of servants, an abundance of cattle and sheep, and all things that men think worth having. How greatly God had increased him and blessed him! He remembers that lonely departure from the home country, and he cannot help contrasting it with his present prosperity.

11-13 Deliver me, I pray thee, from the hand of my brother, from the hand of Esau: for I fear him, lest he will come and smite me, and the mother with the children. And thou saidst, I will surely do thee good, and make thy seed as the sand of the sea, which cannot be numbered for multitude. And he lodged there that same night; and took of that which came to his hand a present for Esau his brother;

There he is, planning again! And this time, perhaps, since he has prayed over the matter, he is planning more wisely than he did before, intending now to try to appease his brother's anger by a munificent 'present for Esau his brother'.

14-16 Two hundred she goats, and twenty he goats, two hundred ewes, and twenty rams, Thirty milch camels with their colts, forty kine, and ten bulls, twenty she asses, and ten foals. And he delivered them into the hand of his servants, every drove by themselves; and said unto his servants, Pass over before me, and put a space betwixt drove and drove.

This was true Oriental policy, in order that there might be time for his brother to look at the present in detail, and see it piece by piece, and so be the more struck with the size of it. Crafty Jacob always had more than enough of something and ability to plan, even when it was not done with wisdom. In this case, I think it was a wise arrangement, for which he is to be commended.

17-19 And he commanded the foremost, saying, When Esau my brother meeteth thee, and asketh thee, saying, Whose art thou? and whither goest thou? and whose are these before thee?

Then thou shalt say, They be thy servant Jacob's; it is a present sent unto my lord Esau: and, behold, also he is behind us. And so commanded he the second, and the third, and all that followed the droves, saying, On this manner shall ye speak unto Esau, when ye find him.

What care he takes about the whole affair! We cannot blame him, under the circumstances; yet, how much grander is the quiet, noble demeanour of Abraham, who trusts in God and leaves matters more in his hands! Yet, alas! even he tried plotting and scheming, more than once, but failed every time he did so.

20-24 And say ye moreover, Behold, thy servant Jacob is behind us. For he said, I will appease him with the present that goeth before me, and afterward I will see his face; peradventure he will accept of me. So went the present over before him: and himself lodged that night in the company. And he rose up that night, and took his two wives, and his two womenservants, and his eleven sons, and passed over the ford Jabbok. And he took them, and sent them over the brook, and sent over that he had. And Jacob was left alone; —

This was a very anxious time for him, the heaviest trial of his life seemed impending. He was dreading it more than he need have done, for God never meant the trouble he feared to come upon him at all. He was trembling under a dark cloud that was to pass over his head without bursting. No tempest of wrath was to break out of it upon him. However, we must admire Jacob in this one respect: with all his thought and care and planning and plotting, he did not neglect prayer. He felt that nothing he could do would be effectual without God's blessing. He had not reached the highest point of faith, though he had gone in the right direction a great deal further than many Christians. He now resolved to have a night of prayer, that he might win deliverance: 'Jacob was left alone.'

24 and there wrestled a man with him until the breaking of the day.

I suppose our Lord Jesus Christ did here, as on many other occasions preparatory to his full incarnation, assume a human form, and came thus to wrestle with the patriarch.

25 And when he saw that he prevailed not against him, he touched the hollow of his thigh; —

Where the column of the leg supports the body, and if that be disjointed, a man has lost all his strength. It was brave of Jacob thus to wrestle, but there was too much of self about it all. It was his own sufficiency that was wrestling with the God-man, Christ Jesus. Now comes the crisis which will make a change in the whole of Jacob's future life: 'He touched the hollow of his thigh.'

25 and the hollow of Jacob's thigh was out of joint, as he wrestled with him.

What can Jacob do now that the main bone of his leg is put out of joint? He cannot even stand up any longer in the great wrestling match. What can he do?

26 And he said, Let me go, for the day breaketh. And he said, I will not let thee go, except thou bless me.

It is evident that, as soon as he felt that he must fall, he grasped the other 'Man' with a kind of death-grip, and would not let him go. Now, in his weakness, he will prevail. While he was so strong, he won not the blessing; but, when he became utter weakness, then did he conquer.

27 And he said unto him, What is thy name? And he said, Jacob.

That is, a supplanter, as poor Esau well knew.

28 And he said, Thy name shall be called no more Jacob, but Israel: —

That is, a prince of God.

28 for as a prince hast thou power with God and with men, and hast prevailed.

Jacob was the prince with the disjointed limb, and that is exactly what a Christian is. He wins, he conquers, when his weakness becomes supreme, and he is conscious of it.

29 And Jacob asked him, and said, Tell me, I pray thee, thy name. And he said, Wherefore is it that thou dost ask after my name? And he blessed him there.

There are limits to all human intercourse with God. We must not go where vain curiosity would lead us, else will he have to say to us, as he did to Jacob, 'Wherefore is it that thou dost ask after my name?'

30 And Jacob called the name of the place Peniel: for I have seen God face to face, and my life is preserved.

How he must have trembled to think that he had the daring, perhaps his fears made him call it the presumption, actually to wrestle with God himself; for, he was conscious now that it was no mere angel, but 'the Angel of the covenant', the Lord himself, with whom he had wrestled.

31 And as he passed over Penuel the sun rose upon him, and he halted upon his thigh.

The memorial of his weakness was to be with him as long as he lived. People would ask, 'How came the halting gait of that princely man?' And the answer would be, 'It was by his weakness that he won his princedom, he became Israel, a prince of God, when his thigh was put out of joint.' How pleased would you and I be to go halting all our days with such weakness as Jacob had, if we might also have the blessing that he thus won!

32 Therefore the children of Israel eat not of the sinew which shrank, which is upon the hollow of the thigh, unto this day: because he touched the hollow of Jacob's thigh in the sinew that shrank.

GENESIS 45:1-13; SONG OF SOLOMON 1:1-7; 3:1-5

Gen. 45:1-2 Then Joseph could not refrain himself before all them that stood by him; and he cried, Cause every man to go out from me. And there stood no man with him, while Joseph made himself known unto his brethren. And he wept aloud: —

Emotion long pent up grows violent; and when at last it does burst forth, it cannot be restrained: 'He wept aloud.'

2-3 and the Egyptians and the house of Pharaoh heard. And Joseph said unto his brethren, I am Joseph; doth my father yet live? And his brethren could not answer him; for they were troubled at his presence.

What a rush of thoughts must have passed through their minds when they remembered all their unkind behaviour toward him! There is no wonder that 'they were troubled at his presence'.

4 And Joseph said unto his brethren, Come near to me, I pray you. —

He pleads with them, he who was far greater than they — a prince among peasants — now prays to them; and is it not wonderful that the Lord Jesus, our infinitely-greater Brother, at times pleads with us, even as he said to the woman at the well, 'Give me to drink'? Joseph said unto his brethren, 'Come near to me, I pray you.'

4-5 And they came near. And he said, I am Joseph your brother, whom ye sold into Egypt. Now therefore be not grieved, nor angry with yourselves, that ye sold me hither: for God did send me before you to preserve life.

'You did very wrong, but I say nothing about that, for I want you to notice how God has over-ruled your action, how your sin has been made to be the means of your preservation and the preservation of many besides: "God did send me before you to preserve life."'

6 For these two years hath the famine been in the land: and yet there are five years, in the which there shall neither be earing nor harvest.

There were to be five more dreary years of utter desolation and want.

7 And God sent me before you to preserve you a posterity in the earth, and to save your lives by a great deliverance.

How wonderfully those two things meet in practical harmony — the free will of man and the predestination of God! Man acts just as freely and just as guiltily as if there were no predestination whatever; and God ordains, arranges, supervises, and overrules, just as accurately as if there were no free will in the universe. There are some purblind people who only believe one or other of these two truths; yet, they are both true, and the one is as true as the other. I believe that much of the theology which is tinged with free will is true, and I know that the teaching which fully proclaims electing love and sovereign grace is also true. You may find much of both these truths in the Scriptures. The fault lies in trying to compress all truth under either of those two heads. These men were verily guilty for selling their brother, yet God was verily wise in permitting him to be sold. The inference which Joseph draws from their misconduct is, of course, an inference of love. Love may not be always logical, but it is sweetly consoling, as it must have been in this case.

8 So now it was not you that sent me hither, but God: and he hath made me a father to Pharaoh, and lord of all his house, and a ruler throughout all the land of Egypt.

See how Joseph traces God's hand in his whole career.

9 Haste ye, and go up to my father, and say unto him, Thus saith thy son Joseph, God hath made me lord of all Egypt: come down unto me, tarry not:

See how love attracts; Joseph must have his brothers near him, now he wants to have his father also near. 'Go up to my father, and say unto him, "Come down unto me."' See how great love turns pleader again; he who said to his brethren, 'Come near to me', sends to his father the message, 'Come down unto me.'

10 And thou shalt dwell in the land of Goshen, and thou shalt be near unto me, thou, and thy children, and thy children's children, and thy flocks, and thy herds, and all that thou hast:

Our common saying, 'Love me, love my dog', is very true. Love me, love even my flocks and my herds. So the blessing of God extends to all that his chosen people have; not only to their children, but to all that they possess.

11-13 And there will I nourish thee; for yet there are five years of famine; lest thou, and thy household, and all that thou hast, come to poverty. And, behold, your eyes see, and the eyes of my brother Benjamin, that it is my mouth that speaketh unto you. And ye shall tell my father of all my glory in Egypt, and of all that ye have seen; and ye shall haste and bring down my father hither.

Love is impatient to have the object of its affection brought near.

Now we will read two short portions out of the Song of Solomon, from which you will see how love evermore craves for nearness to the loved one. The Song opens thus:

S. of S. 1:1-4 The song of songs, which is Solomon's. Let him kiss me with the kisses of his mouth: for thy love is better than wine. Because of the savour of thy good ointments thy name is as ointment poured forth, therefore do the virgins love thee. Draw me, we will run after thee: —

Still is love pleading, you see, but here it is the other side pleading for nearness, the lowly one crying for help to get nearer to the heavenly Bridegroom: 'Draw me, we will run after thee.'

4-5 the king hath brought me into his chambers: we will be glad and rejoice in thee, we will remember thy love more than wine: the upright love thee. I am black, but comely, O ye daughters of Jerusalem, as the tents of Kedar, as the curtains of Solomon.

The spouse was black in herself; sunburnt through her toil and hard suffering, yet lovely in the sight of her Beloved, and comely to look upon 'as the curtains of Solomon'.

6-7 Look not upon me, because I am black, because the sun hath looked upon me: my mother's children were angry with me; they made me the keeper of the vineyards; but mine own vineyard have I not kept. Tell me, O thou whom my soul loveth, where thou feedest, where thou makest thy flock to rest at noon: for why should I be as one that turneth aside by the flocks of thy companions?

Still is there that same craving for nearness to the Beloved. Since we love Christ, we desire to be with him; we cannot bear his absence: 'Tell me, O thou whom my soul loveth, where thou feedest.'

See, dear friends, how this same seeking after the Beloved comes out in another shape in the third chapter of the Song.

S. of S. 3:1 By night on my bed I sought him whom my soul loveth: I sought him, but I found him not.

Sometimes, the most eager search does not at once obtain its end. For wise reasons, Christ sometimes hides himself from his seeking people.

2-5 I will rise now, and go about the city in the streets, and in the broad ways I will seek him whom my soul loveth: I sought him, but I found him not. The watchmen that go about the city found me: to whom I said, Saw ye him whom my soul loveth? It was but a little that I passed from them, but I found him whom my soul loveth: I held him, and would not let him go, until I had brought him into my mother's house, and into the chamber of her that conceived me. I charge you, O ye daughters of Jerusalem, by the roes, and by the hinds of the field, —

'By everything that is timid, and delicate, and pure, and full of love, I charge you, O ye daughters of Jerusalem.'

5 that ye stir not up, nor awake my love, till he please.

'I have found my Beloved, and I would not lose him again; he has come to me, so I will not grieve him, and drive him away.' That is the one of our reading: 'Come near to me, I pray thee; and when thou comest near me, keep by me still.'

GENESIS 45:9-28; JOHN 5:24-44

Gen. 45:9 Haste ye, and go up to my father, and say unto him, Thus saith thy son Joseph, God hath made me lord of all Egypt: come down unto me, tarry not:

Joseph, having made himself known to his brethren, bids them return to their father and bring him down to Egypt to see his long-lost son.

10-11 And thou shalt dwell in the land of Goshen, and thou shalt be near unto me, thou, and thy children, and thy children's children, and thy flocks, and thy herds, and all that thou hast: And there will I nourish thee; for yet there are five years of famine; lest thou, and thy household, and all that thou hast, come to poverty.

It is just like Joseph to speak thus kindly, and to put the invitation so attractively to his father: 'Thou shalt be near unto me.' That would be the greatest joy of all to old Jacob; and this is the greatest joy to a sinner when he comes to Christ, our great Joseph, 'Thou shalt be near unto me.' It is not merely that he gives us the land of Goshen to dwell in, but he promises that we shall be near unto him, and that is best of all.

12-22 And, behold, your eyes see, and the eyes of my brother Benjamin, that it is my mouth that speaketh unto you. And ye shall tell my father of all my glory in Egypt, and of all that ye have seen; and ye shall haste and bring down my father hither. And he fell upon his brother Benjamin's neck, and wept; and Benjamin wept upon his neck. Moreover he kissed all his brethren, and wept upon them: and after that his brethren talked with him. And the fame thereof was heard in Pharaoh's house, saying, Joseph's brethren are come: and it pleased Pharaoh well, and his servants. And Pharaoh said unto Joseph, Say unto thy brethren, This do ye; lade your beasts, and go, get you unto the land of Canaan; And take your father and your households, and come unto me: and I will give you the good of the land of Egypt, and ye shall eat the fat of the land. Now thou art commanded, this do ye; take you wagons out of the land of Egypt for your little ones, and for your wives, and bring your father, and come. Also regard not your stuff; for the good of all the land of Egypt is yours. And the children of Israel did so: and Joseph gave them wagons, according to the commandment of Pharaoh, and gave them provision for the way. To all of them he gave each man changes of raiment; but to Benjamin he gave three hundred pieces of silver, and five changes of raiment.

Benjamin was his full brother, so he loved him best, and gave him most.

23-24 And to his father he sent after this manner; ten asses laden with the good things of Egypt, and ten she asses laden with corn and bread and meat for his father by the way. So he sent his brethren away, and they departed: and he said unto them, See that ye fall not out by the way.

This was a sure sign that Joseph knew his brethren, and they might well recognize him even by that precept, for their consciences must have told them that it had been their common habit to fall out either with or without occasion, so he bids them not to do so.

25-28 And they went up out of Egypt, and came into the land of Canaan unto Jacob their father, and told him, saying, Joseph is yet alive, and he is governor over all the land of Egypt. And Jacob's heart fainted, for he believed them not. And they told him all the words of Joseph, which he had said unto them: and when he saw the wagons which Joseph had sent to carry him, the spirit of Jacob their father revived: And Israel said, It is enough; Joseph my son is yet alive: I will go and see him before I die.

See how quickly the patriarch changes from Jacob into Israel; when his spirit is revived, he becomes Israel.

Now we are going to read in the Gospel according to John, the fifth chapter, beginning at the twenty-fourth verse.

John 5:24 Verily, verily, I say unto you, He that heareth my word, and believeth on him that sent me, hath everlasting life, —

If we truly believe the word of Christ and trust in him who sent his Son into the world, we have at this moment everlasting life.

24 and shall not come into condemnation; but is passed from death unto life.

What a grand verse this is! It is worthy to be written in letters of gold at every street corner; would that we all knew the fulness of its meaning by heartfelt experience!

25-30 Verily, verily, I say unto you, The hour is coming, and now is, when the dead shall hear the voice of the Son of God: and they that hear shall live. For as the Father hath life in himself;

so hath he given to the Son to have life in himself; And hath given him authority to execute judgment also, because he is the Son of man. Marvel not at this: for the hour is coming, in the which all that are in the graves shall hear his voice, And shall come forth; they that have done good, unto the resurrection of life; and they that have done evil, unto the resurrection of damnation. I can of mine own self do nothing: as I hear, I judge: and my judgment is just; because I seek not mine own will, but the will of the Father which hath sent me.

Christ as Mediator did the will of the Father and yet also did his own will, for his will was always the same as his Father's.

31 If I bear witness of myself, my witness is not true.

He did bear witness to himself by his miracles, but that was not the witness upon which he relied, nor was it the only witness to the truth of his mission.

32-40 There is another that beareth witness of me; and I know that the witness which he witnesseth of me is true. Ye sent unto John, and he bare witness unto the truth. But I receive not testimony from man: but these things I say, that ye might be saved. He was a burning and a shining light: and ye were willing for a season to rejoice in his light. But I have greater witness than that of John: for the works which the Father hath given me to finish, the same works that I do, bear witness of me, that the Father hath sent me. And the Father himself, which hath sent me, hath borne witness of me. Ye have neither heard his voice at any time, nor seen his shape. And ye have not his word abiding in you: for whom he hath sent, him ye believe not. Search the scriptures; for in them ye think ye have eternal life: and they are they which testify of me. And ye will not come to me, that ye might have life.

They were great Bible readers, great students of the letter, but they would not come to Christ; and hence the Scriptures themselves became a sepulchre in which they were entombed.

41-44 I receive not honour from men. But I know you, that ye have not the love of God in you. I am come in my Father's name, and ye receive me not: if another shall come in his own name, him ye will receive. How can ye believe, which receive honour one of another, and seek not the honour that cometh from God only?

Some men find it difficult to believe in Christ because they are always seeking honour for themselves; desire for the praise of men often blinds the mind and prejudices the spirit. How boldly our great Master speaks! There is no flattery on his lips. He is the faithful and true Witness, the very Word of God. Oh, that all men would give heed to his message!

GENESIS 49:1-28

Gen. 49:1-2 And Jacob called unto his sons, and said, Gather yourselves together, that I may tell you that which shall befall you in the last days. Gather yourselves together, and hear, ye sons of Jacob; and hearken unto Israel your father.

It must have been a great comfort to the old man to have all his twelve sons with him. What a quiet answer this was to his former unbelief! They were all there, yet he could remember the time when he had said, 'Me have ye bereaved of my children: Joseph is not, and Simeon is not, and ye will take Benjamin away.' Ah! we also shall have in our latter days to chide ourselves for our foolish unbelief. 'Jacob called unto his sons', so he was not bereaved after all. They are all here, Jacob. It falls to the lot of few fathers to have twelve sons, and to fewer still to have all twelve of them gathered about his deathbed. 'Gather yourselves together.' They were to keep together as a family; and shall not the people of God keep together? Come away from the world, beloved, but come close to one another; be one household; be it your delight to assemble around your elder Brother, the Lord Jesus Christ. 'Gather yourselves together, that I may tell you that which shall befall you in the last days.' We are not told nowadays everything about the future, but much of the future is unfolded to us in the great principles of the law and the gospel, and we may learn very much of holy foresight by coming to the oracles of God.

3 Reuben, thou art my firstborn, my might, and the beginning of my strength, the excellency of dignity, and the excellency of power:

The patriarch fixes his eyes on his firstborn; he must say something sharp that would dishonour him, but he does not deny him the rights of birthright. He clothes him with the robes and the jewels of primogeniture, and then he strips him:

4 Unstable as water, thou shalt not excel; because thou wentest up to thy father's bed; then defiledst thou it: he went up to my couch.

So a man may have great opportunities, and yet lose them. Uncontrolled passions may make him very little who otherwise might have been great. Reuben was 'the excellency of dignity and the excellency of power', yet his father had to say to him, 'Thou shalt not excel.'

5 Simeon and Levi —

They stood next according to the order of birth: 'Simeon and Levi' —

5 are brethren; —

They are very much like each other.

5-7 instruments of cruelty are in their habitations. O my soul, come not thou into their secret; unto their assembly, mine honour, be not thou united: for in their anger they slew a man, and in their selfwill they digged down a wall. Cursed be their anger, for it was fierce; and their wrath, for it was cruel: I will divide them in Jacob, and scatter them in Israel.

Hence we do not read of the tribe of Simeon in the blessing of Moses at the end of Deuteronomy; but the Levites had this curse turned into a blessing, for, though they were scattered, yet they were scattered as priests and instructors to the other tribes. Happy is that man who, though he begins with a dark shadow resting upon him, so lives as to turn even that shadow into bright sunlight. Levi gained a blessing at the hands of Moses, one of the richest blessings of any of the tribes. This holy man, Jacob, in dying, did not express himself according to the rules of natural affection, but he yielded himself up to the Spirit of God. Hence, he had to say very much that must have been very bitter for a father to say, and he said it in all faithfulness, being taught of the Spirit concerning things to come.

8 Judah, —

Now the patriarch changes his tone, for he has come to that tribe which would take the birthright, out of which the Christ would come: 'Judah' —

8 thou art he whom thy brethren shall praise: —

They praised God for him; they praised God by him; they praised

God in him. He is the type of Jesus, of whom we can say all this with great emphasis.

8 thy hand shall be in the neck of thine enemies; thy father's children shall bow down before thee.

In the person of David, in the long line of kings of the tribe of Judah, all this came true; and in the person of the great Son of David, the Lord Jesus Christ, all this has come true to a very high degree.

9 Judah is a lion's whelp: from the prey, my son, thou art gone up: he stooped down, he couched as a lion, and as an old lion; who shall rouse him up?

The coat of arms of Judah was a lion couchant, in the fulness of his strength, keeping still, waiting to spring upon his adversary. Our Lord Christ is such a lion today: 'the Lion of the tribe of Judah' couchant, lying down, 'Who shall rouse him up?' Ah! if he be once fully aroused what power will he put forth when he shall spring upon his adversaries?

10 The sceptre shall not depart from Judah, nor a lawgiver from between his feet, until Shiloh come; and unto him shall the gathering of the people be.

Jacob's eyes were dim, but he could see a very long way. He could see to the coming of Christ, the Shiloh, the Pacificator, the Peacemaker; he could see that day when the Jews would cry, 'We have no king but Caesar', for the Shiloh would have come, and the sceptre would have departed from Judah's tribe. 'Unto him shall the gathering of the people be.' Oh, that it might be so today! May many be gathered to Christ! He is the true centre, and we gather unto him. May the divisions of the church be soon healed by a general gathering unto Christ, who alone is the centre of the church. 'Unto him shall the gathering of the people be.'

11-12 Binding his foal unto the vine, and his ass's colt unto the choice vine; he washed his garments in wine, and his clothes in the blood of grapes: His eyes shall be red with wine, and his teeth white with milk.

They were to have a land in which would be milk for babes and wine for strong men; surely this land is 'thy land, O Emmanuel!' What nourishing milk there is in the gospel, and what exhilarating wine for those who know the love of Christ!

13 Zebulun shall dwell at the haven of the sea; and he shall be for an haven of ships; and his border shall be unto Zidon.

When the land was divided by lot, the lot was disposed by God to the complete fulfilment of Jacob's prophecy. Many things may seem to be left to chance, but they are not; the hand of God still guides and controls. This blessing is very suggestive: 'Zebulun shall dwell at the haven of the sea; and he shall be for a haven of ships.' If God puts you by the mind that you are a haven for ships, the Lord, in his providence, fixes your position. See that you turn it to account for the good of others.

14-15 Issachar is a strong ass couching down between two burdens: and he saw that rest was good, and the land that it was pleasant; and bowed his shoulder to bear, and became a servant unto tribute.

Issachar's was a poor case; he was so idle, so fond of rest, that he was willing to become a servant unto tribute. This seems hardly a blessing, yet it was true of Issachar. He liked couching down between two burdens much better than bearing either one of them, yet he had to bow 'his shoulder to bear, and became a servant unto tribute'.

16-17 Dan shall judge his people, as one of the tribes of Israel. Dan shall be a serpent by the way, an adder in the path, that biteth the horse heels, so that his rider shall fall backward.

This tribe would show more cunning than courage; it would excel rather in the strategy of war than in the force of arms. Here the old man paused, and refreshed himself by saying —

18 I have waited for thy salvation, O LORD.

What a happy breathing-space is this! When you and I also are near our journey's end, may we be able to say, as Jacob did, 'I have waited for thy salvation, O Lord.' He could not have said that once. This is the very Jacob who had, in his earlier days, been full of crafty policy and tricks and schemes; but he has done with all that now, and he is able truthfully to say, 'I have waited for thy salvation, O Lord.'

19 Gad, a troop shall overcome him: but he shall overcome at the last.

This has been the blessing of many a child of God — to fight, and apparently to lose the battle, yet to win it at the end. O thou who art striving against sin, or seeking to win souls for Christ, after many disappointments may you be able to clutch this sweet assurance, 'He shall overcome at the last.'

20 Out of Asher his bread shall be fat, and he shall yield royal dainties.

Asher was a tribe that was placed in a very fertile region where everything was crowned with delight. Oh, to have our inheritance where we feed upon the bread of heaven, and where the deep truths of God become to us royal dainties!

21 Naphtali is a hind let loose: he giveth goodly words.

Naphtali was a tribe notable for those that could speak freely, helped of God with a holy freedom in bearing testimony to his truth.

22 Joseph —

Ah, now the patriarch comes to his beloved Joseph, and here the old man lingers long, longer than upon any other of his sons: 'Joseph' —

22 is a fruitful bough, even a fruitful bough by a well; whose branches run over the wall:

The Hebrew puts it: 'Joseph is a son of fruits, even a son of fruits by a well; whose daughters run over the wall.'

23-24 The archers have sorely grieved him, and shot at him, and hated him: But his bow abode in strength, and the arms of his hands were made strong by the hands of the mighty God of Jacob; (from thence is the shepherd, the stone of Israel:)

Joseph is a type of him who is both the Shepherd and the Stone to us. The Shepherd who defends us, provides for us, and dies for us, and the foundation on which we build for time and eternity.

25-28 Even by the God of thy father, who shall help thee; and by the Almighty, who shall bless thee with blessings of heaven above, blessings of the deep that lieth under, blessings of the breasts, and of the womb: The blessings of thy father have prevailed above the blessings of my progenitors unto the utmost bound of the everlasting hills: they shall be on the head of Joseph, and on the crown of the head of him that was separate from his brethren. Benjamin shall ravin as a wolf: in the morning he shall devour the prey, and at night he shall divide the spoil. All these are the twelve tribes of Israel: and this is it that their father spake unto them, and blessed them; every one according to his blessing he blessed them.

All these are the twelve tribes of Israel: and this is it that their father spake unto them, and blessed them; every one according to his blessing he blessed them.

GENESIS 49

Gen. 49:1-3 And Jacob called unto his sons, and said, Gather yourselves together, that I may tell you that which shall befall you in the last days. Gather yourselves together, and hear, ye sons of Jacob; and hearken unto Israel your father. Reuben, thou art my firstborn, my might, and the beginning of my strength, the excellency of dignity, and the excellency of power:

All this was to Reuben's advantage, yet he was spoiled through one fault.

4 Unstable as water, thou shalt not excel; —

So it is clear that the greatest strength and dignity and power will not serve a man, so as to make him excel, if he be unstable. There are many such persons still remaining in the world; their doctrine changes like the moon, and we never know what it is. Their spirit and temper constantly change; their pursuits are sometimes in one direction, and sometimes in another; they are 'everything by starts, and nothing long'; and to each of them it may be said, 'Unstable as water, thou shalt not excel.'

4-7 because thou wentest up to thy father's bed; then defiledst thou it: he went up to my couch. Simeon and Levi are brethren; instruments of cruelty are in their habitations. O my soul, come not thou into their secret; unto their assembly, mine honour, be not thou united: for in their anger they slew a man, and in their selfwill they digged down a wall. Cursed be their anger, for it was fierce; and their wrath, for it was cruel: I will divide them in Jacob, and scatter them in Israel.

It is a very remarkable circumstance, well worthy of notice, that this curse was turned into a real blessing, especially in the case of the tribe of Levi. It is true that they were divided and scattered, like handfuls of salt, throughout the whole of Israel, for they were attendants upon the Lord's priests, and they had cities appointed to them so that, while they did dwell here, and there, and everywhere, it was in order that they might reach the whole of the people and prove a blessing to them. Are any of you labouring under a very serious disadvantage? Does it look to you like a curse? Then pray to God to make it into a blessing. I believe that, often, the worst thing that can happen to Christian men is really the best thing, for, while nature would cry out, 'The clouds are to be dreaded', grace can reply,

> *The clouds ye so much dread*
> *Are big with mercy, and shall break*
> *In blessings on your head.*

8 Judah, thou art he whom thy brethren shall praise: —

His name was praise, and such was his history to be, for David came of that tribe, and great David's greater Son, whom it is our joy to praise.

8 thy hand shall be in the neck of thine enemies; thy father's children shall bow down before thee.

While that was true of Judah, it is still more true of him who sprang out of Judah, even our Lord and King, 'the Lion of the tribe of Judah' [Revelation 5:5].

9 Judah is a lion's whelp: from the prey, my son, thou art gone up: he stooped down, he couched as a lion, and as an old lion; who shall rouse him up?

Our Lord overcame his enemies even in the thicket of this world, and all power is given unto him now that he has 'gone up' again into his glory. Let that man beware who would attack this Lion of the tribe of Judah: 'Who shall rouse him up?' If you persecute his followers, you will rouse him up. If you deny his truth, trample on the doctrine of atonement, and reject his love, you will rouse him up. But beware in that day, for terrible is the King of Judah when he is once aroused. Wherefore, submit yourselves to him: 'Kiss the Son, lest he be angry, and ye perish from the way, when his wrath is kindled but a little' [Psalm 2:12].

10 The sceptre shall not depart from Judah, nor a lawgiver from between his feet, until Shiloh come; and unto him shall the gathering of the people be.

When did the dominion depart from Judah? Not till the Lord Jesus came as the great One. And unto him, to this very day, the people gather, and more and more shall gather in the latter days.

11-12 Binding his foal unto the vine, and his ass's colt unto the choice vine; he washed his garments in wine, and his clothes in the blood of grapes: His eyes shall be red with wine, and his teeth white with milk.

It was literally so with Judah, but it is gloriously so with our Lord to this day. It was his blood which yielded the juice of those rare clusters of the choice vine; and now, with garments dyed with his own blood, he comes from Edom, for he has trodden down his foes, and he cries, 'I have trodden the winepress alone; and of the people there was none with me' [Isaiah 63:3].

13 Zebulun shall dwell at the haven of the sea; and he shall be for an haven of ships; and his border shall be unto Zidon.

So did Zebulun dwell even until the day when our Lord came, for Matthew writes concerning him,

> Now when Jesus had heard that John was cast into prison, he departed into Galilee; and leaving Nazareth, he came and dwelt in Capernaum, which is upon the sea coast, in the borders of Zabulon and Nephthalim: That it might be fulfilled which was spoken by Esaias the prophet, saying, The land of Zabulon, and the land of Nephthalim, by the way of the sea, beyond Jordan, Galilee of the Gentiles; The people which sat in darkness saw

14-15 Issachar is a strong ass couching down between two burdens: And he saw that rest was good, and the land that it was pleasant; and bowed his shoulder to bear, and became a servant unto tribute.

This was a poor character for Issachar to possess; it was a tame-spirited tribe, that loved rest and ease, and therefore did not fight with the common foe. Issachar crouched down between the burdens instead of taking them up and bearing them. God grant that none of us may be of that lazy tribe! I think that I know some who are; they could do a great deal, but they see that rest is good, and the land is pleasant, so they idle away their days.

16-17 Dan shall judge his people, as one of the tribes of Israel. Dan shall be a serpent by the way, an adder in the path, that biteth the horse heels, so that his rider shall fall backward.

Dan is noted among the tribes for its famous leap, capturing that distant part of the country for itself. Here good old Jacob, worn out by what he had already said, exhausted by the ecstasy into which, as a prophet, he had been cast, paused awhile, and panted.

18 I have waited for thy salvation, O LORD.

But he soon resumed his prophecy:

19 Gad, a troop shall overcome him: but he shall overcome at the last.

Many of God's servants belong to this tribe, for their life is spent in conflict. They do not seek it, but it comes to them; and, for a time, they seem to be overcome, yet let them clutch at the promise given by God.

20 Out of Asher his bread shall be fat, and he shall yield royal dainties.

Well fed, and then yielding correspondingly, there are some people who like to have their bread to be fat, but they yield to the King no dainties. Let it not be so with us, but let us both feed well and yield well.

21 Naphtali is a hind let loose: —

The type of what a Christian minister should be — indeed, what every Christian worker should be — 'a hind let loose', one who can say with David, 'O Lord, truly I am thy servant; I am thy servant, and the son of thine handmaid: thou hast loosed my bonds' [Psalm 116:16].

21 he giveth goodly words.

He has liberty in speech, freedom of utterance. He is not in bonds. He is as 'a hind let loose'.

22 Joseph is a fruitful bough, even a fruitful bough by a well; —

Where he can suck up abundant nutriment, —

22 whose branches run over the wall:

He does more than he is expected to do; nothing seems to content him. His 'branches run over the wall'.

23-24 The archers have sorely grieved him, and shot at him, and hated him: But his bow abode in strength, —

You know how sorely Joseph was persecuted by his brethren, yet how the Lord was with him in all his troubles. It appears from these words that he was himself an archer, and that he was not in a hurry to shoot his arrows; his bow remained still. It is the strong who can afford to be quiet. As you go across the village green, a goose will hiss at you, whereas the strong ox lies down calmly and takes no notice of you: 'His bow abode in strength.'

24 and the arms of his hands—

Not only his hands, but the arms of his hands.

24-27 were made strong by the hands of the mighty God of Jacob; (from thence is the shepherd, the stone of Israel:) Even by the God of thy father, who shall help thee; and by the Almighty, who shall bless thee with blessings of heaven above, blessings of the deep that lieth under, blessings of the breasts, and of the womb: The blessings of thy father have prevailed above the blessings of my progenitors unto the utmost bound of the everlasting hills: they shall be on the head of Joseph, and on the crown of the head of him that was separate from his brethren. Benjamin shall ravin as a wolf: in the morning he shall devour the prey, and at night he shall divide the spoil.

Little Benjamin is the last of the tribes.

28-33 All these are the twelve tribes of Israel: and this is it that their father spake unto them, and blessed them; every one according to his blessing he blessed them. And he charged them, and said unto them, I am to be gathered unto my people: bury me with my fathers in the cave that is in the field of Ephron the Hittite, in the cave that is in the field of Machpelah, which is before Mamre, in the land of Canaan, which Abraham bought with the field of Ephron the Hittite for a possession of a buryingplace. There they buried Abraham and Sarah his wife; there they buried Isaac and Rebekah his wife; and there I buried Leah. The purchase of the field and of the cave that is therein was from the children of Heth. And when Jacob had made an end of commanding his sons, he gathered up his feet into the bed, and yielded up the ghost, and was gathered unto his people.

It is a very sweet thing to die with a blessing on your lips, and it is equally good to live in the same spirit. Our Lord Jesus was blessing his disciples when he was taken from them; and since we do not know when we shall be taken away from our relatives, let us be always blessing them. May the Lord, who has blessed us, make us a blessing to others!

DEVOTIONAL THOUGHTS ON THE BIBLE
Charles Haddon Spurgeon

EXODUS

EXODUS 3:1-10

Exod. 3:1 Now Moses kept the flock of Jethro his father in law, the priest of Midian: and he led the flock to the backside of the desert, and came to the mountain of God, even to Horeb.

It must have been a great change for Moses, after forty years in the court of Pharaoh, to be spending another forty years in the wilderness. But it was not waste time; it required the first two periods to make Moses fit for the grand life of the last forty. He must be a prince, and he must be a shepherd, that he might be both a ruler and a shepherd to God's people, Israel. He must be much alone; he must have many solitary communings with his own heart; he must be led to feel his own weakness. And this will be no loss of time to him; he will do more in the last forty years because of the two forties thus spent in preparation. And it is not lost time that a man takes in putting on his harness before he goes to the battle, or that the reaper spends in sharpening his scythe before he cuts down the corn.

2 And the angel of the LORD appeared unto him in a flame of fire out of the midst of a bush: and he looked, and, behold, the bush burned with fire, and the bush was not consumed.

How near God seemed in those ages when he could be beheld in a bush or sitting under an oak! And is he not equally near to us if we are but prepared for his presence? Surely pure eyes are scarce, or sights of God would be more frequent, for the pure in heart shall see God [Matthew 5:8].

3-5 And Moses said, I will now turn aside, and see this great sight, why the bush is not burnt. And when the LORD saw that he turned aside to see, God called unto him out of the midst of the bush, and said, Moses, Moses. And he said, Here am I. And he said, Draw not nigh hither: put off thy shoes from off thy feet, for the place whereon thou standest is holy ground.

God is not to be viewed by curiosity; he is not to be approached by presumption. A holy trembling well becomes the man who would commune with the most holy God. We are not fit for intercourse with God without some measure of preparation. There is something to be put off ere we can behold the Lord.

6 Moreover he said, I am the God of thy father, the God of Abraham, the God of Isaac, and the God of Jacob. And Moses hid his face; for he was afraid to look upon God.

Partly because of the universal superstition that if God appeared to any man, he would surely die; but in Moses' case, perhaps more because of an appreciation of the holiness of God and of his own unworthiness. There is not a man among us but what must do as Moses did if we are in a right state of mind. They that think they are perfect might presume to look, but they that are truly so, as Moses was, would hide their face, as he did, for he was afraid to look upon God.

7 And the LORD said, I have surely seen the affliction of my people which are in Egypt, and have heard their cry by reason of their taskmasters; for I know their sorrows;

Beautiful verse. God had seen, and God had heard, as if their griefs had had two avenues to his heart. God seeth not with eyes and heareth not with ears, as we do, but he speaketh after the manner of men, and he saith by two ways they had reached his very soul: 'I have surely seen the affliction; I have heard their cries'; and then he adds, as if to show the perfection of his sympathy with them: 'I know their sorrows.' Now it is quite true today concerning us and concerning our God, he has seen, he has heard, and he knows — 'I know their sorrows.' When the sorrow is known, then God begins to work. He is no passive spectator of the misery of his chosen, but his hand goes with his heart.

8-9 And I am come down to deliver them out of the hand of the Egyptians, and to bring them up out of that land unto a good land and a large, unto a land flowing with milk and honey; unto the place of the Canaanites, and the Hittites, and the Amorites, and the Perizzites, and the Hivites, and the Jebusites. Now therefore, behold, the cry of the children of Israel is come unto me: —

'Now, therefore, behold, the cry of the children of Israel is come unto me', and when the cry of God's children goes unto him, depend upon it there will be something moving before long. When a father hears the cries of his children, when a mother hears the cry of her babe, it is not long before there will be a movement of the heart and of the hand. I am sure, brethren and sisters, there have been crises in English history which have been entirely due to the prayers of God's people. There have been singular occurrences which the mere reader of history cannot understand, but there are a number still alive who wait upon God in prayer, and they make history. There is more history made in the closet than in the cabinet of the ministry. There is a greater power at the back of the throne than the carnal eye can see, and that power is the cry of God's children.

9-10 and I have also seen the oppression wherewith the Egyptians oppress them. Come now therefore, and I will send thee unto Pharaoh, that thou mayest bring forth my people the children of Israel out of Egypt.

I do not wonder that Moses opened his eyes when he knew what a poor creature he was for God to say, 'Come now, therefore, and I will send thee unto Pharaoh' — the very man whose life was sought by Pharaoh — 'I will send thee unto Pharaoh' — the man that had been rejected by his own people when he took their part — 'that thou mayest bring forth my people, the children of Israel, out of Egypt.' Oh! Let us be ready for any commission. If God were to say that he would build up heaven by the poorest and meanest among us, it would not be for us to draw back. Let him do what he wills with us!

Oh, for a faith to believe that in the midst of our weakness God's strength would appear.

EXODUS 3:1-14; ROMANS 9:1-25

This chapter tells of the appearance of God to Moses in the wilderness. Has he removed from us, brethren? He used to be seen by godly souls by mount and stream and sea; and even bushes were alive and blazing with the indwelt Godhead. Oh, that he would reveal himself to us tonight! I am going to read this chapter with this longing in my heart. I pray that the same longing may be in the heart of every child of God: 'Show me thy face: show me thy face, my God, tonight.'

Exod. 3:1 Now Moses kept the flock of Jethro his father in law, the priest of Midian: and he led the flock to the backside of the desert, and came to the mountain of God, even to Horeb.

There is nothing at all dishonourable about common trade and matters of business. Here is a shepherd who keeps his flock, and God keeps him and reveals himself to him. When God wants a man to lead his people, he seeks for him not among idlers but busy, active men, and God was pleased to show himself more to Moses as a shepherd, than he had ever shown himself to him as a prince in Egypt. I find no glowing Deity in the halls of Pharaoh, but I find the consuming fire manifested in the lone wastes of the desert of Sinai.

2 And the angel of the LORD appeared unto him in a flame of fire out of the midst of a bush: and he looked, and, behold, the bush burned with fire, and the bush was not consumed.

Well might it say, 'behold'. I have seen a bush set alight by a match. It blazed in a moment, but it was gone in another moment; it burned up so fiercely and hastily. But God was pleased to make a poor consumable bush to be the unharmed place of his abiding. He dwells today in the human person of the Saviour. The Godhead is in Christ. He dwells today in the church, which might well enough be consumed by his presence; but it is not consumed. He can come and dwell in my heart and in yours tonight, and yet we shall bear the presence of Deity to the hour of our death. He has a way of so throwing himself into our feebleness that it becomes strong, and that which might otherwise have been destroyed, is even preserved by his presence. 'The bush burned with fire, and was not consumed.'

3-4 And Moses said, I will now turn aside, and see this great sight, why the bush is not burnt. And when the LORD saw that he turned aside to see, God called unto him out of the midst of the bush, and said, Moses, Moses. And he said, Here am I.

Oh, that personal call, that voice from God to the heart! How much we need it. Do you not remember when first the Lord called some of you? Then he says to you tonight, 'I have called thee by my name. Thou art mine.' Own that sweet impeachment, confess that you are his, and say to him, 'For suffering or for service, here am I ready, aye ready, even as Moses was. Here am I.'

5 And he said, Draw not nigh hither: put off thy shoes from off thy feet, for the place whereon thou standest is holy ground.

Stand as a servant stands in the presence of his master in the East. He is not expected to wear in the court of his master the shoes which have trodden in the mire of the world. Now, put off thy cares; put off thy carnal thoughts; put off thyself; put off thy sin. When God is near, solemnity and deep reverence become us. 'The place whereon thou standest is holy ground.'

6 Moreover he said, I am the God of thy father, the God of Abraham, the God of Isaac, and the God of Jacob. And Moses hid his face; for he was afraid to look upon God.

Thou needest not hide thy face if God shall appear to thee, though I am sure thou wilt do it. Thou mayest come boldly. It is thy Father's face: it is the face of one who is reconciled to thee in Christ. Therefore, open thine eyes and look; and may the Lord show himself to thee!

7 And the LORD said, I have surely seen the affliction of my people which are in Egypt, and have heard their cry by reason of their taskmasters; for I know their sorrows;

Now, you troubled ones, are not these verses real music to you? God has seen your afflictions: there are God's eyes. God has heard your cry: there are God's ears. 'I know their sorrows': there is God's mighty understanding. He is thinking about you. He knows all that which tries you tonight.

8-10 And I am come down to deliver them out of the hand of the Egyptians, and to bring them up out of that land unto a good land and a large, unto a land flowing with milk and honey; unto the place of the Canaanites, and the Hittites, and the Amorites, and the Perizzites, and the Hivites, and the Jebusites. Now therefore, behold, the cry of the children of Israel is come unto me: and I have also seen the oppression wherewith the Egyptians oppress them. Come now therefore, —

'Come now therefore' — this was a very extraordinary thing to follow after all that. God has seen the affliction of his people. What then? He says, 'I am come down to deliver them.' What then? Why, the next thing is that he is going to use this trembling man who stands awestruck with his shoes from off his feet in the presence of the still-burning bush. 'Come now, therefore.'

10 and I will send thee unto Pharaoh, that thou mayest bring forth my people the children of Israel out of Egypt.

You have been praying for a blessing. God is going to give it through you. You have been looking east and west and north and south for some deliverer that shall win souls and stir up the church. God calls you to do it. He invites you to undertake this gigantic service, and I think that I see the colour come into your face, and then fly away again. You are ready to faint at the thought of such a charge laid upon you.

11 And Moses said unto God, Who am I, that I should go unto Pharaoh, and that I should bring forth the children of Israel out of Egypt?

Now, catch this —

12 And he said, Certainly I will be with thee; —

What more does Moses want? He said, 'Who am I?' This showed his weakness. God said, 'Never mind who you are. Certainly I will be with thee.' Here was strength enough for him.

12 and this shall be a token unto thee, that I have sent thee: When thou hast brought forth the people out of Egypt, ye shall serve God upon this mountain.

And he did. You know how Sinai trembled while God made it his throne, and how Moses must have been strengthened, when he did exceeding fear and quake before God, when he recollected that this same God had appeared to him, when he was alone in the desert, and had promised that they should worship him there.

13-14 And Moses said unto God, Behold, when I come unto the children of Israel, and shall say unto them, The God of your fathers hath sent me unto you; and they shall say to me, What is his name? what shall I say unto them? And God said unto Moses, I AM THAT I AM: —

That is his name: the infinite, eternal, and unchangeable God.

14 and he said, Thus shalt thou say unto the children of Israel, I AM hath sent me unto you.

Oh, what a glorious commission — to receive it direct from the self-existent God, who is the same for ever and ever, and who only hath immortality. Speak to us tonight, thou great I AM, Jah, Jehovah, God of Abraham, of Isaac, and of Jacob. Speak to this company in this house of prayer tonight, because of Jesus, Joshua, Jehoshua, Jehovah, Jesus. I have tried to show you how that name of Jesus has the name 'Jehovah' hidden away in it. Because of him, draw near to us, O Lord.

The Jews thought that God must certainly save them. They thought they had a birth claim. Were they not the children of Abraham? Surely they had some right to it. This chapter [Romans 9] battles the question of right. No man has any right to the grace of God. The terms are inconsistent. There can be no right to that which is free favour. We are all condemned criminals, and if pardoned, it must be as the result of pure mercy, absolute mercy, for desert there is none in any one of us.

Rom. 9:1-2 I say the truth in Christ, I lie not, my conscience also bearing me witness in the Holy Ghost, That I have great heaviness and continual sorrow in my heart.

He never thought about his unbelieving brethren without the deepest imaginable regret. How far is this from the spirit of those who look upon the ungodly without tears — settle it down as a matter that cannot be altered, and take it as a question of hard fate, but are never troubled about it. Not so the apostle [Paul]. He had great heaviness and continual sorrow in his heart.

3 For I could wish that myself were accursed from Christ for my brethren, my kinsmen according to the flesh:

He had just that self-sacrificing spirit of Moses, that he would lose anything and everything if they might but be saved. And this is the spirit which ought to actuate every church of Christ. The church that is always caring for her own maintenance is no church. The church that would be willing to be destroyed if it could save the sons of men — which feels as if, whatever her shame or sorrow, it would be nothing if she could but save sinners — that church is like the Lord, of whom we read, 'He saved others; himself he cannot save' [Mark 15:31]. Oh! blessed heartbreak over sinful men, which makes men willing to lose everything if they might but bless and win men to Christ! 'My kinsmen', says he, 'according to the flesh'.

4-5 Who are Israelites; to whom pertaineth the adoption, and the glory, and the covenants, and the giving of the law, and the service of God, and the promises; Whose are the fathers, and of whom as concerning the flesh Christ came, who is over all, God blessed for ever. Amen.

What dignity has God put upon ancient Israel! How favoured far beyond any of us in these particulars! They had the light, when the rest of the world was in darkness. Theirs was the law, and theirs the covenant promises. Above all, of them it was, that Christ came. Our Saviour was a Jew. Forever must that race be had in respectful honour, and we must pray for their salvation.

6-7 Not as though the word of God hath taken none effect. For they are not all Israel, which are of Israel: neither, because they are the seed of Abraham, are they all children: but, In Isaac shall thy seed be called.

Now, the apostle is getting to his point. You Jews claim to have the mercy of God because you are of the seed of Abraham; but there is nothing in that, says he, for God made a distinct choice of Isaac to the rejection of Ishmael, as he did afterwards of Jacob, and then Esau was left out.

8 That is, They which are the children of the flesh, these are not the children of God: but the children of the promise are counted for the seed.

Now, Isaac was not the child of Abraham's flesh. He was born according to promise, when his mother was past age, and his father well stricken in years. His was the birth according to the promise, and that is the way the line of grace runs — not according to the flesh, but according to the promise. If, then, all my hope of heaven lies upon my being a child of godly parents, it is an Israelitish hope, and good for nothing. If my hope of heaven lies upon my having been born according to the promise of God — born of his grace and of his power — in that line the covenant stands. God is determined that it shall be so.

9-13 For this is the word of promise, At this time will I come, and Sarah shall have a son. And not only this; but when Rebecca also had conceived by one, even by our father Isaac; (For the children being not yet born, neither having done any good or evil, that the purpose of God according to election might stand, not of works, but of him that calleth;) It was said unto her, The elder shall serve the younger. As it is written, Jacob have I loved, but Esau have I hated.

So, then, there is no claim of birth, for he that had the claim of birth, even Esau, is passed by. There is, indeed, no claim at all, for God gives freely, according to his own will, blessing the sons of men.

14 What shall we say then? Is there unrighteousness with God? God forbid.

There is no unrighteousness in anything that he does; and in the winding up of all affairs, it shall be seen that God was righteous as well as gracious.

15-16 For he saith to Moses, I will have mercy on whom I will have mercy, and I will have compassion on whom I will have compassion. So then it is not of him that willeth, nor of him that runneth, but of God that sheweth mercy.

That is where it must begin. When men are condemned what can they appeal to but the mercy of God? Where is the hope of men but in the sovereignty of the Most High?

17-24 For the scripture saith unto Pharaoh, Even for this same purpose have I raised thee up, that I might shew my power in thee, and that my name might be declared throughout all the earth. Therefore hath he mercy on whom he will have mercy, and whom he will he hardeneth. Thou wilt say then unto me, Why doth he yet find fault? For who hath resisted his will? Nay but, O man, who art thou that repliest against God? Shall the thing formed say to him that formed it, Why hast thou made me thus? Hath not the potter power over the clay, of the same lump to make one vessel unto honour, and another unto dishonour? What if God, willing to shew his wrath, and to make his power known, endured with much longsuffering the vessels of wrath fitted to destruction: And that he might make known the riches of his glory on the vessels of mercy, which he had afore prepared unto glory, Even us, whom he hath called, not of the Jews only, but also of the Gentiles?

There was the sting of it. They could not endure that God should in his divine sovereignty save Gentiles as well as Jews. But he has done so, and he has sent the Gospel to us; while they, having refused it, are left in the darkness which they chose.

25 As he saith also in Osee, I will call them my people, which were not my people; and her beloved, which was not beloved.

Oh! what a splendid verse is this! Let some here who have been far from God until now and never had a gracious thought, nevertheless, hear what he has done and will do again. 'I will call them my people, which were not my people; and her beloved, which was not beloved.'

EXODUS 10:1-20; PSALM 105:25-38

Exod. 10:1-2 And the LORD said unto Moses, Go in unto Pharaoh: for I have hardened his heart, and the heart of his servants, that I might shew these my signs before him: And that thou mayest tell in the ears of thy son, and of thy son's son, what things I have wrought in Egypt, and my signs which I have done among them; that ye may know how that I am the LORD.

God would stamp the early history of Israel with the deep impression of his Godhead. His overthrow of the proud Egyptian king should let Israel know in the very beginning how great a God had chosen her to be his own peculiar portion.

3 And Moses and Aaron came in unto Pharaoh, and said unto him, Thus saith the LORD God of the Hebrews, How long wilt thou refuse to humble thyself before me? let my people go, that they may serve me.

Can you imagine these humble individuals, Moses and Aaron, thus bearding the great king whose word could make their heads to roll upon the sword? They were not afraid, for God was with them; and they who speak in God's stead are traitors if they be not brave. The ambassadors of so great a King must not demean themselves by fear; therefore, right boldly said they to Pharaoh, 'Thus saith the Lord God of the Hebrews, How long wilt thou refuse to humble thyself before me? let my people go, that they may serve me.'

4-6 Else, if thou refuse to let my people go, behold, tomorrow will I bring the locusts into thy coast: And they shall cover the face of the earth, that one cannot be able to see the earth: and they shall eat the residue of that which is escaped, which remaineth unto you from the hail, and shall eat every tree which groweth for you out of the field: And they shall fill thy houses, and the houses of all thy servants, and the houses of all the Egyptians; which neither thy fathers, nor thy fathers' fathers have seen, since the day that they were upon the earth unto this day. And he turned himself, and went out from Pharaoh.

Moses had delivered his message; he had uttered his solemn warning, so he waited no longer in the tyrant's presence.

7 And Pharaoh's servants said unto him, How long shall this man be a snare unto us? let the men go, that they may serve the LORD their God: knowest thou not yet that Egypt is destroyed?

The seven former heavy judgements had so effectually bruised Egypt that the people began to cry against their king for his obstinacy in still further resisting God.

8-9 And Moses and Aaron were brought again unto Pharaoh: and he said unto them, Go, serve the LORD your God: but who are they that shall go? And Moses said, We will go with our young and with our old, with our sons and with our daughters, with our flocks and with our herds will we go; for we must hold a feast unto the LORD.

Pharaoh was inclined to make terms with Moses, but God will have no conditions with men who are rebelling against him. An unconditional surrender is all that God will accept.

10-11 And he said unto them, Let the LORD be so with you, as I will let you go, and your little ones: look to it; for evil is before you. Not so: go now ye that are men, and serve the LORD; for that ye did desire. And they were driven out from Pharaoh's presence.

See how proud, how stout-hearted towards evil is this wicked and foolish king. When his people appeal to him to yield, he only does so for a moment, and then he drives out the messengers of God in anger.

12-17 And the LORD said unto Moses, Stretch out thine hand over the land of Egypt for the locusts, that they may come up upon the land of Egypt, and eat every herb of the land, even all that the hail hath left. And Moses stretched forth his rod over the land of Egypt, and the LORD brought an east wind upon the land all that day, and all that night; and when it was morning, the east wind brought the locusts. And the locusts went up over all the land of Egypt, and rested in all the coasts of Egypt: very grievous were they; before them there were no such locusts as they, neither after them shall be such. For they covered the face of the whole earth, so that the land was darkened; and they did eat every herb of the land, and all the fruit of the trees which the hail had left: and there remained not any green thing in the trees, or in the herbs of the field, through all the land of Egypt. Then Pharaoh called for Moses and Aaron in haste; and he said, I have sinned against the LORD your God, and against you. Now therefore forgive, I pray thee, my sin only this once, and intreat the LORD your God, that he may take away from me this death only.

See how he is obliged to come to his knees at length. He will be up again soon, for his heart is not humbled, though he is eating his own words. An unhumbled heart is not subdued by judgements; it is so apparently, but really it is still a heart of stone.

18-20 And he went out from Pharaoh, and intreated the LORD. And the LORD turned a mighty strong west wind, which took away the locusts, and cast them into the Red sea; there remained not one locust in all the coasts of Egypt. But the LORD hardened Pharaoh's heart, so that he would not let the children of Israel go.

God kept his grace back from him, so that he relapsed into his natural state of obduracy. Pharaoh is the great mirror of pride and obstinacy; I wonder whether we have a Pharaoh here.

Now let us turn to Psalm 105 and see further what God did against this proud Pharaoh.

Ps. 105:25-28 He turned their heart to hate his people, to deal subtilly with his servants. He sent Moses his servant; and Aaron whom he had chosen. They shewed his signs among them, and wonders in the land of Ham. He sent darkness, and made it dark; and they rebelled not against his word.

So cowed were they by that awful darkness, that for a time they seemed to repent of their rebellion against the Lord.

29-30 He turned their waters into blood, and slew their fish. Their land brought forth frogs in abundance, in the chambers of their kings.

Though the fish could not live, the frogs could. When good was taken away, evil came. What a strange succession of miracles was this — the fish slain, but the frogs multiplied!

31-34 He spake, and there came divers sorts of flies, and lice in all their coasts. He gave them hail for rain, and flaming fire in their land. He smote their vines also and their fig trees; and brake the trees of their coasts. He spake, and the locusts came, and caterpillers, and that without number,

There is great sublimity in this expression. God had only to speak, and whole battalions of devouring locusts and caterpillars seemed to leap out of the earth or to drop from the clouds: 'He spake, and the locusts came, and caterpillars, and that without number.'

35-37 And did eat up all the herbs in their land, and devoured the fruit of their ground. He smote also all the firstborn in their land, the chief of all their strength. He brought them forth also with silver and gold: and there was not one feeble person among their tribes.

It was a notable miracle that, after all the oppression they had endured, they should be in such a state of health that 'there was not one feeble person among their tribes'. When God makes his people march, he puts them into marching trim.

38 Egypt was glad when they departed: for the fear of them fell upon them.

Yet this was the mighty nation whose proud king had defied the Lord. At last, they had had enough of the combat; they were glad that the people of God should retire out of their land, and they themselves bowed low before him. May we be taught humility of heart, so that we can sing this hymn:

Sovereign Ruler, Lord of all,
Prostrate at thy feet I fall;
Hear, oh, hear my earnest cry;
Frown not, lest I faint and die!

EXODUS 12:1-20

Exod. 12:1-2 And the LORD spake unto Moses and Aaron in the land of Egypt saying, This month shall be unto you the beginning of months: it shall be the first month of the year to you.

God thinks a great deal of the redemption of his people. When he redeemed them out of their Egyptian bondage, he took care that the mighty deed should be worthily commemorated. Thenceforth, the Jewish year was to begin with the celebration of the national deliverance; and now, when any of us are converted to God, and so are set free from the slavery of sin, we should reckon that then we really begin to live. All the previous part of our life has been wasted, but when we are brought truly to know God, through faith in our Lord and Saviour Jesus Christ, then have we realized, indeed, what life is. The month of our conversion should be to us the beginning of months, the first month of the year to us.

3-4 Speak ye unto all the congregation of Israel, saying, In the tenth day of this month they shall take to them every man a lamb, according to the house of their fathers, a lamb for an house: And if the household be too little for the lamb, let him and his neighbour next unto his house take it according to the number of the souls; every man according to his eating shall make your count for the lamb.

The worship of God must be rendered in an orderly manner, with due thoughtfulness and preparation. This paschal supper was not to be celebrated in any fashion that the people might choose, but they were to take time to have the lamb properly examined, that it might be found perfect in every respect, and that everything might be set in order so that the feast should be observed with due reverence and solemnity. Let us take care that we act thus in all our devotions. Let us never rush to prayer or hasten to praise. Let us pause awhile and think what we are about to do, lest we offer the sacrifice of fools and so cause the Lord to bid us take back that which we have brought to put upon his altar without due thoughtfulness.

5 Your lamb shall be without blemish, a male of the first year: ye shall take it out from the sheep, or from the goats:

It was to be a type of Christ, and therefore, it must be the best that they had. It must be in the prime of its strength, otherwise it would not be a fit emblem of the 'strong Son of God' whose mighty love moved him to give himself to death for us.

6-10 And ye shall keep it up until the fourteenth day of the same month: and the whole assembly of the congregation of Israel shall kill it in the evening. And they shall take of the blood, and strike it on the two side posts and on the upper door post of the houses, wherein they shall eat it. And they shall eat the flesh in that night, roast with fire, and unleavened bread; and with bitter herbs they shall eat it. Eat not of it raw, nor sodden at all with water, but roast with fire; his head with his legs, and with the purtenance thereof. And ye shall let nothing of it remain until the morning; and that which remaineth of it until the morning ye shall burn with fire.

Everything was to be done exactly according to God's order; the alteration of the slightest detail would have spoiled it all. I wish that all Christians would remember this rule with regard to the ordinances of God's house. They are not for us to make, or for us to alter, but for us to keep.

11 And thus shall ye eat it; with your loins girded, your shoes on your feet, and your staff in your hand; and ye shall eat it in haste: it is the LORD's passover.

They were thus to exercise an act of faith. Why were they to eat in haste but that they expected soon to be gone? They were to stand like travellers who are starting upon a journey, believing that God was about to set them free. Oh, that we would always exercise faith in all our devotions, for without faith it must ever be impossible to please God.

12-13 For I will pass through the land of Egypt this night, and will smite all the firstborn in the land of Egypt, both man and beast; and against all the gods of Egypt I will execute judgment:

I am the LORD. And the blood shall be to you for a token upon the houses where ye are: and when I see the blood, I will pass over you, —

What a grand gospel statement that is! When the sinner sees the blood, it is for his comfort, but it is God's sight of the blood that is, after all, the grand thing; and when is it that he does not see it?

13-20 and the plague shall not be upon you to destroy you, when I smite the land of Egypt. And this day shall be unto you for a memorial; and ye shall keep it a feast to the LORD throughout your generations; ye shall keep it a feast by an ordinance for ever. Seven days shall ye eat unleavened bread; even the first day ye shall put away leaven out of your houses: for whosoever eateth leavened bread from the first day until the seventh day, that soul shall be cut off from Israel. And in the first day there shall be an holy convocation, and in the seventh day there shall be an holy convocation to you; no manner of work shall be done in them, save that which every man must eat, that only may be done of you. And ye shall observe the feast of unleavened bread; for in this selfsame day have I brought your armies out of the land of Egypt: therefore shall ye observe this day in your generations by an ordinance for ever. In the first month, on the fourteenth day of the month at even, ye shall eat unleavened bread, until the one and twentieth day of the month at even. Seven days shall there be no leaven found in your houses: for whosoever eateth that which is leavened, even that soul shall be cut off from the congregation of Israel, whether he be a stranger, or born in the land. Ye shall eat nothing leavened; in all your habitations shall ye eat unleavened bread.

Thus we see God instituting a commemoration of the deliverance of his people out of Egypt. How much more ought you and I, with joyful gladness, to remember the deliverance of our soul from the slavery of sin and Satan! Let us never forget it. I should like to refresh the memories of bygone times with you who know the Lord; the Lord help you now, with deepest gratitude, to recollect the day when first you saw your Saviour and the yoke was taken from your neck and the burden from your shoulder. Glory be to the delivering Lord!

EXODUS 12:1-27

Exod. 12:1-2 And the LORD spake unto Moses and Aaron in the land of Egypt saying, This month shall be unto you the beginning of months: it shall be the first month of the year to you.

And for this reason: now, as a nation, they were to begin their separate history, separate in existence from all the rest of mankind.

3-4 Speak ye unto all the congregation of Israel, saying, In the tenth day of this month they shall take to them every man a lamb, according to the house of their fathers, a lamb for an house: And if the household be too little for the lamb, let him and his neighbour next unto his house take it according to the number of the souls; every man according to his eating shall make your count for the lamb.

The separation of the lamb was to take place some four days before the time of its slaughter. Probably it was kept in the house. According to the Jewish tradition it was so, and they would hear it bleating, and be reminded of the purpose for which it was to be slain.

5 Your lamb shall be without blemish, a male of the first year: ye shall take it out from the sheep, or from the goats:

You know what a type this is of Christ, 'without blemish', offered up for us in the very fulness of his strength, in the prime and glory of his manhood, giving himself up to be our paschal Lamb, 'the Lamb of God'.

6 And ye shall keep it up until the fourteenth day of the same month: and the whole assembly of the congregation of Israel shall kill it in the evening.

Just as the sun went down, or just before it set for the evening. There is also the marginal reading 'between the two evenings'. The even before the sun set, was the first, and then the daylight after the sun set was the second evening.

7 And they shall take of the blood, and strike it on the two side posts and on the upper door post of the houses, wherein they shall eat it.

Not on the threshold, lest it should be trodden upon; and woe be unto the man who shall trample upon the blood of Christ! On the two side posts and on the lintel was placed the mark indicating that God had redeemed the inmates of that house with blood.

8-9 And they shall eat the flesh in that night, roast with fire, and unleavened bread; and with bitter herbs they shall eat it. Eat not of it raw, nor sodden at all with water, but roast with fire; his head with his legs, and with the purtenance thereof.

And they shall eat the flesh in that night, roast with fire, and unleavened bread; and with bitter herbs they shall eat it. 'Eat not of it raw, nor sodden at all with water, but roast with fire; his head with his legs, and with the purtenance thereof.' We are to have a whole Christ, with his head of wisdom and his heart of love, the walk and conversation of Christ, and all the inward secret life and grace of Christ all to be ours.

10 And ye shall let nothing of it remain until the morning; and that which remaineth of it until the morning ye shall burn with fire.

Not a bone was to be left for the Egyptians to treat with dishonour, but all was to be consumed.

11-12 And thus shall ye eat it; with your loins girded, your shoes on your feet, and your staff in your hand; and ye shall eat it in haste: it is the LORD's passover. For I will pass through the land of Egypt this night, and will smite all the firstborn in the land of Egypt, both man and beast; and against all the gods of Egypt I will execute judgment: I am the LORD.

All those false gods had been smitten in the different plagues; and now, inasmuch as the Egyptians regarded the firstborn in the family with veneration, the last stroke was about to be struck, and Pharaoh and all his subjects would stagger under the tremendous blow.

13 And the blood shall be to you for a token upon the houses where ye are: —

Oh that we would all look upon the blood of Jesus as a token — a token of divine love in giving the well-Beloved to die for us, a token that justice has had its due, a token that we are perfectly secure for ever!

13 and when I see the blood, I will pass over you, —

It is God's view of the blood of Christ which is the all-important matter. When he looks at Christ upon the cross and is satisfied with the atonement that he there offered, the Lord passes over all those for whom Christ died as a Substitute.

13-15 and the plague shall not be upon you to destroy you, when I smite the land of Egypt. And this day shall be unto you for a memorial; and ye shall keep it a feast to the LORD throughout your generations; ye shall keep it a feast by an ordinance for ever. Seven days shall ye eat unleavened bread; even the first day ye shall put away leaven out of your houses:

for whosoever eateth leavened bread from the first day until the seventh day, that soul shall be cut off from Israel.

He who was cut off from Israel was, therefore, no partaker in the redemption purchased by blood. He who is not purged from hypocrisy may say what he likes, but the blood will not save him unless he repents. There must be the putting away of this leaven of the Pharisees, which is hypocrisy, or else even the blood of atonement will not avail.

16 And in the first day there shall be an holy convocation, and in the seventh day there shall be an holy convocation to you; no manner of work shall be done in them, save that which every man must eat, that only may be done of you.

What rest this brought into the houses of the Israelites! There was not only deliverance from the plagues, but there was also rest from all manner of work. Herein is the blessedness of the blood of the Lamb; when it comes to the home and the heart of the believer, it gives him rest of soul, while others are toiling in vain to get relief by their own works.

17-25 And ye shall observe the feast of unleavened bread; for in this selfsame day have I brought your armies out of the land of Egypt: therefore shall ye observe this day in your generations by an ordinance for ever. In the first month, on the fourteenth day of the month at even, ye shall eat unleavened bread, until the one and twentieth day of the month at even. Seven days shall there be no leaven found in your houses: for whosoever eateth that which is leavened, even that soul shall be cut off from the congregation of Israel, whether he be a stranger, or born in the land. Ye shall eat nothing leavened; in all your habitations shall ye eat unleavened bread. Then Moses called for all the elders of Israel, and said unto them, Draw out and take you a lamb according to your families, and kill the passover. And ye shall take a bunch of hyssop, and dip it in the blood that is in the bason, and strike the lintel and the two side posts with the blood that is in the bason; and none of you shall go out at the door of his house until the morning. For the LORD will pass through to smite the Egyptians; and when he seeth the blood upon the lintel, and on the two side posts, the LORD will pass over the door, and will not suffer the destroyer to come in unto your houses to smite you. And ye shall observe this thing for an ordinance to thee and to thy sons for ever. And it shall come to pass, when ye be come to the land which the LORD will give you, according as he hath promised, that ye shall keep this service.

What? Were they never to forget the slaying of the lamb and the sprinkling of the blood? No, never. Not when they came to Canaan, to the land that flowed with milk and honey, and when God had wrought other great marvels for them? No, never; and the highest honour that we shall ever have will be this, to be able truthfully to sing:

A monument of grace,
A sinner saved by blood.

26-27 And it shall come to pass, when your children shall say unto you, What mean ye by this service? That ye shall say, It is the sacrifice of the LORD's passover, who passed over the houses of the children of Israel in Egypt, when he smote the Egyptians, and delivered our houses. And the people bowed the head and worshipped.

EXODUS 13:21-22; 14

We are going to read once more the familiar story of how the Lord relieved his people from the power of Egypt after he had brought them out of the house of bondage.

Exod. 13:21-22; 14:1-2 And the LORD went before them by day in a pillar of a cloud, to lead them the way; and by night in a pillar of fire, to give them light; to go by day and night: He took not away the pillar of the cloud by day, nor the pillar of fire by night, from before the people. And the LORD spake unto Moses, saying, Speak unto the children of Israel, that they turn and encamp before Pihahiroth, between Migdol and the sea, over against Baalzephon: before it shall ye encamp by the sea.

It might have been sufficient for the pillar of cloud to move that way; but, it was really such an extraordinary thing for the Lord to lead the people right down to the sea that he gave a special command, as well as the movement of the cloud. That Moses himself might not be staggered by what would seem to him to be such strange guidance, the Lord tells him what to say to the people and then gives him this explanation:

3-4 For Pharaoh will say of the children of Israel, They are entangled in the land, the wilderness hath shut them in. And I will harden Pharaoh's heart, that he shall follow after them; and I will be honoured upon Pharaoh, and upon all his host; that the Egyptians may know that I am the LORD. And they did so.

Those four words, 'And they did so', though they are very short and very simple words, express a great deal. Oh, that it might always be said of all of us whenever God commands us to do anything, 'And they did so.'

5 And it was told the king of Egypt that the people fled: and the heart of Pharaoh and of his servants was turned against the people, and they said, Why have we done this, that we have let Israel go from serving us?

Nothing but the grace of God will truly humble men. These Egyptians had been crushed by terrible plagues into a false kind of humility, but they were soon as proud as ever. Nothing but the omnipotent grace of God can really subdue a proud and stubborn heart.

6-8 And he made ready his chariot, and took his people with him: And he took six hundred chosen chariots, and all the chariots of Egypt, and captains over every one of them. And the LORD hardened the heart of Pharaoh king of Egypt, and he pursued after the children of Israel: and the children of Israel went out with an high hand.

They were resolute and brave as long as they realized that God was with them; and the Egyptians behind them were bold and proud although God was not with them. There were two high hands that day: the high hand of the proud, puny Pharaoh and the high hand of the ever-blessed omnipotent Jehovah.

9-10 But the Egyptians pursued after them, all the horses and chariots of Pharaoh, and his horsemen, and his army, and overtook them encamping by the sea, beside Pihahiroth, before Baalzephon. And when Pharaoh drew nigh, the children of Israel lifted up their eyes, and, behold, the Egyptians marched after them; and they were sore afraid: —

Forgetting what God had done for them, and promised to them, they became timid at the sight of their old master. They knew the cruelty of the Egyptians in time of war, and their hearts failed them.

10 and the children of Israel cried out unto the LORD.

Ah, dear friends, if they had cried to the Lord in true believing prayer, they would have been worthy of commendation; but they did not do so. They cried out unto the Lord in an unbelieving complaint, as the next verse plainly shows:

11-12 And they said unto Moses, Because there were no graves in Egypt, hast thou taken us away to die in the wilderness? wherefore hast thou dealt thus with us, to carry us forth out of Egypt? Is not this the word that we did tell thee in Egypt, saying, Let us alone, that we may serve the Egyptians? For it had been better for us to serve the Egyptians, than that we should die in the wilderness.

What cowards they were, and how faint-hearted! Were these the people that were to conquer Canaan? Were these God's chosen people? Ah, judge them not, for you and I have often been quite as faint-hearted and quite as fickle as they were. May God forgive us as he again and again forgave them!

13-15 And Moses said unto the people, Fear ye not, stand still, and see the salvation of the LORD, which he will shew to you to day: for the Egyptians whom ye have seen to day, ye shall see them again no more for ever. The LORD shall fight for you, and ye shall hold your peace. And the LORD said unto Moses, Wherefore criest thou unto me? speak unto the children of Israel, that they go forward:

Moses was no doubt praying in his heart though it is not recorded that he uttered any words in prayer; but it was not the time for prayer, it was the time for action. When people sometimes say when they know their duty, 'We will make it a matter of prayer', they generally mean that they will try to find some excuse for not doing it. You need not pray about any matter when you know what you ought to do. Go and do it.

16-20 But lift thou up thy rod, and stretch out thine hand over the sea, and divide it: and the children of Israel shall go on dry ground through the midst of the sea. And I, behold, I will harden the hearts of the Egyptians, and they shall follow them: and I will get me honour upon Pharaoh, and upon all his host, upon his chariots, and upon his horsemen. And the Egyptians shall know that I am the LORD, when I have gotten me honour upon Pharaoh, upon his chariots, and upon his horsemen. And the angel of God, which went before the camp of Israel, removed and went behind them; and the pillar of the cloud went from before their face, and stood behind them: And it came between the camp of the Egyptians and the camp of Israel; and it was a cloud and darkness to them, but it gave light by night to these: so that the one came not near the other all the night.

God was like a wall of fire between them and their enemies, so that they had no cause for fear even though the Egyptians were so near.

21-25 And Moses stretched out his hand over the sea; and the LORD caused the sea to go back by a strong east wind all that night, and made the sea dry land, and the waters were divided.

And the children of Israel went into the midst of the sea upon the dry ground: and the waters were a wall unto them on their right hand, and on their left. And the Egyptians pursued, and went in after them to the midst of the sea, even all Pharaoh's horses, his chariots, and his horsemen. And it came to pass, that in the morning watch the LORD looked unto the host of the Egyptians through the pillar of fire and of the cloud, and troubled the host of the Egyptians, And took off their chariot wheels, that they drave them heavily: so that the Egyptians said, Let us flee from the face of Israel; for the LORD fighteth for them against the Egyptians.

They were now in the midst of the sea between the two high walls of water, and before they could flee see what happened to them.

26-31 And the LORD said unto Moses, Stretch out thine hand over the sea, that the waters may come again upon the Egyptians, upon their chariots, and upon their horsemen. And Moses stretched forth his hand over the sea, and the sea returned to his strength when the morning appeared; and the Egyptians fled against it; and the LORD overthrew the Egyptians in the midst of the sea. And the waters returned, and covered the chariots, and the horsemen, and all the host of Pharaoh that came into the sea after them; there remained not so much as one of them. But the children of Israel walked upon dry land in the midst of the sea; and the waters were a wall unto them on their right hand, and on their left. Thus the LORD saved Israel that day out of the hand of the Egyptians; and Israel saw the Egyptians dead upon the sea shore. And Israel saw that great work which the LORD did upon the Egyptians: and the people feared the LORD, and believed the LORD, and his servant Moses.

And well they might [fear and believe]! Yet how soon they murmured both against the Lord and against Moses!

HOSEA 2:14-15; EXODUS 15:1-21

We will begin with reading Hosea 2:14-15.

Hosea 2:14-15 Therefore, behold, I will allure her, and bring her into the wilderness, and speak comfortably unto her. And I will give her her vineyards from thence, and the valley of Achor for a door of hope: and she shall sing there, as in the days of her youth, and as in the day when she came up out of the land of Egypt.

Now I want you to hear how she did sing in the days of her youth, in the day when she came up out of the land of Egypt. Turn to Exodus 15 where we have the joyful song of the emancipated chosen nation.

Exod. 15:1-10 Then sang Moses and the children of Israel this song unto the LORD, and spake, saying, I will sing unto the LORD, for he hath triumphed gloriously: the horse and his rider hath he thrown into the sea. The LORD is my strength and song, and he is become my salvation: he is my God, and I will prepare him an habitation; my father's God, and I will exalt him. The LORD is a man of war: the LORD is his name. Pharaoh's chariots and his host hath he cast into the sea: his chosen captains also are drowned in the Red sea. The depths have covered them: they sank into the bottom as a stone. Thy right hand, O LORD, is become glorious in power: thy right hand, O LORD, hath dashed in pieces the enemy. And in the greatness of thine excellency thou hast overthrown them that rose up against thee: thou sentest forth thy wrath, which consumed them as stubble. And with the blast of thy nostrils the waters were gathered together, the floods stood upright as an heap, and the depths were congealed in the heart of the sea. The enemy said, I will pursue, I will overtake, I will divide the spoil; my lust shall be satisfied upon them; I will draw my sword, my hand shall destroy them. Thou didst blow with thy wind, the sea covered them: they sank as lead in the mighty waters.

They were all noise and bluster and boast, but observe the sublime attitude of God, how readily he eased himself of his adversaries: 'Thou didst blow with thy wind, the sea covered them: they sank as lead in the mighty waters.'

11-14 Who is like unto thee, O LORD, among the gods? who is like thee, glorious in holiness, fearful in praises, doing wonders? Thou stretchedst out thy right hand, the earth swallowed them. Thou in thy mercy hast led forth the people which thou hast redeemed: thou hast guided them in thy strength unto thy holy habitation. The people shall hear, and be afraid: sorrow shall take hold on the inhabitants of Palestina.

That is, the heathen nations who, at that time, inhabited the land of Palestine: 'Sorrow shall take hold on the inhabitants of Palestina.'

15 Then the dukes of Edom shall be amazed; the mighty men of Moab, trembling shall take hold upon them; all the inhabitants of Canaan shall melt away.

This great deed of God would be told, and told again, all over Palestine; and the inhabitants would feel that their end was come, for who could stand against Israel's mighty God?

16 Fear and dread shall fall upon them; by the greatness of thine arm they shall be as still as a stone; till thy people pass over, O LORD, till the people pass over, which thou hast purchased.

And how still they were! All the forty years that the Israelites were in the wilderness, they were scarcely ever attacked; and even then, it was not by the inhabitants of Canaan, but by the wandering Bedouin tribe of the Amalekites, who slew the hindmost of them. It was wonderful that no troops ever came out of Egypt to molest God's people after the destruction at the Red Sea; neither out of Canaan did any come to block their way. When God strikes, he makes his adversaries dread all future conflicts.

17-21 Thou shalt bring them in, and plant them in the mountain of thine inheritance, in the place, O LORD, which thou hast made for thee to dwell in, in the Sanctuary, O LORD, which thy hands have established. The LORD shall reign for ever and ever. For the horse of Pharaoh went in with his chariots and with his horsemen into the sea, and the LORD brought again the waters of the sea upon them; but the children of Israel went on dry land in the midst of the sea. And Miriam the prophetess, the sister of Aaron, took a timbrel in her hand; and all the women went out after her with timbrels and with dances. And Miriam answered them, Sing ye to the LORD, for he hath triumphed gloriously; the horse and his rider hath he thrown into the sea.

They sang as in an oratorio: Miriam singing the solo and all the women joining in the jubilant chorus; and well might they rejoice after the great deliverance which the Lord had wrought for them.

EXODUS 15; JEREMIAH 7:21-26

Exod. 15:1 Then sang Moses and the children of Israel this song unto the LORD, and spake, saying, I will sing unto the LORD, for he hath triumphed gloriously: the horse and his rider hath he thrown into the sea.

Note, that they were singing, singing a very loud and triumphant song; and you would have thought that they would have kept on singing for the next forty years. It was such a triumph, such a deliverance. God's arm was made so bare before their eyes, that you would have thought that their jubilation would have lasted throughout a lifetime, at the least. On the contrary, it lasted a very little while. Yet what a song it was that they sang! 'I will sing unto the Lord, for he hath triumphed gloriously: the horse and his rider hath he thrown into the sea.' What a song of triumph that is which is sung by souls saved from sin and death and hell by the great atoning sacrifice of Christ! Oh, when we first realize that we are redeemed by the precious blood of Christ, we do, indeed, 'feel like singing all the time', for our sins are washed away, and we have a notion that we shall always keep on singing till we join in the song of the glorified in heaven. So it ought to be; but, alas, from sad experience we know that it is not so! However, the song of Moses and the children of Israel goes on:

2 The LORD is my strength and song, and he is become my salvation: he is my God, and I will prepare him an habitation; my father's God, and I will exalt him.

The heart is prompted by gratitude to think of doing something for God. It thinks of preparing him a habitation, but what habitation shall we prepare for him whom the heaven of heavens cannot contain? All that we can possibly do is too little for the greatness of his grace and his glory. 'Thou didst well that it was in thine heart', said the Lord to David, though he might not prepare God a habitation. It is well that it is in our heart today to do some little thing for the glory of God. As an old Puritan says, 'we give for love-tokens a cracked sixpence, or a flower that soon fades'. It is accepted as a love-token, not for its intrinsic value but as an emblem of what our heart feels and would do if it could. Even so it is with the Lord and the service his people seek to render to him. He takes our trifles and makes much of them.

3-5 The LORD is a man of war: the LORD is his name. Pharaoh's chariots and his host hath he cast into the sea: his chosen captains also are drowned in the Red sea. The depths have covered them: they sank into the bottom as a stone.

And this is what has happened to all the powers that were against us. Our sins, where are they? Has not the Lord cast them into the depths of the sea? Yes, blessed be his name for ever! We, like Israel on the other side of the Red Sea, praise the Lord that we have escaped out of the hand of the oppressor, and that Pharaoh holds us as servants no longer. To the Lord alone is due the glory of our deliverance.

6-8 Thy right hand, O LORD, is become glorious in power: thy right hand, O LORD, hath dashed in pieces the enemy. And in the greatness of thine excellency thou hast overthrown them that rose up against thee: thou sentest forth thy wrath, which consumed them as stubble. And with the blast of thy nostrils the waters were gathered together, the floods stood upright as an heap, and the depths were congealed in the heart of the sea.

What cannot God do? The liquid becomes solid; nature itself changes when the God of nature puts forth his power. Trust thou in God, and he will do wonders for thee also, as he did for his ancient people Israel.

9 The enemy said, I will pursue, I will overtake, I will divide the spoil; my lust shall be satisfied upon them; I will draw my sword, my hand shall destroy them.

How the powers of darkness rage and rave! What a flurry they are in! What big words they speak! What cruel designs they harbour against God's people! See how still and calm is the Lord amid all their raging.

10 Thou didst blow with thy wind, the sea covered them: they sank as lead in the mighty waters.

God has only to use his breath to blow upon them, and away they go, and all their boastings, too. One word from the mouth of God can destroy all our doubts and fears. The breath of his Spirit can sink all our enemies, and make us sing for joy of heart at our great deliverance.

11-13 Who is like unto thee, O LORD, among the gods? who is like thee, glorious in holiness, fearful in praises, doing wonders? Thou stretchedst out thy right hand, the earth swallowed them. Thou in thy mercy hast led forth the people which thou hast redeemed: thou hast guided them in thy strength unto thy holy habitation.

The song becomes prophetic. All joy gets to be prophetic; at least, the joy of earth when once it is touched with the live coal from off the heavenly altar. We begin to praise God 'for all the grace we have not tasted yet', as Israel here does. They praise the Lord for leading his people through the wilderness, and bringing them unto his holy habitation, even while they are only at the beginning of their journey.

14 The people —

That is, the Canaanites, —

14-15 shall hear, and be afraid: sorrow shall take hold on the inhabitants of Palestina. Then the dukes of Edom shall be amazed; the mighty men of Moab, trembling shall take hold upon them; all the inhabitants of Canaan shall melt away.

When they hear of the great things that Jehovah has done for his people, they shall feel that the day of their doom is come. Who can stand against so mighty a God? Yet there are some, in our day, whose hearts are stouter and harder than the hearts of the dukes of Edom and the mighty men of Moab. They hear of God's judgements upon the wicked, and of the terrible doom of the ungodly, and yet they dare to defy the Lord and to continue in their evil ways.

16-18 Fear and dread shall fall upon them; by the greatness of thine arm they shall be as still as a stone; till thy people pass over, O LORD, till the people pass over, which thou hast purchased. Thou shalt bring them in, and plant them in the mountain of thine inheritance, in the place, O LORD, which thou hast made for thee to dwell in, in the Sanctuary, O LORD, which thy hands have established. The LORD shall reign for ever and ever.

How grandly that last note must have pealed forth from the hundreds of thousands of male voices! The women must also have sung it with the utmost conceivable joy as they struck their timbrels, and danced before the Lord.

19-22 For the horse of Pharaoh went in with his chariots and with his horsemen into the sea, and the LORD brought again the waters of the sea upon them; but the children of Israel went on dry land in the midst of the sea. And Miriam the prophetess, the sister of Aaron, took a timbrel in her hand; and all the women went out after her with timbrels and with dances. And Miriam answered them, Sing ye to the LORD, for he hath triumphed gloriously; the horse and his rider hath he thrown into the sea. So Moses brought Israel from the Red sea, and they went out into the wilderness of Shur; and they went three days in the wilderness, and found no water.

At first, they were afraid of too much water, from the waves of the sea; now they are afraid of too little. Will their songs be over in three days? Ah, yea! At the end of the third day they came to some springs of water, but they were brackish or bitter.

23-24 And when they came to Marah, they could not drink of the waters of Marah, for they were bitter: therefore the name of it was called Marah. And the people murmured —

Ah, these singers had sadly changed their notes! Where are the timbrels now? 'The people murmured' —

24-27 against Moses, saying, What shall we drink? And he cried unto the LORD; and the LORD shewed him a tree, which when he had cast into the waters, the waters were made sweet: there he made for them a statute and an ordinance, and there he proved them, And said, If thou wilt diligently hearken to the voice of the LORD thy God, and wilt do that which is right in his sight, and wilt give ear to his commandments, and keep all his statutes, I will put none of these diseases upon thee, which I have brought upon the Egyptians: for I am the LORD that healeth thee. And they came to Elim, —

They did not stop long at Marah, probably only a few hours.

27 where were twelve wells of water, and threescore and ten palm trees: and they encamped there by the waters.

That Elim must have been prepared on purpose for Israel. Twelve springs of water — that was the number of the tribes. Threescore and ten palm trees that was the number of the elders. I do not wonder that Moses noted these numbers. It must have seemed remarkable that, long before they came there, there were the wells and there were the palm trees all ready for their encampment. It was most significant that these things should have been prepared according to the number of the children of Israel; but everything else is arranged by the same rule. When the Lord divided the people, he set the bounds of the nations according to the number of the children of Israel. It is by this line that he builds his church still. It is according to his thoughts of his own people that he rules everything in his providence.

Jer. 7:21-22 Thus saith the LORD of hosts, the God of Israel; Put your burnt offerings unto your sacrifices, and eat flesh. For I spake not unto your fathers, nor commanded them in the day that I brought them out of the land of Egypt, concerning burnt offerings or sacrifices:

You have heard what God said to them when they came out of Egypt.

23-26 But this thing commanded I them, saying, Obey my voice, and I will be your God, and ye shall be my people: and walk ye in all the ways that I have commanded you, that it may be well unto you. But they hearkened not, nor inclined their ear, but walked in the counsels and in the imagination of their evil heart, and went backward, and not forward. Since the day that your fathers came forth out of the land of Egypt unto this day I have even sent unto you all my servants the prophets, daily rising up early and sending them: Yet they hearkened not unto me, nor inclined their ear, but hardened their neck: they did worse than their fathers.

God grant that these words may never be a truthful description of us!

Oh, may we keep the covenant of our God and walk before him with a holy, reverent fear and serve him all our days! Amen.

EXODUS 16:1-5,11-36; NUMBERS 11:1-10

Exod. 16:1-2 And they took their journey from Elim, and all the congregation of the children of Israel came unto the wilderness of Sin, which is between Elim and Sinai, on the fifteenth day of the second month after their departing out of the land of Egypt. And the whole congregation of the children of Israel murmured against Moses and Aaron in the wilderness:

They have been only about six weeks in the wilderness, and already they are up in arms against their leaders. Remember that we have the same kind of people to deal with as Moses and Aaron had. The children of Israel were no better than any other nation; and I do not think they were any worse. We may take them as a fair average of human nature, which is a discontented, rebellious thing in the best of circumstances.

3 And the children of Israel said unto them, Would to God we had died by the hand of the LORD in the land of Egypt, when we sat by the flesh pots, and when we did eat bread to the full; for ye have brought us forth into this wilderness, to kill this whole assembly with hunger.

They forgot all about the brick-making and the whips and the iron bondage, and they recollected nothing but the fleshpots of Egypt. Ah, me! how soon, when we escape from a great trial, we forget it! The present much smaller one seems far heavier than that which is past.

4 Then said the LORD unto Moses, Behold, I will rain bread from heaven for you; and the people shall go out and gather a certain rate every day, that I may prove them, whether they will walk in my law, or no.

See God's answer to man's murmuring. They send up their complaint, and he promises to rain bread down from above. It is a blessed story on God's part all along: a rain of mercy for a smoke of complaining.

5 And it shall come to pass, that on the sixth day they shall prepare that which they bring in; and it shall be twice as much as they gather daily.

Now let us read at the eleventh verse.

11-12 And the LORD spake unto Moses, saying, I have heard the murmurings of the children of Israel: —

'I have heard them.' God always does hear. Oh, his wonderful patience! If he took no notice of the murmurers, or punished them for their wickedness, we should have no cause for wonder; but he is long-suffering, even to those who do not deserve his pity.

12 speak unto them, saying, At even ye shall eat flesh, and in the morning ye shall be filled with bread; and ye shall know that I am the LORD your God.

'There shall be no mistake about who I am. I will work this miracle in such a God-like style, and on such a divine scale, that ye shall know that I am Jehovah your God.'

13-16 And it came to pass, that at even the quails came up, and covered the camp: and in the morning the dew lay round about the host. And when the dew that lay was gone up, behold, upon the face of the wilderness there lay a small round thing, as small as the hoar frost on the ground. And when the children of Israel saw it, they said one to another, It is manna: for they wist not what it was. And Moses said unto them, This is the bread which the LORD hath given you to eat. This is the thing which the LORD hath commanded, Gather of it every man according to his eating, an omer for every man, —

About two pints and a half, I think; according to some calculations, two quarts, or thereabouts. There would be more sustenance in it than in a half-quarter loaf of bread *per diem*: 'An omer for every man.'

16-18 according to the number of your persons; take ye every man for them which are in his tents. And the children of Israel did so, and gathered, some more, some less. And when they did mete it with an omer, he that gathered much had nothing over, and he that gathered little had no lack; they gathered every man according to his eating.

God meant it to be so; not every man according to his avarice, that he might save any of it, but 'every man according to his eating'. God took care that neither should feebleness be stinted nor should greed have any excess.

19-22 And Moses said, Let no man leave of it till the morning. Notwithstanding they hearkened not unto Moses; but some of them left of it until the morning, and it bred worms, and stank: and

Moses was wroth with them. And they gathered it every morning, every man according to his eating: and when the sun waxed hot, it melted. And it came to pass, that on the sixth day they gathered twice as much bread, two omers for one man: and all the rulers of the congregation came and told Moses.

He had told them that it would be so, but they evidently did not accept the message that he had delivered to them as the very Word of Jehovah their God; so that, when it was fulfilled, it struck them with wonder, and they 'came and told Moses'.

23 And he said unto them, This is that which the LORD hath said, —

How often could that answer be made to us! God hears our prayer, and we run and say, 'What a wonderful thing! God has heard my prayer.' 'This is that which the Lord hath said.' Is it a strange thing that what Jehovah has said is proved to be true, and is it a subject for surprise that he should keep his promise? You dishonour God when you talk after this fashion.

23 To morrow is the rest of the holy sabbath unto the LORD: —

And yet the Sabbath had not been instituted according to law, which proves that its foundation lay deeper and earlier than the promulgation of the Ten Commandments; it is bound up with the essential arrangement of time since the creation: 'This is that which the Lord hath said, Tomorrow is the rest of the holy sabbath unto the Lord.'

23-27 bake that which ye will bake to day, and seethe that ye will seethe; and that which remaineth over lay up for you to be kept until the morning. And they laid it up till the morning, as Moses bade: and it did not stink, neither was there any worm therein. And Moses said, Eat that to day; for to day is a sabbath unto the LORD: to day ye shall not find it in the field. Six days ye shall gather it; but on the seventh day, which is the sabbath, in it there shall be none. And it came to pass, that there went out some of the people on the seventh day for to gather, and they found none.

They might have expected it to be so; but they would not believe, and as they would not believe, they must needs put the Word of God to the test. But it endures the trial; it is always true. Oh, that men would, in a believing spirit test the Word of God, instead of doing it after this skeptical fashion!

28-31 And the LORD said unto Moses, How long refuse ye to keep my commandments and my laws? See, for that the LORD hath given you the sabbath, therefore he giveth you on the sixth day the bread of two days; abide ye every man in his place, let no man go out of his place on the seventh day. So the people rested on the seventh day. And the house of Israel called the name thereof Manna: —

Or, 'What is it?' It was something too wonderful to be understood and they kept the expression of their wonderment as the name of their bread from heaven. When they first saw it, they exclaimed, 'Man-hu?' 'Man-hu?' 'What is it?' 'What is it?' Thus it received its Hebrew name, manna; but God called it, 'Bread from heaven.'

31-33 and it was like coriander seed, white; and the taste of it was like wafers made with honey. And Moses said, This is the thing which the LORD commandeth, Fill an omer of it to be kept for your generations; that they may see the bread wherewith I have fed you in the wilderness, when I brought you forth from the land of Egypt. And Moses said unto Aaron, Take a pot, and put an omer full of manna therein, and lay it up before the LORD, to be kept for your generations.

This production, which would not keep a single day under ordinary circumstances, would keep for two days to supply the needs of the Sabbath, and it would keep for generations as a memorial of God's goodness to his chosen people during their forty years' wanderings through the wilderness. We may be quite sure that Aaron would not have kept a stinking thing laid up before the Lord.

34-36 As the LORD commanded Moses, so Aaron laid it up before the Testimony, to be kept. And the children of Israel did eat manna forty years, until they came to a land inhabited; they did eat manna, until they came unto the borders of the land of Canaan. Now an omer is the tenth part of an ephah.

Now I want you to read in the Book of Numbers. Further on in the history of the children of Israel, when the people had been long in the wilderness, the same kind of thing happened again.

Num. 11:1 And when the people complained, it displeased the LORD: —

Interpreters cannot make out what they had to complain of. The curse of labour had been removed; they did not earn their bread with the sweat of their face, for it fell from heaven every day. They were at no expense for clothing; and though they journeyed, their feet did not swell. I suppose that they complained of the weather. It was too cold; it was too hot; it was too wet; it was too dry. They complained when they stood still; they were much too long in a place. They complained when they marched; they moved too often. In fact, they were very like ourselves; they often complained most when they had least to complain of. Discontent is chronic to our humanity, and I do not believe that the poorest are the most discontented. It is often the very reverse. When a man is put in a place where be has nothing to complain of, especially if he is an Englishman, he feels quite out of place. He must have something to grumble at, something or other to be a grievance, or else he is not happy. 'When the people complained, it displeased the Lord.'

1 and the LORD heard it; and his anger was kindled; and the fire of the LORD burnt among them, and consumed them that were in the uttermost parts of the camp.

He could hear their first murmurings, as they were new to the wilderness: they were hungry; they were thirsty; and the Lord pitied them. But now, when there was no reason for their complaining, his fire in terrible judgement visited his people, on account of their rebellion and murmuring against the goodness of God.

2-4 And the people cried unto Moses; and when Moses prayed unto the LORD, the fire was quenched. And he called the name of the place Taberah: because the fire of the LORD burnt among them. And the mixt multitude that was among them fell a lusting: —

All evil seems to begin there, among 'the mixt multitude', as it does among those church members who are unconverted and among those people who try to hold with the hare and run with the hounds — those who want to be Christians and worldlings, too.

4 and the children of Israel also wept again, and said, Who shall give us flesh to eat?

Even the true people of God caught the infection of the scum that was mixed with them, and they fell weeping, and said, —

5 We remember the fish, which we did eat in Egypt freely; the cucumbers, and the melons, and the leeks, and the onions, and the garlick:

Fine stuff that to recollect! 'Why!' say you, 'you have read before something very much like that.' I am reading another record; but there is no originality in grumbling; it is always the same old thing over again. You might well suppose that I was reading in the Book of Exodus, but I am not; there are many years in between. He who sitteth down with a discontented hand to paint a picture will paint the same picture that he painted before. There is no originality in the murmuring, although they put in a few new touches. Before, it was the flesh pots that they remembered; now, in addition to the flesh, there are these savoury vegetables, 'the cucumbers, and the melons, and the leeks, and the onions, and the garlick'.

6 But now our soul is dried away: there is nothing at all, beside this manna, before our eyes.

Here they pour contempt upon the bread of angels, upon the food of heaven, upon the venison of God. Oh, what will men not complain of?

7 And the manna was as coriander seed, and the colour thereof as the colour of bdellium.

A fine white colour, like a pearl.

8 And the people went about, and gathered it, and ground it in mills, or beat it in a mortar, and baked it in pans, and made cakes of it: and the taste of it was as the taste of fresh oil.

At first they thought it was like wafers made with honey. Getting more used to it, they, perhaps, described it quite as accurately, but not quite so sweetly; they said it was like fresh oil, and there is no better taste than that. Oil, by the time it comes to us, has usually a rank and rancid taste; but in the oil countries it is delicious; and he who has bread and a drop or two of oil, will find himself not ill supplied with a dinner. 'The taste of it was as the taste of fresh oil.'

9 And when the dew fell upon the camp in the night, the manna fell upon it.

God took care to preserve his precious gift, encasing each single particle of it within a drop of dew, which gave it freshness. And when truth comes to us encased in the dew of the Spirit, how sweet is its taste! May it be so to us whenever we feed on Christ!

10 Then Moses heard the people weep throughout their families, every man in the door of his tent: and the anger of the LORD was kindled greatly; Moses also was displeased.

And no wonder; meek man as he was, they vexed his gracious spirit by their perpetual murmurings. As we read this sad story, let us, as in a glass, see ourselves; and let us deeply repent of our murmuring and complaining, and henceforth sing,

> *I will praise thee every day!*
> *Now thine anger's turn'd away.*

EXODUS 20:1-17, 2 KINGS 17:23-41

Exod. 20:1-3 And God spake all these words, saying, I am the LORD thy God, which have brought thee out of the land of Egypt, out of the house of bondage. Thou shalt have no other gods before me.

God is the only God, and no other object of worship is to be tolerated for a moment.

4-6 Thou shalt not make unto thee any graven image, or any likeness of any thing that is in heaven above, or that is in the earth beneath, or that is in the water under the earth. Thou shalt not bow down thyself to them, nor serve them: for I the LORD thy God am a jealous God, visiting the iniquity of the fathers upon the children unto the third and fourth generation of them that hate me; And shewing mercy unto thousands of them that love me, and keep my commandments.

Here we are forbidden to worship God under any similitude whatever. The first command forbids the worship of another God; the second strictly forbids us to worship anything which our eyes can see, under the pretense that we are worshipping God thereby. This is another offense and much more common than the first; and it is often pleaded, 'Oh, we do not worship these things; we worship God whom these represent.' But here it is strictly forbidden to represent God under any form or substance whatsoever and to make that an object of worship.

7 Thou shalt not take the name of the LORD thy God in vain; for the LORD will not hold him guiltless that taketh his name in vain.

A reverence for the very name of God is demanded, and all things that are connected with his worship are to be kept sacred.

8-11 Remember the sabbath day, to keep it holy. Six days shalt thou labour, and do all thy work: But the seventh day is the sabbath of the LORD thy God: in it thou shalt not do any work, thou, nor thy son, nor thy daughter, thy manservant, nor thy maidservant, nor thy cattle, nor thy stranger that is within thy gates: For in six days the LORD made heaven and earth, the sea, and all that in them is, and rested the seventh day: wherefore the LORD blessed the sabbath day, and hallowed it.

It is good for us that we make the Sabbath a day of rest — a day of holy worship — a day of drawing near unto God. Thus far, we have the first table, containing the duties towards God. The rest inscribed on the second table are our duties towards man.

12-14 Honour thy father and thy mother: that thy days may be long upon the land which the LORD thy God giveth thee. Thou shalt not kill. Thou shalt not commit adultery.

These commandments take a far wider sweep than the mere words. 'Thou shalt not kill' includes the doing of anything by which life may be shortened as well as taken away. It includes anger — every evil wish and every malicious passion. And, 'Thou shalt not commit adultery' includes every form of unchastity and impurity.

15-17 Thou shalt not steal. Thou shalt not bear false witness against thy neighbour. Thou shalt not covet thy neighbour's house, thou shalt not covet thy neighbour's wife, nor his manservant, nor his maidservant, nor his ox, nor his ass, nor any thing that is thy neighbour's.

It was the tenth commandment that convicted the apostle Paul, for he says, 'I had not known sin… except the law had said, "Thou shalt not covet"' [Romans 7:7]. When men break the other commandments they often break this one first.

2 Kings 17:23-24 Until the LORD removed Israel out of his sight, as he had said by all his servants the prophets. So was Israel carried away out of their own land to Assyria unto this day. And the king of Assyria brought men from Babylon, and from Cuthah, and from Ava, and from Hamath, and from Sepharvaim, and placed them in the cities of Samaria instead of the children of Israel: and they possessed Samaria, and dwelt in the cities thereof.

It was a part of the tactics of the Assyrian empire to take people away from their original location and colonize them in other places — to shift them to another land; so that while the Israelites were taken to Babylon, numbers of those who had lived round about Babylon were brought to live in the Samaritan province, in order that nationalities might thus be broken down and patriotism might expire, thus making it easier for the Assyrian tyrant to govern the land.

25-27 And so it was at the beginning of their dwelling there, that they feared not the LORD: therefore the LORD sent lions among them, which slew some of them. Wherefore they spake to the king of Assyria, saying, The nations which thou hast removed, and placed in the cities of Samaria, know not the manner of the God of the land: therefore he hath sent lions among them, and, behold, they slay them, because they know not the manner of the God of the land. Then the king of Assyria commanded, saying, Carry thither one of the priests whom ye brought from thence; and let them go and dwell there, and let him teach them the manner of the God of the land.

He did not care one single farthing himself what religion they were of; but, if they did not happen to have a religion to suit the country, 'Well, then, send one of the priests who used to live there who can teach them what it is.' According to his notions, they could take it up just when they liked.

28-31 Then one of the priests whom they had carried away from Samaria came and dwelt in Bethel, and taught them how they should fear the LORD. Howbeit every nation made gods of their own, and put them in the houses of the high places which the Samaritans had made, every nation in their cities wherein they dwelt. And the men of Babylon made Succothbenoth, and the men of Cuth made Nergal, and the men of Hamath made Ashima, And the Avites made Nibhaz and Tartak, and the Sepharvites burnt their children in fire to Adrammelech and Anammelech, the gods of Sepharvaim.

It would answer no practical purpose if I were to explain the meaning of the names of these various gods. They were some of them of brute forms. Their worship was generally attended with the most lascivious rites, and especially the worship of Molech or Moloch, who is mentioned under two different forms here. He was a god whose worship was consummated with the most dreadful cruelties, for children were

32-38 So they feared the LORD, and made unto themselves of the lowest of them priests of the high places, which sacrificed for them in the houses of the high places. They feared the LORD, and served their own gods, after the manner of the nations whom they carried away from thence. Unto this day they do after the former manners: they fear not the LORD, neither do they after their statutes, or after their ordinances, or after the law and commandment which the LORD commanded the children of Jacob, whom he named Israel; With whom the LORD had made a covenant, and charged them, saying, Ye shall not fear other gods, nor bow yourselves to them, nor serve them, nor sacrifice to them: But the LORD, who brought you up out of the land of Egypt with great power and a stretched out arm, him shall ye fear, and him shall ye worship, and to him shall ye do sacrifice. And the statutes, and the ordinances, and the law, and the commandment, which he wrote for you, ye shall observe to do for evermore; and ye shall not fear other gods. And the covenant that I have made with you ye shall not forget; neither shall ye fear other gods.

How this warning comes over and over and over again! 'Hear, O Israel. The Lord thy God is one God.' The worship of anything else under any pretext whatsoever, besides the one ever-blessed trinity in unity is for ever forbidden to us.

39-41 But the LORD your God ye shall fear; and he shall deliver you out of the hand of all your enemies. Howbeit they did not hearken, but they did after their former manner. So these nations feared the LORD, and served their graven images, both their children, and their children's children: as did their fathers, so do they unto this day.

Trying, as far us ever they could, to link the old idolatries with the worship of the true God, which thing is the most loathsome in the sight of Most High.

EXODUS 25:10-22

Exod. 25:10-11 And they shall make an ark of shittim wood: two cubits and a half shall be the length thereof, and a cubit and a half the breadth thereof, and a cubit and a half the height thereof. And thou shalt overlay it with pure gold, within and without shalt thou overlay it, and shalt make upon it a crown of gold round about.

The ark of the covenant was the most sacred object in the tabernacle in the wilderness. It stood at the extreme end of the holy of holies. It was the place over which the bright shining light, called the Shekinah, which was the token of the presence of God, shone forth. The ark was, doubtless, typical of our Lord Jesus Christ. It was a sacred chest made to contain the law. Blessed are they who know the law in Christ. Outside of Christ, the law condemns. In Christ, it becomes a blessed guide to us. This ark was made of wood, perhaps to typify the human nature of our blessed Lord; but it was of unrotting wood, acacia, which resists the worm; and truly, in him there was no corruption in life, by way of sin, and no corruption sullied him in death, when he slept for a while in the grave. Wood is a thing that grows out of the earth, even as Jesus sprang up like a root out of a dry ground.

But the ark must be made of the best kind of wood — unrotting and untainted. Yet the ark, though made of wood, did not appear to be so, for it was completely overlaid with pure gold; so everywhere, the Deity, or if you will, the perfect righteousness of Jesus Christ could be seen. The ark was of shittim wood, yet it was an ark of gold; and he, who was truly man was just as truly God, blessed be his holy name. Round about the top of this ark there was a crown of gold. How glorious is Christ in his mediation, as covering the law and preserving it within himself! He is King, glorious in holiness, and honoured in the midst of his people.

12-14 And thou shalt cast four rings of gold for it, and put them in the four corners thereof; and two rings shall be in the one side of it, and two rings in the other side of it. And thou shalt make staves of shittim wood, and overlay them with gold. And thou shalt put the staves into the rings by the sides of the ark, that the ark may be borne with them.

The rings were, of course, for the staves to pass through, and the staves were for the priests to carry the ark as it moved from place to place. It went with the children of Israel in all their journeys; and our Lord Jesus is always with us. He goes with us wherever we go and tarries with us wherever we abide. Though his glorified person is in heaven, yet his presence is not restricted to any one place; as he said to his disciples, 'Lo, I am with you aways, even unto the end of the world' [Matthew 28:20].

15 The staves shall be in the rings of the ark: they shall not be taken from it.

So that it was always ready to be moved.

16 And thou shalt put into the ark the testimony which I shall give thee.

That is to say, the two tables of stone were to be put into the ark of the covenant.

17 And thou shalt make a mercy seat of pure gold: two cubits and a half shall be the length thereof, and a cubit and a half the breadth thereof.

It exactly fitted upon the top of the ark and, so, completely covered whatever was put within. It was of pure gold. This, perhaps, was the most important part of this very important article of the tabernacle furniture. It was the mercy seat, the cover that hid the law, the place where God promised to meet with his people.

18-20 And thou shalt make two cherubims of gold, of beaten work shalt thou make them, in the two ends of the mercy seat. And make one cherub on the one end, and the other cherub on the other end: even of the mercy seat shall ye make the cherubims on the two ends thereof. And the cherubims shall stretch forth their wings on high, covering the mercy seat with their wings, and their faces shall look one to another; toward the mercy seat shall the faces of the cherubims be.

They were part and parcel of the mercy seat; they were made of the same precious metal and all formed one piece. They may represent the angels, who stand desiring to look into the mysteries of God, and they may also represent the church, which is all of a piece with Christ, for ever one with him.

21-22 And thou shalt put the mercy seat above upon the ark; and in the ark thou shalt put the testimony that I shall give thee. And there I will meet with thee, and I will commune with thee from above the mercy seat, from between the two cherubims which are upon the ark of the testimony, of all things which I will give thee in commandment unto the children of Israel.

It was the meeting place of God and men, where the law was covered with a solid plate of gold; so is Jesus the meeting place between God and sinners, where the law is covered with his perfect righteousness.

EXODUS 29:38-46; ISAIAH 53

Exod. 29:38 Now this is that which thou shalt offer upon the altar; two lambs of the first year day by day continually.

Remember, as long as there was a Jewish state, the morning and the evening were to open and to close with the sacrifice of a lamb.

39-42 The one lamb thou shalt offer in the morning; and the other lamb thou shalt offer at even: And with the one lamb a tenth deal of flour mingled with the fourth part of an hin of beaten oil; and the fourth part of an hin of wine for a drink offering. And the other lamb thou shalt offer at even, and shalt do thereto according to the meat offering of the morning, and according to the drink offering thereof, for a sweet savour, an offering made by fire unto the LORD. This shall be a continual burnt offering throughout your generations at the door of the tabernacle of the congregation before the LORD: where I will meet you, to speak there unto thee.

See, the lamb is the place of meeting; God comes to his people as his people come to him, with the morning, and with the evening lamb.

43 And there I will meet with the children of Israel, and the tabernacle shall be sanctified by my glory.

God's glory is in the lamb: it is there he is pleased to manifest himself in the glory of his infinite grace to his people.

44-46 And I will sanctify the tabernacle of the congregation, and the altar: I will sanctify also both Aaron and his sons, to minister to me in the priest's office. And I will dwell among the children of Israel, and will be their God. And they shall know that I am the LORD their God, that brought them forth out of the land of Egypt, that I may dwell among them: I am the LORD their God.

Not without the lamb, you see; that morning and evening sacrifice must be the token and the way of God's dealing with his people.

Now concerning this same lamb, we will read Isaiah 53. Blessed passage — I hope you all know it by heart; it should be like the alphabet to every child. See how it begins.

Isa. 53:1 Who hath believed our report? and to whom is the arm of the LORD revealed?

This is the continual cry of the men of God. The sent ones of God who come to bear testimony of the Lamb of God have no easy time of it. With broken heart they have to go to their Master, and say, 'Who hath believed our report? and to whom is the arm of the Lord revealed?'

2 For he shall grow up before him as a tender plant, and as a root out of a dry ground: he hath no form nor comeliness; and when we shall see him, there is no beauty that we should desire him.

Carnal minds never did see beauty in Christ, and never will. Christ as the great sacrifice is always rejected.

3-5 He is despised and rejected of men; a man of sorrows, and acquainted with grief: and we hid as it were our faces from him; he was despised, and we esteemed him not. Surely he hath borne our griefs, and carried our sorrows: yet we did esteem him stricken, smitten of God, and afflicted. But he was wounded for our transgressions, he was bruised for our iniquities: the chastisement of our peace was upon him; and with his stripes we are healed.

Blessed be his name. Some of us can say that with great delight: 'With his stripes we are healed.'

6-7 All we like sheep have gone astray; we have turned every one to his own way; and the LORD hath laid on him the iniquity of us all. He was oppressed, and he was afflicted, yet he opened not his mouth: he is brought as a lamb to the slaughter, and as a sheep before her shearers is dumb, so he openeth not his mouth.

'He was oppressed and he was afflicted, yet he opened not his mouth.' Our blessed Master — there are his seven cries upon the cross, but not one word of murmuring, no complaint against his enemies — 'He opened not his mouth: he is brought as the lamb to the slaughter, and as a sheep before her shearers is dumb, so he openeth not his mouth.'

8-10 He was taken from prison and from judgment: and who shall declare his generation? for he was cut off out of the land of the living: for the transgression of my people was he stricken. And he made his grave with the wicked, and with the rich in his death; because he had done no violence, neither was any deceit in his mouth. Yet it pleased the LORD to bruise him; he hath put him to grief: when thou shalt make his soul an offering for sin, he shall see his seed, he shall prolong his days, and the pleasure of the LORD shall prosper in his hand.

'Yet it pleased the Lord to bruise him.' If ever there was a man whom God should have protected from every sorrow and guarded from every stroke of injustice, it was Jesus; and unless it was for sins not his own he suffered, unless it was as a substitute for man, it was the most unjust of all heard of injustices that Christ should die at all.

11-12 He shall see of the travail of his soul, and shall be satisfied: by his knowledge shall my righteous servant justify many; for he shall bear their iniquities. Therefore will I divide him a portion with the great, and he shall divide the spoil with the strong; because he hath poured out his soul unto death: and he was numbered with the transgressors; and he bare the sin of many, and made intercession for the transgressors.

'He shall see of the travail of his soul.' Oh! what a joy is this to us! He did not travail in vain. His pangs were as of a travailing woman; but the birth, the glorious birth that comes of it in the salvation of multitudes — this is his recompense.

EXODUS 32:1-29

Exod. 32:1 And when the people saw that Moses delayed to come down out of the mount, the people gathered themselves together unto Aaron, and said unto him, Up, make us gods, which shall go before us; for as for this Moses, the man that brought us up out of the land of Egypt, we wot not what is become of him.

They wanted something to look at — something visible that they could adore. It was not that they meant to cease to worship Jehovah, but they intended to worship him under some tangible symbol. That is the great fault of Ritualists and Romanists, they aim at worshipping God, but they must do so through some sign, some symbol, some cross, some crucifix, or something or other that they can see.

2-3 And Aaron said unto them, Break off the golden earrings, which are in the ears of your wives, of your sons, and of your daughters, and bring them unto me. And all the people brake off the golden earrings which were in their ears, and brought them unto Aaron.

People are often very generous in their support of a false religion; and, to make idol gods, they will sacrifice their most precious treasures, as these idolaters willingly gave their golden earrings.

4 And he received them at their hand, and fashioned it with a graving tool, after he had made it a molten calf: and they said, These be thy gods, O Israel, which brought thee up out of the land of Egypt.

No doubt they copied the Egyptian god, which was in the form of a bull, which the Holy Spirit, by the pen of Moses, here calls a calf. The psalmist probably also alludes to it when he speaks of 'an ox or a bullock that hath horns and hoofs'. It seems strange that these people should have thought of worshipping the living God under such a symbol as that.

5 And when Aaron saw it, he built an altar before it; and Aaron made proclamation, and said, To morrow is a feast to the LORD.

'To Jehovah'. They intended to worship Jehovah under the form of a bull — the image of strength. Other idolaters go further, and worship Baal and various false gods; but, between the worship of a golden calf and the worship of false gods, there is very little choice; and, between the idolatry of the heathen and popery, there is about as much difference as there is between six and half a dozen.

6 And they rose up early on the morrow, and offered burnt offerings, and brought peace offerings; and the people sat down to eat and to drink, and rose up to play.

It was usual to worship false gods with music and dancing and with orgies of drunkenness and obscene rites, and the Israelites fell into the same evils as they had seen among their neighbours.

7 And the LORD said unto Moses, —

Just in the midst of his hallowed communion, the Lord said to him:

7 Go, get thee down; for thy people, which thou broughtest out of the land of Egypt, have corrupted themselves:

God would not own them as his people. He called them Moses' people: 'thy people, which thou broughtest out of the land of Egypt, have corrupted themselves'.

8-10 They have turned aside quickly out of the way which I commanded them: they have made them a molten calf, and have worshipped it, and have sacrificed thereunto, and said, These be thy gods, O Israel, which have brought thee up out of the land of Egypt. And the LORD said unto Moses, I have seen this people, and, behold, it is a stiffnecked people: Now therefore let me alone, that my wrath may wax hot against them, and that I may consume them: and I will make of thee a great nation.

For Moses began at once to pray for the people — to interpose between God and the execution of his righteous wrath; and therefore, the Lord said to him, 'Let me alone ... that I may consume them.'

11 And Moses besought the LORD his God, and said, LORD, why doth thy wrath wax hot against thy people, —

See how he dares even to say to God, 'They are thy people, though they have acted so wickedly. "Why doth thy wrath wax hot against thy people?"'

11-13 which thou hast brought forth out of the land of Egypt with great power, and with a mighty hand? Wherefore should the Egyptians speak, and say, For mischief did he bring them out, to slay them in the mountains, and to consume them from the face of the earth? Turn from thy fierce wrath, and repent of this evil against thy people. Remember Abraham, Isaac, and Israel, thy servants, to whom thou swarest by thine own self, and saidst unto them, I will multiply your seed as the stars of heaven, and all this land that I have spoken of will I give unto your seed, and they shall inherit it for ever.

Moses pleaded the covenant which the Lord had made with Abraham, Isaac, and Israel, and there is no plea like that. Although it might have been to his own personal interest that the people should be destroyed, Moses would not have it so; and he pleaded with God, for the sake of his own honour, his faithfulness, and his truth, not to run back from the word which he had spoken.

14-15 And the LORD repented of the evil which he thought to do unto his people. And Moses turned, and went down from the mount, —

Does it not seem sad for Moses to have to go down from the immediate presence of God, and to stand among the idolatrous and rebellious people in the camp? Yet that is often the lot of those whom God employs as his servants. They have, as it were, to come down from heaven to fight with hell upon earth.

15-17 and the two tables of the testimony were in his hand: the tables were written on both their sides; on the one side and on the other were they written. And the tables were the work of God, and the writing was the writing of God, graven upon the tables. And when Joshua heard the noise of the people as they shouted, he said unto Moses, There is a noise of war in the camp.

For Joshua was a younger man than Moses, and also a soldier, so his ear was quicker to hear what he took to be 'a noise of war in the camp'.

18 And he said, It is not the voice of them that shout for mastery, neither is it the voice of them that cry for being overcome: but the noise of them that sing do I hear.

Moses knew that it was not a battle cry either of the victors or the vanquished but the song of idolatrous worshippers.

19 And it came to pass, as soon as he came nigh unto the camp, that he saw the calf, and the dancing: and Moses' anger waxed hot, and he cast the tables out of his hands, and brake them beneath the mount.

In righteous indignation, he preserved those sacred tablets from the profane touch of the polluted people, by dashing them to fragments in his holy anger.

20 And he took the calf which they had made, and burnt it in the fire, and ground it to powder, and strawed it upon the water, and made the children of Israel drink of it.

Think of the courage of this one man, to go single handed right into the middle of the idolaters' camp, and deal thus with their precious god!

21-24 And Moses said unto Aaron, What did this people unto thee, that thou hast brought so great a sin upon them? And Aaron said, Let not the anger of my lord wax hot: thou knowest the people, that they are set on mischief. For they said unto me, Make us gods, which shall go before us: for as for this Moses, the man that brought us up out of the land of Egypt, we wot not what is become of him. And I said unto them, Whosoever hath any gold, let them break it off. So they gave it me: then I cast it into the fire, and there came out this calf.

Which was a lie. Aaron was a poor weak-minded creature, easily persuaded to do wrong; and when his stronger-minded and more gracious brother was absent, he became the willing tool of the idolatrous people. And yet Aaron is called, by the psalmist, 'the saint of the Lord', and so he was, taking him as a whole. One black spot, on the face of a fair man, does not prove him to be a black man; and so, one sin, in the life of a man who is usually holy, does not put him among the ungodly.

25-28 And when Moses saw that the people were naked; (for Aaron had made them naked unto their shame among their enemies:) Then Moses stood in the gate of the camp, and said, Who is on the LORD's side? let him come unto me. And all the sons of Levi gathered themselves together unto him. And he said unto them, Thus saith the LORD God of Israel, Put every man his sword by his side, and go in and out from gate to gate throughout the camp, and slay every man his brother, and every man his companion, and every man his neighbour. And the children of Levi did according to the word of Moses: —

The rebellious, the idolatrous, the men who had defied the authority of God, were to be summarily executed on the spot.

28-29 and there fell of the people that day about three thousand men. For Moses had said, Consecrate yourselves today to the LORD, even every man upon his son, and upon his brother; that he may bestow upon you a blessing this day.

Such a colossal crime as that must be expiated before the Lord could again bless the chosen race.

EXODUS 32

Exod. 32:1 And when the people saw that Moses delayed to come down out of the mount, the people gathered themselves together unto Aaron, and said unto him, Up, make us gods, which shall go before us; for as for this Moses, the man that brought us up out of the land of Egypt, we wot not what is become of him.

What a terrible speech to be made by the people whom God had chosen to be his own! 'Make us gods. Make our Creator.' How could that be?

2 And Aaron said unto them, Break off the golden earrings, which are in the ears of your wives, of your sons, and of your daughters, and bring them unto me.

Poor Aaron! He never had the backbone of his brother Moses. He was a better speaker; but oh, the poverty of his heart! He yields to the will of these idolatrous people and bows to their wicked behests at once.

3 And all the people brake off the golden earrings which were in their ears, and brought them unto Aaron.

Idolaters spare no expense; there is many a worshipper of a god of wood or mud who gives more to that idol than professing Christians give to the cause of the one living and true God. It is sad that it should be so.

4 And he received them at their hand, and fashioned it with a graving tool, after he had made it a molten calf: and they said, These be thy gods, O Israel, which brought thee up out of the land of Egypt.

This was an Egyptian idolatry, the worship of God under the fashion of an ox, the emblem of strength; but God is not to be worshipped under emblems at all. What a poor representation of God any emblem must be!

5 And when Aaron saw it, he built an altar before it; and Aaron made proclamation, and said, To morrow is a feast to the LORD.

They were going to worship Jehovah under the emblem of an ox. This is what you will hear idolaters say; they do not worship the image, they say, but the true God under that image. Yet that is expressly forbidden under the second commandment.

6 And they rose up early on the morrow, and offered burnt offerings, and brought peace offerings; and the people sat down to eat and to drink, and rose up to play.

Lascivious games were sure to accompany idolatrous worship, for idolatry always leads to filthiness in some form or other, as if it were inevitable.

7 And the LORD said unto Moses, Go, get thee down; for thy people, which thou broughtest out of the land of Egypt, have corrupted themselves:

How startled Moses must have been when Jehovah said this to him!

8-9 They have turned aside quickly out of the way which I commanded them: they have made them a molten calf, and have worshipped it, and have sacrificed thereunto, and said, These be thy gods, O Israel, which have brought thee up out of the land of Egypt. And the LORD said unto Moses, I have seen this people, and, behold, it is a stiffnecked people:

Moses perhaps begins to lift his voice in prayer, and God says:

10 Now therefore let me alone, that my wrath may wax hot against them, and that I may consume them: and I will make of thee a great nation.

'I will keep my promise to Abraham by destroying these rebels, and taking thee, his true descendant, and fulfilling the covenant in thee.'

11-13 And Moses besought the LORD his God, and said, LORD, why doth thy wrath wax hot against thy people, which thou hast brought forth out of the land of Egypt with great power, and with a mighty hand? Wherefore should the Egyptians speak, and say, For mischief did he bring them out, to slay them in the mountains, and to consume them from the face of the earth? Turn from thy fierce wrath, and repent of this evil against thy people. Remember Abraham, Isaac, and Israel, thy servants, to whom thou swarest by thine own self, and saidst unto them, I will multiply your seed as the stars of heaven, and all this land that I have spoken of will I give unto your seed, and they shall inherit it for ever.

What a brave prayer this was! Here is a wrestling Moses, true son of wrestling Israel. He brings his arguments to bear upon Jehovah when he is angry, and he succeeds in turning aside the Lord's wrath.

14-15 And the LORD repented of the evil which he thought to do unto his people. And Moses turned, and went down from the mount, —

An unhappy, broken-hearted man, going from the closest communion with God down into the midst of a wicked people.

15-17 and the two tables of the testimony were in his hand: the tables were written on both their sides; on the one side and on the other were they written. And the tables were the work of God, and the writing was the writing of God, graven upon the tables. And when Joshua heard the noise of the people as they shouted, he said unto Moses, There is a noise of war in the camp.

Joshua had probably waited lower down, and he met Moses in his descent. He heard with the quick ears of a soldier, and his thoughts went that way.

18-19 And he said, It is not the voice of them that shout for mastery, neither is it the voice of them that cry for being overcome: but the noise of them that sing do I hear. And it came to pass, as soon as he came nigh unto the camp, that he saw the calf, and the dancing: and Moses' anger waxed hot, and he cast the tables out of his hands, and brake them beneath the mount.

This is he who had been praying to God, and saying, 'Why doth thy wrath wax hot against thy people?' Now he is in deep sympathy with God, and he is himself angry with the idolaters. He cannot help it when he begins to see their sin. Before, he had only thought of the people, but now he looks at their sin. When you see sin, if you are a man of God, your wrath waxes hot, and you get into sympathy with that holy God who cannot be otherwise than indignant at iniquity wherever it may be.

20 And he took the calf which they had made, and burnt it in the fire, and ground it to powder, and strawed it upon the water, and made the children of Israel drink of it.

See the power of this one man who has God at his back and God in him. While the people are dancing around their idol, he tears it down, grinds it to powder, and says, 'You shall drink it every one of you.' Why, there are millions to one; but what cares he about their millions? God is with him, and he is God's servant; and therefore, they all tremble before him.

21-24 And Moses said unto Aaron, What did this people unto thee, that thou hast brought so great a sin upon them? And Aaron said, Let not the anger of my lord wax hot: thou knowest the people, that they are set on mischief. For they said unto me, Make us gods, which shall go before us: for as for this Moses, the man that brought us up out of the land of Egypt, we wot not what is become of him. And I said unto them, Whosoever hath any gold, let them break it off. So they gave it me: then I cast it into the fire, and there came out this calf.

That was a lie, for he had made the calf and shaped it himself. Aaron had not any backbone nor any principle; he could not be stout-hearted for God. What a poor little man he seems by the side of his great brother! How he shrivels up under the rebuke of Moses!

25 And when Moses saw that the people were naked; (for Aaron had made them naked unto their shame among their enemies:)

Moses does not spare Aaron, he lays at his door the guilt of the great sin he had committed: 'Aaron had made them naked unto their shame among their enemies.'

26-27 Then Moses stood in the gate of the camp, and said, Who is on the LORD's side? let him come unto me. And all the sons of Levi gathered themselves together unto him. And he said unto them, Thus saith the LORD God of Israel, Put every man his sword by his side, and go in and out from gate to gate throughout the camp, and slay every man his brother, and every man his companion, and every man his neighbour.

This is the man who pleaded for them on the top of the mount. See how he acts in the sight of their sin; by divine authority, he smites them right and left. Possibly, those who were slain were the men who refused to drink the water on which the powder had been sprinkled or those who continued in rebellion against the Lord.

28-30 And the children of Levi did according to the word of Moses: and there fell of the people that day about three thousand men. For Moses had said, Consecrate yourselves today to the LORD, even every man upon his son, and upon his brother; that he may bestow upon you a blessing this day. And it came to pass on the morrow, that Moses said unto the people, Ye have sinned a great sin: and now I will go up unto the LORD; peradventure I shall make an atonement for your sin.

I will be bound to say that this was said after a sleepless night. The people's sin is now so vividly before him that he begins to feel that God will be just if he punishes them and does not grant them any forgiveness; so he goes, once more, up that steep climb to the top of Sinai with a trembling heart and with only a 'peradventure' on his lip.

31-32 And Moses returned unto the LORD, and said, Oh, this people have sinned a great sin, and have made them gods of gold. Yet now, if thou wilt forgive their sin—; —

There he broke down, he could not finish that sentence.

32 and if not, blot me, I pray thee, out of thy book which thou hast written.

'Let me die in their stead!' But God could not accept one man in the stead of another. There *is* a great Substitute, ordained of old, but he is more than man, and therefore he can stand in the sinner's stead.

33-35 And the LORD said unto Moses, Whosoever hath sinned against me, him will I blot out of my book. Therefore now go, lead the people unto the place of which I have spoken unto thee: behold, mine Angel shall go before thee: nevertheless in the day when I visit I will visit their sin upon them. And the LORD plagued the people, because they made the calf, which Aaron made.

Moses had only half success in pleading for the people; they were not to die as yet, but God declared that he would visit their sin upon them.

DEVOTIONAL THOUGHTS ON THE BIBLE
Charles Haddon Spurgeon

LEVITICUS

LEVITICUS 16:1-31; HEBREWS 9:1-22

Lev. 16:1-2 And the LORD spake unto Moses after the death of the two sons of Aaron, when they offered before the LORD, and died; And the LORD said unto Moses, Speak unto Aaron thy brother, that he come not at all times into the holy place within the vail before the mercy seat, which is upon the ark; that he die not: for I will appear in the cloud upon the mercy seat.

The way into the heavenly places was not yet made manifest; the inner shrine, called the holy of holies, was specially guarded from human access. No one could have said in those days, 'Let us come boldly unto the throne of grace', for only the high priest could approach the mercy seat at all, and he must go within the vail strictly in accordance with the instructions given to Moses by the Lord. Nadab and Abihu appear to have entered into the presence of God wrongfully. They had probably been drinking, for there was a command afterwards given that no priest should drink wine or strong drink when he went into the house of the Lord. God in his righteous anger slew these young men at once, and now, lest any others should intrude into the secret place of communion, a law was given to tell when and how man might approach his God.

3 Thus shall Aaron come into the holy place: with a young bullock for a sin offering, and a ram for a burnt offering.

There is no access to God except by sacrifice; there never was, and there never can be any way to God for sinful man except by sacrifice.

4 He shall put on the holy linen coat, and he shall have the linen breeches upon his flesh, and shall be girded with a linen girdle, and with the linen mitre shall he be attired: these are holy garments; therefore shall he wash his flesh in water, and so put them on.

Our great High Priest offered himself without spot to God. He is himself without sin; but, the Jewish high priest must make himself typically pure, by putting on the snow white garments of holy service, and before doing so, he must wash himself with water, that he might come before God acceptably. None might approach the holy God with impurities upon them.

5-6 And he shall take of the congregation of the children of Israel two kids of the goats for a sin offering, and one ram for a burnt offering. And Aaron shall offer his bullock of the sin offering, which is for himself, and make an atonement for himself, and for his house.

These priests were sinful; therefore, they must first themselves be purged from guilt before they could come nigh to God, but the true High Priest of God, our Lord Jesus, needed to offer no sacrifice for himself, for he was pure and without blemish or stain of sin.

7 And he shall take the two goats, and present them before the LORD at the door of the tabernacle of the congregation.

These two goats were not for himself but for the people. You must regard them as if they were but one offering, for it needed both of them to set forth the divine plan by which sin is put away: one was to die, and the other was typically to bear away the sin of the people.

8 And Aaron shall cast lots upon the two goats; one lot for the LORD, and the other lot for the scapegoat.

One goat was to show how sin is put away in reference to God by sacrifice, and the other goat was to show how it is put away in reference to us, God's people, by being carried into oblivion.

9-14 And Aaron shall bring the goat upon which the LORD's lot fell, and offer him for a sin offering. But the goat, on which the lot fell to be the scapegoat, shall be presented alive before the LORD, to make an atonement with him, and to let him go for a scapegoat into the wilderness. And Aaron shall bring the bullock of the sin offering, which is for himself, and shall make an atonement for himself, and for his house, and shall kill the bullock of the sin offering which is for himself: And he shall take a censer full of burning coals of fire from off the altar before the LORD, and his hands full of sweet incense beaten small, and bring it within the vail: And he shall put the incense upon the fire before the LORD, that the cloud of the incense may cover the mercy seat that is upon the testimony, that he die not: And he shall take of the blood of the bullock, and sprinkle it with his finger upon the mercy seat eastward; and before the mercy seat shall he sprinkle of the blood with his finger seven times.

This was his first entrance within the vail, with holy incense to denote the acceptance which Christ has with God, though he is always well-beloved and dear and precious to his Father. This incense sent up a cloud that veiled the glory of the Shekinah which shone between the wings of the two cherubims, and so the high priest was better able to bear the wondrous brilliance by which God revealed his presence. When Aaron had thus filled the place with the sweetly perfumed smoke, he took the blood of the bullock of the sin offering and carefully sprinkled it seven times on the mercy seat and on the ground around the mercy seat. What a mercy it is for you and me that the spot where we meet with God is a place where the blood of the great sacrifice has been sprinkled, aye, and that the ground of our meeting with God, the place on which the mercy seat rests, has also the blood mark upon it!

15 Then shall he kill the goat of the sin offering, that is for the people, and bring his blood within the vail, and do with that blood as he did with the blood of the bullock, and sprinkle it upon the mercy seat, and before the mercy seat:

Twice, you see, is the holy place thus besprinkled, first with the blood of the bullock and then with that of the goat.

16 And he shall make an atonement for the holy place, because of the uncleanness of the children of Israel, and because of their transgressions in all their sins: and so shall he do for the tabernacle of the congregation, that remaineth among them in the midst of their uncleanness.

If God is to dwell in the midst of sinful men, it can only be through the blood of the atonement. Twice seven times were the holy place and the tabernacle to be sprinkled with blood, as though to indicate a double perfectness of efficacy of the preparation for God's dwelling among sinful men.

17-19 And there shall be no man in the tabernacle of the congregation when he goeth in to make an atonement in the holy place, until he come out, and have made an atonement for himself, and for his household, and for all the congregation of Israel. And he shall go out unto the altar that is before the LORD, and make an atonement for it; and shall take of the blood of the bullock, and of the blood of the goat, and put it upon the horns of the altar round about. And he shall sprinkle of the blood upon it with his finger seven times, and cleanse it, and hallow it from the uncleanness of the children of Israel.

Even this altar, to which we bring our prayers and our thank-offerings, has sin upon it. There is some defilement even in the salt water of our penitent tears; there is some unbelief even in our most acceptable faith; there is some want of holiness about our holiest things. We are unclean by nature and by practice, too. What could we do without the sprinkling of the blood? See how the Lord insisted upon it in the case of his ancient people, yet there are some in these modern times who deride it. God forgive their blasphemy!

20-21 And when he hath made an end of reconciling the holy place, and the tabernacle of the congregation, and the altar, he shall bring the live goat: And Aaron shall lay both his hands upon the head of the live goat, and confess over him all the iniquities of the children of Israel, and all their transgressions in all their sins, putting them upon the head of the goat, and shall send him away by the hand of a fit man into the wilderness:

Notice the 'all' in this twenty-first verse: 'Aaron shall lay both his hands upon the head of the live goat, and confess over him all the iniquities of the children of Israel, and all their transgressions in all their sins, putting them upon the head of the goat, and shall send him away by the hand of a fit man into the wilderness.' This was the second part of the atonement, showing, not sacrifice, but the effect of sacrifice and explaining what becomes of sin after the sacrifice has been accepted and the blood has been presented within the vail.

22-25 And the goat shall bear upon him all their iniquities unto a land not inhabited: and he shall let go the goat in the wilderness. And Aaron shall come into the tabernacle of the congregation, and shall put off the linen garments, which he put on when he went into the holy place, and shall leave them there: And he shall wash his flesh with water in the holy place, and put on his garments, and come forth, and offer his burnt offering, and the burnt offering of the people, and make an atonement for himself, and for the people. And the fat of the sin offering shall he burn upon the altar.

Only the fat of it, the best of it, was burnt upon the altar, for sin offerings were not acceptable to God. They were regarded as being filled with impurity by reason of the sin which they brought to mind; for this reason, the bullock and the goat of the sin offering had to be burnt without the camp: 'Wherefore Jesus also, that he might sanctify the people with his own blood, suffered without the gate' [Hebrews 13:12], as our sin offering. Yet, inasmuch as the fat was accepted upon the altar, so is Christ, even as our sin offering, acceptable before God.

26-27 And he that let go the goat for the scapegoat shall wash his clothes, and bathe his flesh in water, and afterward come into the camp. And the bullock for the sin offering, and the goat for the sin offering, whose blood was brought in to make atonement in the holy place, shall one carry forth without the camp; and they shall burn in the fire their skins, and their flesh, and their dung.

All must be burnt; and the last is mentioned because it more strikingly sets forth the impurity of the sin connected with the sin offering. All must be burnt right up; there must not be a particle of the sin offering left unconsumed.

28 And he that burneth them shall wash his clothes, and bathe his flesh in water, and afterward he shall come into the camp.

Everything that has to do with God's service must be clean and purified by fire and purified by water. An atonement cannot be made by that which is itself defiled; it must be without spot or wrinkle or any such thing before it can put sin away. This is the virtue of Christ's atonement, for he was altogether without sin of any kind.

29-31 And this shall be a statute for ever unto you: that in the seventh month, on the tenth day of the month, ye shall afflict your souls, and do no work at all, whether it be one of your own country, or a stranger that sojourneth among you: For on that day shall the priest make an atonement for you, to cleanse you, that ye may be clean from all your sins before the LORD. It shall be a sabbath of rest unto you, and ye shall afflict your souls, by a statute for ever.

This shows what sacredness the Lord attached to the great day of atonement and gives us more than a hint of the preciousness of our Lord's atoning work for us.

Now let us turn to the Epistle to the Hebrews and see how the apostle spiritualizes the services of the Mosaic dispensation.

Heb. 9:1 Then verily the first covenant had also ordinances of divine service, and a worldly sanctuary.

An external sanctuary, a material structure, and therefore belonging to this world.

2 For there was a tabernacle made; the first, wherein was the candlestick, and the table, and the shewbread; which is called the sanctuary.

Or, 'the Holy Place'.

3-8 And after the second veil, the tabernacle which is called the Holiest of all; Which had the golden censer, and the ark of the covenant overlaid round about with gold, wherein was the golden pot that had manna, and Aaron's rod that budded, and the tables of the covenant; And over it the cherubims of glory shadowing the mercyseat; of which we cannot now speak particularly. Now when these things were thus ordained, the priests went always into the first tabernacle, accomplishing the service of God. But into the second went the high priest alone once every year, not without blood, which he offered for himself, and for the errors of the people: The Holy Ghost this signifying, that the way into the holiest of all was not yet made manifest, while as the first tabernacle was yet standing:

Notice especially those words, 'not without blood'. There could be no approach to God under the old dispensation without the shedding of blood, and there is no access to the Lord now without the precious blood of Christ.

9-22 Which was a figure for the time then present, in which were offered both gifts and sacrifices, that could not make him that did the service perfect, as pertaining to the conscience; Which stood only in meats and drinks, and divers washings, and carnal ordinances, imposed on them until the time of reformation. But Christ being come an high priest of good things to come, by a greater and more perfect tabernacle, not made with hands, that is to say, not of this building; Neither by the blood of goats and calves, but by his own blood he entered in once into the holy place, having obtained eternal redemption for us. For if the blood of bulls and of goats, and the ashes of an heifer sprinkling the unclean, sanctifieth to the purifying of the flesh: How much more shall the blood of Christ, who through the eternal Spirit offered himself without spot to God, purge your conscience from dead works to serve the living God? And for this cause he is the mediator of the new testament, that by means of death, for the redemption of the transgressions that were under the first testament, they which are called might receive the promise of eternal inheritance. For where a testament is, there must also of necessity be the death of the testator. For a testament is of force after men are dead: otherwise it is of no strength at all while the testator liveth. Whereupon neither the first testament was dedicated without blood. For when Moses had spoken every precept to all the people according to the law, he took the blood of calves and of goats, with water, and scarlet wool, and hyssop, and sprinkled both the book, and all the people, Saying, This is the blood of the testament which God hath enjoined unto you. Moreover he sprinkled with blood both the tabernacle, and all the vessels of the ministry. And almost all things are by the law purged with blood; and without shedding of blood is no remission.

That is the great gospel truth that was set forth by all the sacrifices under the law: 'without shedding of blood is no remission'.

LEVITICUS 25:1-7,17-22; DEUTERONOMY 15:1-18

Lev. 25:1-2 And the LORD spake unto Moses in mount Sinai, saying, Speak unto the children of Israel, and say unto them, When ye come into the land which I give you, then shall the land keep a sabbath unto the LORD.

The Jews had much rest provided for them. If they had had faith enough to obey God's commands, they might have been the most favoured of people, but they were not a spiritual people, and the Lord often had to lament their disobedience as in the words recorded by Isaiah: 'O that thou hadst hearkened to my commandments! then had thy peace been as a river, and thy righteousness as the waves of the sea' [Isaiah 48:18].

3-4 Six years thou shalt sow thy field, and six years thou shalt prune thy vineyard, and gather in the fruit thereof; But in the seventh year shall be a sabbath of rest unto the land, a sabbath for the LORD: —

Think of a Sabbath a year long, in which nothing was to be done but to worship God and, so, to rest!

4-5 thou shalt neither sow thy field, nor prune thy vineyard. That which groweth of its own accord of thy harvest thou shalt not reap, neither gather the grapes of thy vine undressed: for it is a year of rest unto the land.

A restful period in a restful land: all land to have rest and yet to have fruitfulness in that rest, the rest of a garden, not the rest of a task. Thus is it oftentimes with God's people: when they rest most, they work best; and while they are resting, they are bearing fruit unto God.

6-7 And the sabbath of the land shall be meat for you; for thee, and for thy servant, and for thy maid, and for thy hired servant, and for thy stranger that sojourneth with thee. And for thy cattle, and for the beast that are in thy land, shall all the increase thereof be meat.

There was to be no private property in the spontaneous produce of that year. It was free to everybody; free even to the cattle, which might go and eat what they would and where they would.

17-21 Ye shall not therefore oppress one another; but thou shalt fear thy God: for I am the LORD your God. Wherefore ye shall do my statutes, and keep my judgments, and do them; and ye shall dwell in the land in safety. And the land shall yield her fruit, and ye shall eat your fill, and dwell therein in safety. And if ye shall say, What shall we eat the seventh year? behold, we shall not sow, nor gather in our increase: Then I will command my blessing upon you in the sixth year, and it shall bring forth fruit for three years.

Not merely for the one year of rest but fruit for three years.

22 And ye shall sow the eighth year, and eat yet of old fruit until the ninth year; until her fruits come in ye shall eat of the old store.

They were to have enough for the year of rest and for the next year in which the harvest was growing and still to have something over for the ninth year. They scarcely could want as much as that, but God would give them more than they actually needed, exceeding abundantly above what they asked or even thought. That Sabbatical year had other blessings connected with it.

Let us read about them in the Book of Deuteronomy, chapter fifteen.

Deut. 15:1-2 At the end of every seven years thou shalt make a release. And this is the manner of the release: Every creditor that lendeth ought unto his neighbour shall release it; he shall not exact it of his neighbour, or of his brother; because it is called the LORD's release.

What a wonderful title for it, 'the Lord's release'!

3 Of a foreigner thou mayest exact it again: but that which is thine with thy brother thine hand shall release;

How was a man to pay when he did not sow or reap during the Sabbatical year? The foreigner did not observe the year of rest; consequently he was bound to pay, and it was only fair that he should do so; but for the Israelite, who carried out the divine law, there was provision made if he was in debt.

4 Save when there shall be no poor among you; —

If there were no poor, then there would be no need for this law.

4-6 for the LORD shall greatly bless thee in the land which the LORD thy God giveth thee for an inheritance to possess it: Only if thou carefully hearken unto the voice of the LORD thy God, to observe to do all these commandments which I command thee this day. For the LORD thy God blesseth thee, as he promised thee: —

That little clause, 'as he promised thee', is worth noticing. This is the rule of God; he deals with us 'according to promise'.

6 and thou shalt lend unto many nations, but thou shalt not borrow; and thou shalt reign over many nations, but they shall not reign over thee.

If God's people had done his will, they would have been like their language; it is observed of the Hebrew, by some, that it borrows nothing from other tongues but lends many words to various languages.

7-9 If there be among you a poor man of one of thy brethren within any of thy gates in thy land which the LORD thy God giveth thee, thou shalt not harden thine heart, nor shut thine hand from thy poor brother: But thou shalt open thine hand wide unto him, and shalt surely lend him sufficient for his need, in that which he wanteth. Beware that there be not a thought in thy wicked heart, saying, The seventh year, the year of release, is at hand; and thine eye be evil against thy poor brother, and thou givest him nought; and he cry unto the LORD against thee, and it be sin unto thee.

Moses, moved by the Spirit of God, anticipates what would very naturally occur to many: 'Then I shall not lend anywhere near the seventh year; if I do, I shall lose it, for I must release my debtor then.' The hardhearted would be sure to make this their evil excuse for lending nothing. But here the Hebrew is warned against such wicked thoughts, lest, refusing to lend to his poor brother for this cause, the needy one should cry to God, and it should be accounted sin on the part of the merciless refuser.

10-11 Thou shalt surely give him, and thine heart shall not be grieved when thou givest unto him: because that for this thing the LORD thy God shall bless thee in all thy works, and in all that thou puttest thine hand unto. For the poor shall never cease out of the land: —

They would have done so; they might have done so, if the rule of God had been kept; but, inasmuch as he foresaw that it never would be kept, he also declared, 'the poor shall never cease out of the land'.

11 therefore I command thee, saying, Thou shalt open thine hand wide unto thy brother, to thy poor, and to thy needy, in thy land.

See how God calls them, not 'the poor', but 'thy poor' and 'thy needy'. The church of God should feel a peculiar property in the poor and needy, as if they were handed over, in the love of Christ, to his people that they might care for them.

12 And if thy brother, an Hebrew man, or an Hebrew woman, be sold unto thee, and serve thee six years; then in the seventh year thou shalt let him go free from thee.

He might be under an apprenticeship of servitude for six years, but the seventh year was to be a year of rest to him, as it was a year of release to debtors, and of rest to the land.

13 And when thou sendest him out free from thee, thou shalt not let him go away empty:

To begin life again with nothing at all in his pocket.

14 Thou shalt furnish him liberally out of thy flock, and out of thy floor, and out of thy winepress: of that wherewith the LORD thy God hath blessed thee thou shalt give unto him.

Who would think of finding such a law as that on the statute book? Where is there such a law under any governor but God? The theocracy would have made a grand government for Israel if Israel had but been able to walk before God in faith and obedience.

15 And thou shalt remember that thou wast a bondman in the land of Egypt, and the LORD thy God redeemed thee: therefore I command thee this thing to day.

The remembrance of their own deliverance out of Egyptian bondage was to make them merciful and kind to their own bondservants.

16-18 And it shall be, if he say unto thee, I will not go away from thee; because he loveth thee and thine house, because he is well with thee; Then thou shalt take an aul, and thrust it through his ear unto the door, and he shall be thy servant for ever. And also unto thy maidservant thou shalt do likewise. It shall not seem hard unto thee, when thou sendest him away free from thee; for he hath been worth a double hired servant to thee, in serving thee six years: and the LORD thy God shall bless thee in all that thou doest.

He has had no pay; he has been always at his work; he has been worth two ordinary hired labourers; let him go, therefore, and let him not go away empty.

DEVOTIONAL THOUGHTS ON THE BIBLE

Charles Haddon Spurgeon

NUMBERS

NUMBERS 4:1-33

Num. 4:1-2 And the LORD spake unto Moses and unto Aaron, saying, Take the sum of the sons of Kohath from among the sons of Levi, after their families, by the house of their fathers,

There were three families, those of Kohath, Gershon, and Merari, and to each of these families a different service was allotted. First, they were to be numbered. 'The Lord knoweth them that are his', and he takes count of all his people.

3 From thirty years old and upward even until fifty years old, all that enter into the host, to do the work in the tabernacle of the congregation.

They were to take up this work as a warfare; for, though it was a peaceful work, yet it is described as being a warfare: and he who serves the Lord, though that service be perfect peace, will not serve him without finding it to be also a warfare.

4 This shall be the service of the sons of Kohath in the tabernacle of the congregation, about the most holy things:

They were to have to do with the most holy place, to carry it, and to carry the vessels of it, a very honourable position.

5-6 And when the camp setteth forward, Aaron shall come, and his sons, and they shall take down the covering vail, and cover the ark of testimony with it: And shall put thereon the covering

NUMBERS 4

of badgers' skins, and shall spread over it a cloth wholly of blue, and shall put in the staves thereof.

These Kohathites might not so take the ark as to handle it, much less might they ever look at it. But the priests, and the sons of Aaron, went in first, and after carefully covering the holy place, they covered up the sacred ark with a cloth of blue. Blue was the token of holiness — of separation. Hence, every Israelite wore a border of blue upon his garment; but this, which was the symbol of the divine presence, was 'all of blue'. It is all holiness. We wear, alas! but a border of blue, but this holy thing was 'all of blue'.

7 And upon the table of shewbread they shall spread a cloth of blue, and put thereon the dishes, and the spoons, and the bowls, and covers to cover withal: and the continual bread shall be thereon:

When they moved the sacred table, the bread was always there; twelve cakes for the twelve tribes, for the bread of God's house is never lacking.

8-10 And they shall spread upon them a cloth of scarlet, and cover the same with a covering of badgers' skins, and shall put in the staves thereof. And they shall take a cloth of blue, and cover the candlestick of the light, and his lamps, and his tongs, and his snuffdishes, and all the oil vessels thereof, wherewith they minister unto it: And they shall put it and all the vessels thereof within a covering of badgers' skins, and shall put it upon a bar.

There were means for handling these vessels without touching them. I mean, the ark had staves, and the vessels were put upon a bar for carrying them.

11 And upon the golden altar they shall spread a cloth of blue, and cover it with a covering of badgers' skins, and shall put to the staves thereof:

A type of the holiness veiled in our Lord's humanity, the badger skin made apparent the simplicity, the poverty, the humility of our Lord, covering evermore that wondrous cloth of blue.

12-13 And they shall take all the instruments of ministry, wherewith they minister in the sanctuary, and put them in a cloth of blue, and cover them with a covering of badgers' skins, and shall put them on a bar: And they shall take away the ashes from the altar, and spread a purple cloth thereon:

A royal altar is this, always grand and glorious in our eyes, covered with a purple cloth.

14-20 And they shall put upon it all the vessels thereof, wherewith they minister about it, even the censers, the fleshhooks, and the shovels, and the basons, all the vessels of the altar; and they shall spread upon it a covering of badgers' skins, and put to the staves of it. And when Aaron and his sons have made an end of covering the sanctuary, and all the vessels of the sanctuary, as the camp is to set forward; after that, the sons of Kohath shall come to bear it: but they shall not touch any holy thing, lest they die. These things are the burden of the sons of Kohath in the tabernacle of the congregation. And to the office of Eleazar the son of Aaron the priest pertaineth the oil for the light, and the sweet incense, and the daily meat offering, and the anointing oil, and the oversight of all the tabernacle, and of all that therein is, in the sanctuary, and in the vessels thereof. And the LORD spake unto Moses and unto Aaron saying, Cut ye not off the tribe of the families of the Kohathites from among the Levites: But thus do unto them, that they may live, and not die, when they approach unto the most holy things: Aaron and his sons shall go in, and appoint them every one to his service and to his burden: But they shall not go in to see when the holy things are covered, lest they die.

This is a very awful thing; I mean, something which should produce a great awe and solemnity in our hearts. These men were chosen to carry the vessels of the most holy place, yet they must never see them. They must be covered up by the hands of the priest; they must never touch them. They must bear them by their staves, or upon the bar upon which they were placed. Oh, how terrible a thing it is to draw near to God! The Lord our God is a jealous God. He will be served with holy reverence or not at all. Hence, he says to Moses and Aaron, 'Take care that you do not lead these men into any mistake. You go in first, and point out to each man what he is to carry. See that all is covered up, for if you do not, they may die in their work. Do not be accessories to their act, and bring upon them this terrible judgment.' I often wish that God's people would be careful not to cause sin in any of his servants when they are engaged in the divine ministry. Perhaps in preaching, or otherwise, there may be something done which vexes the Holy Spirit and causes trouble and sin. And, oh! he who stands in the holy place and bears the holiest of the vessels needs to fear and tremble before God. He needs to ask his brethren to see that they do nothing which might inadvertently cause him to sin.

21-24 And the LORD spake unto Moses, saying, Take also the sum of the sons of Gershon, throughout the houses of their fathers, by their families; From thirty years old and upward until fifty years old shalt thou number them; all that enter in to perform the service, to do the work in the tabernacle of the congregation. This is the service of the families of the Gershonites, to serve, and for burdens:

They were to bear the external coverings of the holy place. The most holy place was in the custody of the Kohathites; but the Gershonites were to carry as follows:

25-28 And they shall bear the curtains of the tabernacle, and the tabernacle of the congregation, his covering, and the covering of the badgers' skins that is above upon it, and the hanging for the door of the tabernacle of the congregation, And the hangings of the court, and the hanging for the door of the gate of the court, which is by the tabernacle and by the altar round about, and their cords, and all the instruments of their service, and all that is made for them: so shall they serve. At the appointment of Aaron and his sons shall be all the service of the sons of the Gershonites, in all their burdens, and in all their service: and ye shall appoint unto them in charge all their burdens. This is the service of the families of the sons of Gershon in the tabernacle of the congregation: and their charge shall be under the hand of Ithamar the son of Aaron the priest.

There was a wise division of labour. I wish we had the same kind of thing in every church, and that every member occupied himself in that to which God has appointed him. But there are some who want to do what they cannot do, and who do not care to do what they can do.

29-32 As for the sons of Merari, thou shalt number them after their families, by the house of their fathers; From thirty years old and upward even unto fifty years old shalt thou number them, every one that entereth into the service, to do the work of the tabernacle of the congregation. And this is the charge of their burden, according to all their service in the tabernacle of the congregation; the boards of the tabernacle, and the bars thereof, and the pillars thereof, and sockets thereof, And the pillars of the court round about, and their sockets, and their pins, and their cords, with all their instruments, and with all their service: and by name ye shall reckon the instruments of the charge of their burden.

They had the heaviest load to carry, but they were the more numerous. They carried the solid columns upon which the covering of the tabernacle rested. And notice that they had also to carry the pins. Sometimes, God's servants dislike carrying pins. They feel themselves too big, but blessed is that servant who, in his place, can be content to carry 'their sockets, and their pins, and their cords, with all their instruments'.

33 This is the service of the families of the sons of Merari, according to all their service, in the tabernacle of the congregation, under the hand of Ithamar the son of Aaron the priest.

NUMBERS 8:5-22

Num. 8:5-6 And the LORD spake unto Moses, saying, Take the Levites from among the children of Israel, and cleanse them.

These men were to be the servants of God; they are the type of God's elect — a people set apart unto divine service, to be zealous for good works. 'Take the Levites from among the children of Israel, and cleanse them.' That is just the way that God the Holy Ghost takes Christians out of the main of mankind and cleanses them.

7-8 And thus shalt thou do unto them, to cleanse them: Sprinkle water of purifying upon them, and let them shave all their flesh, and let them wash their clothes, and so make themselves clean. Then let them take a young bullock with his meat offering, even fine flour mingled with oil, and another young bullock shalt thou take for a sin offering.

There are still, typically, these three things in the cleansing of God's people — the blood, the water, and the razor. There is blood, the emblem of the putting away of sin by Christ's atoning sacrifice; the water, typical of the Holy Ghost, by whom the power of sin is overcome; and then that razor, cutting off that which grows of the flesh; that which was their beauty and their glory is all taken away from them. There are some of God's people who have not felt much of that razor; but if they are to serve God perfectly, it must be used. 'Let them shave all their flesh.'

9-12 And thou shalt bring the Levites before the tabernacle of the congregation: and thou shalt gather the whole assembly of the children of Israel together: And thou shalt bring the Levites before the LORD: and the children of Israel shall put their hands upon the Levites: And Aaron shall offer the Levites before the LORD for an offering of the children of Israel, that they may execute the service of the LORD. And the Levites shall lay their hands upon the heads of the bullocks: and thou shalt offer the one for a sin offering, and the other for a burnt offering, unto the LORD, to make an atonement for the Levites.

There is no true way of serving God without the atonement. Leave that out, and you have left out the vital part of the whole. What service can we render to the Most High if we begin by disloyalty to him whom God has set forth to be the propitiation for sin, even his dear Son?

13-14 And thou shalt set the Levites before Aaron, and before his sons, and offer them for an offering unto the LORD. Thus shalt thou separate the Levites from among the children of Israel: and the Levites shall be mine.

We are to offer up to God our spirit, soul, and body, which is our reasonable service; and if we be indeed God's children, we are to feel that, henceforth, we are not our own, for we are bought with a price. We belong wholly to God; all that we are, and all that we have, is to be his through life and in death and throughout eternity.

15 And after that shall the Levites go in to do the service of the tabernacle of the congregation: and thou shalt cleanse them, and offer them for an offering.

An offering must be presented for us before we can offer ourselves as an offering unto God.

16 For they are wholly given unto me from among the children of Israel; —

Listen to this, you who trust that you are made like unto the elder Brother, and the firstborn from among the creatures of God:

16-18 instead of such as open every womb, even instead of the firstborn of all the children of Israel, have I taken them unto me. For all the firstborn of the children of Israel are mine, both man and beast: on the day that I smote every firstborn in the land of Egypt I sanctified them for myself. And I have taken the Levites for all the firstborn of the children of Israel.

God's people are the elect; they have escaped from death. In that day when the sword of the Lord was drawn, they were shielded by the blood of the lamb sprinkled on the lintel and on the two side posts; and henceforth, because they have been thus preserved, they belong unto the Lord.

19-22 And I have given the Levites as a gift to Aaron and to his sons from among the children of Israel, to do the service of the children of Israel in the tabernacle of the congregation, and to make an atonement for the children of Israel: that there be no plague among the children of Israel, when the children of Israel come nigh unto the sanctuary. And Moses, and Aaron, and all the congregation of the children of Israel, did to the Levites according unto all that the LORD commanded Moses concerning the Levites, so did the children of Israel unto them. And the Levites were purified, and they washed their clothes; and Aaron offered them as an offering before the LORD; and Aaron made an atonement for them to cleanse them. And after that went the Levites in to do their service in the tabernacle of the congregation before Aaron, and before his sons: as the LORD had commanded Moses concerning the Levites, so did they unto them.

How instructive all this is to us! We are not to begin blunderingly to serve God while we are yet in our sins — before we have been sprinkled with the blood — before we have been washed in the water which flowed with the blood — before we have felt that razor that takes away from us all our own pride and glory. No; but when all that is done, then there is to be no delay: 'After that went the Levites in to do their service.'

NUMBERS 9

Num. 9:1-2 And the LORD spake unto Moses in the wilderness of Sinai, in the first month of the second year after they were come out of the land of Egypt, saying, Let the children of Israel also keep the passover at his appointed season.

I should almost fear that they had omitted the keeping of the Passover for a year. There was a first celebration of it when they came out of Egypt; but then it was not so much a type as a matter of fact. It was the thing itself, not the remembrance of the coming out of Egypt, but the actual coming out, the Exodus. One would gather from this command of the Lord that, on the first anniversary of that memorable season, the children of Israel had omitted its observance, and hence Jehovah said to Moses, 'Let the children of Israel also keep the passover at his appointed season.' If this conjecture is correct, it is very significant that a rite which belonged to the law, and was therefore to pass away, was so soon neglected — and certainly it was afterwards neglected for many, many years; whereas, the great memorial ordinance of the Christian dispensation, the Lord's supper, was not neglected even when Christians were under fierce persecution from the Jews or other nations. When the observance of that rite among the heathen was pretty sure to bring death, yet Christians met together on the first day of the week, and continually broke bread in remembrance of their Lord's death, even as we do to this day. I suppose that the supper, which is the memorial of Christ our Passover, has never been altogether neglected throughout the world but has been a matter of constant observation in the church of Christ and shall be 'till he come'.

3-7 In the fourteenth day of this month, at even, ye shall keep it in his appointed season: according to all the rites of it, and according to all the ceremonies thereof, shall ye keep it. And Moses spake unto the children of Israel, that they should keep the passover. And they kept the passover on the fourteenth day of the first month at even in the wilderness of Sinai: according to all that the LORD commanded Moses, so did the children of Israel. And there were certain men, who were defiled by the dead body of a man, that they could not keep the passover on that day: and they came before Moses and before Aaron on that day: And those men said unto him, We are defiled by the dead body of a man: wherefore are we kept back, that we may not offer an offering of the LORD in his appointed season among the children of Israel?

They were in a great difficulty. They were commanded to come to the Passover; they sinned if they did not come, but they had defiled themselves, either through accident or of necessity, and if they came thus to the Passover, they would be committing sin; so either way, they were in an ill case. There must be somebody to bury the dead. I suppose that these persons had fulfilled that necessary office, and there had not been time for them to purge themselves from the ceremonial defilement involved in the touching of the dead; so, what were they to do?

8 And Moses said unto them, Stand still, and I will hear what the LORD will command concerning you.

Oh, how wisely we should give advice if we would never decide till we had prayed about the matter! Possibly, we think ourselves so experienced and so well acquainted with the mind of God that we can answer offhand; or, peradventure, we think that we need not consult the Lord at all, but that our own opinion will be sufficient guide. Moses was greater and wiser than we are, yet he said to these men, 'Stand still, and I will hear what Jehovah will command concerning you.'

9-12 And the LORD spake unto Moses, saying, Speak unto the children of Israel, saying, If any man of you or of your posterity shall be unclean by reason of a dead body, or be in a journey afar off, yet he shall keep the passover unto the LORD. The fourteenth day of the second month at even they shall keep it, and eat it with unleavened bread and bitter herbs. They shall leave none of it unto the morning, nor break any bone of it: according to all the ordinances of the passover they shall keep it.

So, provision was made for the holding of a second Passover, that persons who were defiled at the first observance might have the opportunity to keep the feast a month afterwards.

13 But the man that is clean, and is not in a journey, and forbeareth to keep the passover, even the same soul shall be cut off from among his people: because he brought not the offering of the LORD in his appointed season, that man shall bear his sin.

What a solemn sentence that is! Let me read it apart from its connection: 'Because he brought not the offering of the Lord in his appointed season, that man shall bear his sin.' You see, the great offering of the Lord, the atoning sacrifice of our Lord Jesus Christ, is the only way by which sin can be put away; and if any man will not bring that, in other words, if he will not believe in Jesus, then here is his certain doom, 'that man shall bear his sin'. No more terrible judgement can be pronounced upon any one of us than this, 'that man shall bear his sin'. 'If ye believe not that I am he', said Christ, 'ye shall die in your sins' [John 8:24].

14 And if a stranger shall sojourn among you, and will keep the passover unto the LORD; according to the ordinance of the passover, and according to the manner thereof, so shall he do: ye shall have one ordinance, both for the stranger, and for him that was born in the land.

Now comes another subject: —

15-16 And on the day that the tabernacle was reared up the cloud covered the tabernacle, namely, the tent of the testimony: and at even there was upon the tabernacle as it were the appearance of fire, until the morning. So it was alway: the cloud covered it by day, and the appearance of fire by night.

This was the sign of the presence of God in the midst of that vast canvas city. I suppose that the great cloud rose up from the most holy place, and probably covered the whole camp of the tribes, so that it shielded them from the fierceness of the sun, while at night the entire region was lit up by this marvelous illumination. The chosen nation had the pillar of cloud by day, for a shelter, and the pillar of fire by night, for a light. God's presence acts upon us in much the same way as the cloudy fiery pillar acted upon Israel:

> *He hath been my joy in woe,*
> *Cheer'd my heart when it was low,*
> *And, with warnings softly sad,*
> *Calm'd my heart when it was glad.*

We get shelter from the fierce heat of the world's day and deliverance also from the darkness of the world's night through our Lord's gracious presence.

17-20 And when the cloud was taken up from the tabernacle, then after that the children of Israel journeyed: and in the place where the cloud abode, there the children of Israel pitched their tents. At the commandment of the LORD the children of Israel journeyed, and at the commandment of the LORD they pitched: as long as the cloud abode upon the tabernacle they rested in their tents. And when the cloud tarried long upon the tabernacle many days, then the children of Israel kept the charge of the LORD, and journeyed not. And so it was, when the cloud was a few days upon the tabernacle; according to the commandment of the LORD they abode in their tents, and according to the commandment of the LORD they journeyed.

Happy people to be thus divinely guided! They could never tell when they would have to be on the move; they had no abiding city. When their tents were pitched, and they were just getting comfortably settled, perhaps that very morning the pillar of cloud moved; and at other times, when they desired to be marching, it stood still. They could never be certain of staying long in any one place. It is just so with you and with me; our Lord intends to keep us with a loose hold on all things here below. We cannot tell what changes may come to any one of us; therefore, reckon on nothing that God has not plainly promised. Be certain of nothing but uncertainty, and always expect the unexpected. You cannot tell between here and heaven where your Guide may take you; happy will you be if you can truly say that you desire ever to follow where the Lord leads.

21-23 And so it was, when the cloud abode from even unto the morning, and that the cloud was taken up in the morning, then they journeyed: whether it was by day or by night that the cloud was taken up, they journeyed. Or whether it were two days, or a month, or a year, that the cloud tarried upon the tabernacle, remaining thereon, the children of Israel abode in their tents, and journeyed not: but when it was taken up, they journeyed. At the commandment of the LORD they rested in the tents, and at the commandment of the LORD they journeyed: they kept the charge of the LORD, at the commandment of the LORD by the hand of Moses.

So may each one of us ever be divinely guided!

Let the fiery cloudy pillar
Lead me all my journey thru.

NUMBERS 19; PSALM 51

Num. 19:1 And the LORD spake unto Moses and unto Aaron, saying,

This ordinance was not given to Moses on Mount Sinai, but in the wilderness of Paran, after the people had broken their covenant with God and were condemned to die. You know that ninetieth Psalm — that dolorous dirge which we read at funerals — called, 'A prayer of Moses the man of God'. Well might he write that Psalm, for he lived among a generation of people who were all doomed to die within a short time, and to die in the wilderness. This ordinance was especially appointed to meet the cases of those who were rendered unclean by the frequent deaths which occurred. There was to be a simple and easy way of purification for them; and the teaching of this chapter to us is

NUMBERS 19 — Charles Haddon Spurgeon

that, inasmuch as we dwell in a sinful world, there needs to be some simple and ready method of cleansing us, that we may be able to draw near to God.

2-3 This is the ordinance of the law which the LORD hath commanded, saying, Speak unto the children of Israel, that they bring thee a red heifer without spot, wherein is no blemish, and upon which never came yoke: And ye shall give her unto Eleazar the priest, that he may bring her forth without the camp, and one shall slay her before his face:

This was not a usual sacrifice, for the beasts offered were as a rule males; but this was to be a special sacrifice. It was not to be killed by the priest, as other sacrificial offerings were; but the Lord said, 'One shall slay her before his face.'

4 And Eleazar the priest shall take of her blood with his finger, and sprinkle of her blood directly before the tabernacle of the congregation seven times:

This makes it a sacrifice; otherwise, it scarcely deserves the name.

5-6 And one shall burn the heifer in his sight; her skin, and her flesh, and her blood, with her dung, shall he burn: And the priest shall take cedar wood, and hyssop, and scarlet, and cast it into the midst of the burning of the heifer.

All was to be burnt, and then the ashes, the essence and product of it, were to be preserved to make the water of purification needed to remove those constant defilements which fell upon the people of the camp. So, the merits of our Lord Jesus Christ, which are the very essence of him, are perpetually preserved for the removal of our daily pollution. There was also the essence of cedar wood, that is, the emblem of fragrant immortality, for cedar was an unrotting wood, 'and hyssop, and scarlet'. There must be the humble hyssop used, yet there must be some degree of royalty about the sacrifice, as the scarlet colour imported. All this is mixed with the blood and the flesh and the skin of the creature, to make the ashes of purification.

7 Then the priest shall wash his clothes, and he shall bathe his flesh in water, and afterward he shall come into the camp, and the priest shall be unclean until the even.

What a strange sacrifice was this, for even when it was offered it seemed to make unclean all those who had anything to do with it!

8-9 And he that burneth her shall wash his clothes in water, and bathe his flesh in water, and shall be unclean until the even. And a man that is clean —

Now we come to the merit of Christ, for who is clean except Christ?

9 shall gather up the ashes of the heifer, and lay them up without the camp in a clean place, and it shall be kept for the congregation of the children of Israel for a water of separation: it is a purification for sin.

This ceremony does not represent the putting away of sin, that typified in the slaying of the victims, but it represents that daily cleansing which the children of God need, the perpetual efficacy of the merit of Christ, for this red heifer was probably killed only once in the wilderness. According to Jewish tradition, there never have been more than six killed. I cannot tell whether that is true or not, but certainly the ashes of one single beast would last for a long time if they were only to be mixed with water, and then the water to be sprinkled upon the unclean. So this ordinance is meant to represent the standing merit, the perpetual purifying of believers by the sacrifice of Christ, enabling them to come to the worship of God and to mingle with holy men, and even with holy angels, without defiling them. In the fullest sense, it may be said of our Lord's atoning sacrifice, 'It is a purification for sin.'

10 And he that gathereth the ashes of the heifer shall wash his clothes, and be unclean until the even: and it shall be unto the children of Israel, and unto the stranger that sojourneth among them, for a statute for ever.

That was the remedy ordained by the Lord for purifying the defiled; now notice what made this remedy so necessary.

11-12 He that toucheth the dead body of any man shall be unclean seven days. He shall purify himself with it on the third day, and on the seventh day he shall be clean: but if he purify not himself the third day, then the seventh day he shall not be clean.

I wonder whether that is a revelation of our being justified through the resurrection of Christ, which took place on the third day after his death, and then our being brought into perfect rest, which represents the seventh day, through the wondrous purifying of our great Sacrifice, the Lamb of God.

13-14 Whosoever toucheth the dead body of any man that is dead, and purifieth not himself, defileth the tabernacle of the LORD; and that soul shall be cut off from Israel: because the water of separation was not sprinkled upon him, he shall be unclean; his uncleanness is yet upon him. This is the law, when a man dieth in a tent: all that come into the tent, and all that is in the tent, shall be unclean seven days.

Think, dear friends, what a solemn and yet what an irksome ordinance this must have been! Why, according to this regulation, Joseph could not have gone to see his father, Jacob, and to be present at his death, without being defiled. You could not have watched over your consumptive child or have nursed your dying mother, without becoming defiled, if you had been subject to this law; and everything that was in the tent, or in the house, became defiled, too.

15-16 And every open vessel, which hath no covering bound upon it, is unclean. And whosoever toucheth one that is slain with a sword in the open fields, or a dead body, or a bone of a man, or a grave, shall be unclean seven days.

This law was indeed a yoke of bondage which our fathers were not able to bear. It was meant to teach us how easily we can be defiled. Anywhere they went, these people might touch a bone or touch a grave, and then they were defiled, and you and I, watch as carefully as we may, will find ourselves touching some of the dead works of sin and becoming defiled. It is a happy circumstance for us that there is the means of purification always at hand; we may ever go to the precious blood of Jesus and may once again be washed clean and be made fit to go up to the house of the Lord.

17-22 And for an unclean person they shall take of the ashes of the burnt heifer of purification for sin, and running water shall be put thereto in a vessel: And a clean person shall take hyssop, and dip it in the water, and sprinkle it upon the tent, and upon all the vessels, and upon the persons that were there, and upon him that touched a bone, or one slain, or one dead, or a grave: And the clean person shall sprinkle upon the unclean on the third day, and on the seventh day: and on the seventh day he shall purify himself, and wash his clothes, and bathe himself in water, and shall be clean at even. But the man that shall be unclean, and shall not purify himself, that soul shall be cut off from among the congregation, because he hath defiled the sanctuary of the LORD: the water of separation hath not been sprinkled upon him; he is unclean. And it shall be a perpetual statute unto them, that he that sprinkleth the water of separation shall wash his clothes; and he that toucheth the water of separation shall be unclean until even. And whatsoever the unclean person toucheth shall be unclean; and the soul that toucheth it shall be unclean until even.

This ordinance was partly sanitary. The Egyptians were accustomed to keep their dead in their houses, preserved as mummies. No Jew could do that, for he would be defiled. Other nations were accustomed to bury their dead, as we once did, within the city walls, or round their own places of worship, as if to bring death as near as they could to themselves. No Jew could do this, for he was defiled if he even passed over a grave; so they were driven to what God intended they should have, that is, extramural interments, and to keep the graveyard as far as they could away from the abodes of the living. The spiritual meaning of this regulation is that we must watch with great care against every occasion for sin; and, inasmuch as there will be these occasions and we shall be defiled, we must constantly go to the Lord with a prayer like that of David in Psalm 51.

Ps. 51:1 Have mercy upon me, O God, according to thy loving-kindness: according unto the multitude of thy tender mercies blot out my transgressions.

There may be some people who think themselves so holy that they cannot join in this psalm. I can, for one, and I believe that there are many of you who can join with me. Just let us for the time being forget all others, and let us come, each one for himself or herself, with David's language on our lips or in our hearts so far as it applies to our individual case.

2-19 Wash me throughly from mine iniquity, and cleanse me from my sin. For I acknowledge my transgressions: and my sin is ever before me. Against thee, thee only, have I sinned, and done this evil in thy sight: that thou mightest be justified when thou speakest, and be clear when thou judgest. Behold, I was shapen in iniquity; and in sin did my mother conceive me. Behold, thou desirest truth in the inward parts: and in the hidden part thou shalt make me to know wisdom. Purge me with hyssop, and I shall be clean: wash me, and I shall be whiter than snow.

NUMBERS 21   *Charles Haddon Spurgeon*

Make me to hear joy and gladness; that the bones which thou hast broken may rejoice. Hide thy face from my sins, and blot out all mine iniquities. Create in me a clean heart, O God; and renew a right spirit within me. Cast me not away from thy presence; and take not thy holy spirit from me. Restore unto me the joy of thy salvation; and uphold me with thy free spirit. Then will I teach transgressors thy ways; and sinners shall be converted unto thee. Deliver me from bloodguiltiness, O God, thou God of my salvation: and my tongue shall sing aloud of thy righteousness. O Lord, open thou my lips; and my mouth shall shew forth thy praise. For thou desirest not sacrifice; else would I give it: thou delightest not in burnt offering. The sacrifices of God are a broken spirit: a broken and a contrite heart, O God, thou wilt not despise. Do good in thy good pleasure unto Zion: build thou the walls of Jerusalem. Then shalt thou be pleased with the sacrifices of righteousness, with burnt offering and whole burnt offering: then shall they offer bullocks upon thine altar.

NUMBERS 21:1-9; JOHN 3:1-15

Num. 21:1-4 And when king Arad the Canaanite, which dwelt in the south, heard tell that Israel came by the way of the spies; then he fought against Israel, and took some of them prisoners. And Israel vowed a vow unto the LORD, and said, If thou wilt indeed deliver this people into my hand, then I will utterly destroy their cities. And the LORD hearkened to the voice of Israel, and delivered up the Canaanites; and they utterly destroyed them and their cities: and he called the name of the place Hormah. And they journeyed from mount Hor by the way of the Red sea, to compass the land of Edom: and the soul of the people was much discouraged because of the way.

They were not allowed to go through the land of Edom, they had therefore to turn round, and go right away from the land where they one day hoped to dwell, and the road was a particularly trying one, over hot and burning sand, 'and the soul of the people was much discouraged because of the way'. Sometimes, God's own people, when they find that they are not so far advanced in the divine life as they thought they were, when they find old sins reviving, and when troubles multiply upon them, get 'discouraged because of the way'. If this is our experience, let us not fall into the sin into which these Israelites fell, but even in our discouragement let us turn to our God.

5 And the people spake against God, and against Moses, Wherefore have ye brought us up out of Egypt to die in the wilderness? for there is no bread, neither is there any water; and our soul loatheth this light bread.

One gets tired, in reading of the wanderings of Israel in the wilderness, of this parrot cry, 'Wherefore have ye brought us up out of Egypt?' For nearly forty years, this was their cry whenever they met with any sort of difficulty. How weary God must have been of their cry, and how weary of them too! And now it was raised because they had been fed with 'angels' food' which they called 'light bread'. It was easy of digestion, healthful, and the very best kind of food for them in the wilderness; but they wanted something more substantial, something that had a coarser flavour about it, more of earth and less of heaven. There is no satisfying an unregenerate heart. If we had all the blessings of this life, we should still be vying for more.

6-9 And the LORD sent fiery serpents among the people, and they bit the people; and much people of Israel died. Therefore the people came to Moses, and said, We have sinned, for we have spoken against the LORD, and against thee; pray unto the LORD, that he take away the serpents from us. And Moses prayed for the people. And the LORD said unto Moses, Make thee a fiery serpent, and set it upon a pole: and it shall come to pass, that every one that is bitten, when he looketh upon it, shall live. And Moses made a serpent of brass, and put it upon a pole, and it came to pass, that if a serpent had bitten any man, when he beheld the serpent of brass, he lived.

Like a true mediator, he was always ready — even when they had most insulted him, and grieved his meek and quiet spirit — still to bow the knee, and intercede with the Lord on their behalf. The people implored him to ask that the serpents might be taken away from them; but, apparently, they still continued to trouble them. However, if God does not answer prayer in one way, he does in another. The fervent prayer of a righteous man may not prevail in the particular direction in which it is offered, but it 'availeth much' in some direction or other. Just as when the mists ascend they may not fall upon the very spot from which they rose, but they fall somewhere, and true prayer is never lost, it cometh back in blessing, if not according to our mind, yet according to another mind that is kinder and wiser than our own.

John 3:1-3 There was a man of the Pharisees, named Nicodemus, a ruler of the Jews: The same came to Jesus by night, and said unto him, Rabbi, we know that thou art a teacher come from God: for no man can do these miracles that thou doest, except God be with him. Jesus answered and said unto him, Verily, verily, I say unto thee, Except a man be born again, he cannot see the kingdom of God.

There must be a new birth because a new name is absolutely necessary for the discernment of spiritual things. The natural man cannot comprehend spiritual things; they must be spiritually discerned. The new birth is therefore necessary, that we may have a spirit within us which can see or understand the kingdom of God; but, until a man is born again, 'he cannot see the kingdom of God'.

4-5 Nicodemus saith unto him, How can a man be born when he is old? can he enter the second time into his mother's womb, and be born? Jesus answered, Verily, verily, I say unto thee, Except a man be born of water and of the Spirit, he cannot enter into the kingdom of God.

We understand the passage to mean, 'Water, that is, the Spirit'; but it may refer to the purifying influence of the Word as symbolized by water. I do not think that baptism is referred to here at all.

6 That which is born of the flesh is flesh; —

Parents may be the most devout people who ever lived, but that which is born of them is only flesh.

6 and that which is born of the Spirit is spirit.

It is only then, as we are born of the Spirit of God that there is any spiritual life in us whatsoever.

7-8 Marvel not that I said unto thee, Ye must be born again. The wind bloweth where it listeth, and thou hearest the sound thereof, but canst not tell whence it cometh, and whither it goeth: so is every one that is born of the Spirit.

He undergoes a mysterious change; he becomes a new man; he enters into a new life which others cannot comprehend. Though they hear the sound of it, they cannot tell whence this man's new life comes or whither it goes. He has become a spiritual person, not comprehended of natural men.

9-10 Nicodemus answered and said unto him, How can these things be? Jesus answered and said unto him, Art thou a master of Israel, and knowest not these things?

'So learned in the law of God, art thou ignorant of the Spirit of God? Hast thou read the law so many times and yet not found out that natural births and outward washings are of no avail in spiritual things?'

11-12 Verily, verily, I say unto thee, We speak that we do know, and testify that we have seen; and ye receive not our witness. If I have told you earthly things, and ye believe not, how shall ye believe, if I tell you of heavenly things?

If, at the very entrance to the kingdom of heaven, you say, 'How can these things be?' what will you say if I take you into the central metropolis of truth and introduce you to the great King himself?

13-15 And no man hath ascended up to heaven, but he that came down from heaven, even the Son of man which is in heaven. And as Moses lifted up the serpent in the wilderness, even so must the Son of man be lifted up: That whosoever believeth in him should not perish, but have eternal life.

DEVOTIONAL THOUGHTS ON THE BIBLE
Charles Haddon Spurgeon

DEUTERONOMY

DEUTERONOMY 6:1-23

Deut. 6:1-2 Now these are the commandments, the statutes, and the judgments, which the LORD your God commanded to teach you, that ye might do them in the land whither ye go to possess it: That thou mightest fear the LORD thy God, to keep all his statutes and his commandments, which I command thee, thou, and thy son, and thy son's son, all the days of thy life; and that thy days may be prolonged.

Obedience to God should arise from the fear of him, or from a holy awe of God felt in the heart, for all true religion must be heart work. It is not the bare action alone at which God looks, but at the motive — at the spirit which dictates it. Hence it is always put, 'That thou mightest fear the Lord thy God, to keep all his statutes and his commandments.' Neither are we to be content with keeping commands ourselves. It is the duty of parents to seek the good of their children — to seek that thy son and thy son's son should walk in the ways of God all their lives. May God grant us never to be partakers of the spirit of those who think that they have no need to look after the religion of their children — who seem as if they left it to a blind fate. May we care for them with this care that our son and our son's son should walk before the Lord all the days of their life.

3 Hear therefore, O Israel, and observe to do it; that it may be well with thee, and that ye may increase mightily, as the LORD God of thy fathers hath promised thee, in the land that floweth with milk and honey.

It seems, according to the old covenant, that temporal prosperity was appended as a blessing to the keeping of God's commandments. It has been sometimes said that while prosperity was the blessing of the old covenant, adversity is the blessing of the new. And there is some truth in that statement, 'for whom the Lord loveth he chasteneth', and yet is it true that the best thing for a man is that he should walk in the commands of God. There is a sense in which we do make the best of both worlds when we seek the love of God. When we seek first the kingdom of God and his righteousness, other things are added to us; so that it is not without meaning to us that the Lord here promises temporal blessings to his people.

4 Hear, O Israel: The LORD our God is one LORD:

This is the great doctrine that we learn, both from the Old, and from the New Testament, there is one LORD. And this great truth has been burnt into the Jews by their long chastisement, and whatever other mistakes they make, you never find them making a mistake about this: 'The LORD our God is one LORD.' May we be kept always from all idolatry — from all worship of anything else, except the living God. The sacred unity of the divine trinity may we hold fast evermore.

5 And thou shalt love the LORD thy God with all thine heart, and with all thy soul, and with all thy might.

It is not a little love that God deserves, nor is it a little love that he will accept. He blesses us with all his heart and all his might, and after that fashion are we to love him.

6-7 And these words, which I command thee this day, shall be in thine heart: And thou shalt teach them diligently unto thy children, and shalt talk of them when thou sittest in thine house, and when thou walkest by the way, and when thou liest down, and when thou risest up.

The Word of God is not for some particular place called a church or a meeting house. It is for all places, all times, and all occupations. I wish that we had more of this talking over of God's Word when we sit by the way or when we walk.

8 And thou shalt bind them for a sign upon thine hand, and they shall be as frontlets between thine eyes.

With thee in all thine actions — with thee in all thy thoughts — conspicuously with thee — not out of ostentation but through thine obedience to become apparent unto all men.

9-12 And thou shalt write them upon the posts of thy house, and on thy gates. And it shall be, when the LORD thy God shall have brought thee into the land which he sware unto thy fathers, to Abraham, to Isaac, and to Jacob, to give thee great and goodly cities, which thou buildedst not, And houses full of all good things, which thou filledst not, and wells digged, which thou diggedst not, vineyards and olive trees, which thou plantedst not; when thou shalt have eaten and be full; Then beware lest thou forget the LORD, which brought thee forth out of the land of Egypt, from the house of bondage.

Pride is the peculiar sin of prosperity, and pride stands side by side with forgetfulness of God. Instead of remembering whence our mercies came, we begin to thank ourselves for these blessings, and God is forgotten. I remember one of whom it was said that he was a self-made man, and he adored his Creator, and I may say that there are a great many persons who do just that. They believe that they have made themselves, and so they worship themselves. Be it ours to remember that it is God who giveth us strength to get wealth or to get position, and therefore, unto him be all the honour of it, and never let him be forgotten.

13-15 Thou shalt fear the LORD thy God, and serve him, and shalt swear by his name. Ye shall not go after other gods, of the gods of the people which are round about you; (For the LORD thy God is a jealous God among you) —

He will have the heart all to himself. Two Gods he cannot endure. Of false gods, there may be many: of the true God there can be but one, and he is a jealous God.

15-19 lest the anger of the LORD thy God be kindled against thee, and destroy thee from off the face of the earth. Ye shall not tempt the LORD your God, as ye tempted him in Massah. Ye shall diligently keep the commandments of the LORD your God, and his testimonies, and his statutes, which he hath commanded thee. And thou shalt do that which is right and good in the sight of the LORD: that it may be well with thee, and that thou mayest go in and possess the good land which the LORD sware unto thy fathers, To cast out all thine enemies from before thee, as the LORD hath spoken.

Now, this covenant of works they break, as we also have long ago broken ours. Blessed be God, our salvation now hangs on another covenant which cannot fail nor break down — the covenant of grace. Yet, still, now that we become the Lord's children, we are put under the discipline of the Lord's house, and these words might not unfitly set forth what is the discipline of the Lord's house towards his own children, namely, that he does bless us when we walk in his ways and that he will walk contrary to us if we walk contrary to him. He keeps a rod in his house, and in love he uses that upon his best beloved ones. 'You only have I known of all the nations of the earth; therefore, I will punish you for your iniquities.' He will not kill his children, nor treat them as a judge treats a criminal, for they are not under the law but under grace; but he will chasten them and treat them as a father chasteneth his child — out of love. Oh! that we might have grace to walk before him with a holy, childlike fear, that so we may walk always in the light of his countenance.

20-23 And when thy son asketh thee in time to come, saying, What mean the testimonies, and the statutes, and the judgments, which the LORD our God hath commanded you? Then thou shalt say unto thy son, We were Pharaoh's bondmen in Egypt; and the LORD brought us out of Egypt with a mighty hand: And the LORD shewed signs and wonders, great and sore, upon Egypt, upon Pharaoh, and upon all his household, before our eyes: And he brought us out from thence, that he might bring us in, to give us the land which he sware unto our fathers.

And cannot we tell our children what God has done for us — how he brought us out of our spiritual captivity and how in his almighty love, he has brought us into his church and will surely bring us into the glory above? May God grant us grace to speak about these things without diffidence and with great confidence to tell our children of what he has done.

DEUTERONOMY 6

Deut. 6:1 Now these are the commandments, the statutes, and the judgments, which the LORD your God commanded to teach you, that ye might do them in the land whither ye go to possess it:

God's commandments are to be taught, but they are also to be practised: 'which the Lord your God commanded to teach you, that ye might do them'. And it is this doing of them that is the hard part of the work. It is not easy always to teach them; a man needs the Spirit of God if he is to teach them aright, but practice is harder than preaching. May God grant us grace, whenever we hear his Word, to do it!

2 That thou mightest fear the LORD thy God, to keep all his statutes and his commandments, which I command thee, thou, and thy son, and thy son's son, all the days of thy life; and that thy days may be prolonged.

The fear of God must always be a practical power in our lives: 'that thou mightest fear the Lord thy God, to keep all his statutes and his commandments'. And that practical fear should lead us into obedience in detail; we ought so to study God's Word that we endeavour 'to keep all his statutes and his commandments'. A slipshod obedience is disobedience. We must be careful and watchful to know the divine will, and in all respects to carry it out. You who are his children, dwelling in such a household, and with such a Father, it well becomes you to be obedient children.

Nay, it is not only for us to obey the command of the Lord our God, but we should pray till the rest of the verse also comes true: 'thou, and thy son, and thy son's son', our children and our children's children. I am sure that, if we love God, we shall long that our children and our children's children may love him too. If your trade has supported you and brought you in a competence, you will naturally wish to bring your son up to it. But, on a far higher platform, if God has been a good God to you, your deepest desire will be that your son and your son's son should serve the same divine Master through all the days of their life. 'That thy days may be prolonged.' God does not give long life to all his people; yet, in obedience to God is the most probable way of securing long life. There are also many of God's saints who are spared in times of pestilence or who are delivered by an act of faith out of great dangers. That ancient declaration of God often comes true in these latter times: 'As the days of a tree are the days of my people, and mine elect shall long enjoy the work of their hands' [Isaiah 65:22]. At any rate, you who love the Lord shall live out your days, whereas the wicked shall not live out half their days. You shall complete the circle of life, whether it be a great circle or a little one; with long life will God satisfy you, and show you his salvation [Psalm 91:16].

The passage which now follows is held in very great esteem by the Jewish people even down to this day. They repeat it frequently, for it forms part of their morning and evening services.

3-4 Hear therefore, O Israel, and observe to do it; that it may be well with thee, and that ye may increase mightily, as the LORD God of thy fathers hath promised thee, in the land that floweth with milk and honey. Hear, O Israel: The LORD our God is one LORD:

There is but one God. This is the very basis of our faith; we know nothing of 'gods many and lords many'. Yet it is the triune God whom we worship; we are not less Unitarians in the highest meaning of that word because we are Trinitarians. We are not less believers in the one living and true God because we worship Father, Son, and Holy Spirit.

5 And thou shalt love the LORD thy God with all thine heart, and with all thy soul, and with all thy might.

Does not this show what is the very nature of God? God is love, for he commands us to love him. There was never an earthly prince or king, whom I have heard of, in whose statute book it was written, 'Thou shalt love the king.' No; it is only in the statute book of him who is the Lord of life and love that we read such a command as this. To my mind it seems a very blessed privilege for us to be permitted to love One so great as God is. Here it is we find our heaven. It is a command, but we regard it rather as a loving, tender invitation to the highest bliss: 'Thou shalt love the Lord thy God with all thine heart' — that is, intensely; 'and with all thy soul' — that is, most sincerely, most lovingly; 'and with all thy might' — that is, with all thy energy, with every faculty, with every possibility of thy nature.

6 And these words, which I command thee this day, shall be in thine heart:

Oh, how blessed to have them written on the heart by the Holy Spirit. We can never get them there except he who made the heart anew shall engrave upon these fleshy tablets the divine precepts.

7 And thou shalt teach them diligently unto thy children, —

Christian parent, have you done this? 'Thou shalt' not only teach them, but 'teach them diligently unto thy children'.

7 and shalt talk of them when thou sittest in thine house, and when thou walkest by the way, and when thou liest down, and when thou risest up.

Our common talk should be much more spiritual than it often is. There is no fear of degrading sacred subjects by the frequent use of them; the fear lies much the other way, lest by a disuse of them we come to forget them. This blessed book, the holy Word of God, is a fit companion for your leisure as well as for your labour, for the time of your sleeping and the time of your waking. It will bless you in your private meditations, and equally cheer the social hearth, and comfort you when in mutual friendship you speak the one with the other. Those who truly love God greatly love his holy Word.

8 And thou shalt bind them for a sign upon thine hand, —

They shall be thy practical guide, at thy fingers' ends, as it were.

8 and they shall be as frontlets between thine eyes.

Thou shalt see *by* them, thou shalt see *with* them, thou shalt see *through* them.

9 And thou shalt write them upon the posts of thy house, and on thy gates.

I could almost wish that this were literally fulfilled much more often than it is. I was charmed, in many a Swiss village, to see a text of Scripture carved on the door post. A text hung up in your houses may often speak when you are silent. We cannot do anything that shall be superfluous in the way of making known the Word of God.

10-12 And it shall be, when the LORD thy God shall have brought thee into the land which he sware unto thy fathers, to Abraham, to Isaac, and to Jacob, to give thee great and goodly cities, which thou buildedst not, and houses full of all good things, which thou filledst not, and wells digged, which thou diggedst not, vineyards and olive trees, which thou plantedst not; when thou shalt have eaten and be full; Then beware lest thou forget the LORD, which brought thee forth out of the land of Egypt, from the house of bondage.

Bread eaten is soon forgotten. How often we act like dogs that will take the bones from our hand and then forget the hand that gave them! It should not be so with us. All our spiritual mercies, and many of our temporal ones, are very much like the inheritance of Israel in the land of Canaan: wells that they did not dig and vineyards which they did not plant. Our blessings come from sources that are beyond our own industry and skill; they are the fruits of the holy inventiveness of God and the splendour and fulness of his thoughtfulness towards his poor children. Let us not forget him, since evidently he never forgets us.

13-15 Thou shalt fear the LORD thy God, and serve him, and shalt swear by his name. Ye shall not go after other gods, of the gods of the people which are round about you; (For the LORD thy God is a jealous God among you) lest the anger of the LORD thy God be kindled against thee, and destroy thee from off the face of the earth.

Our God is a jealous God. One said to a Puritan, 'Why be so precise?' and he replied, 'Because I serve a precise God.' God has done so much for us in order to win our hearts that he ought to have them altogether for himself. When he has them all, it is all too little; but to divide our heart is to grieve his Spirit and sorely to vex him.

16-24 Ye shall not tempt the LORD your God, as ye tempted him in Massah. Ye shall diligently keep the commandments of the LORD your God, and his testimonies, and his statutes, which he hath commanded thee. And thou shalt do that which is right and good in the sight of the LORD: that it may be well with thee, and that thou mayest go in and possess the good land which the LORD sware unto thy fathers, To cast out all thine enemies from before thee, as the LORD hath spoken. And when thy son asketh thee in time to come, saying, What mean the testimonies, and the statutes, and the judgments, which the LORD our God hath commanded you? Then thou shalt say unto thy son, We were Pharaoh's bondmen in Egypt; and the LORD brought us out of Egypt with a mighty hand: And the LORD shewed signs and wonders, great and sore, upon Egypt, upon Pharaoh, and upon all his household, before our eyes: and he brought us out from thence, that he might bring us in, to give us the land which he sware unto our fathers. And the LORD commanded us to do all these statutes, to fear the LORD our God, for our good always, that he might preserve us alive, as it is at this day.

Oh, friends, it will be well when our boys and girls ask us questions like this and when we can give such answers! The great lack of the age in which we live is obedience to God. 'Modern thought' has flung off obedience to divine revelation; and even in matters relating to social morality, many men reject all idea of anything being commanded of God; they only judge by what appears to them to be either pleasurable or profitable. What is most needed just now is that we ourselves, and those about us, become really conscious of the greatness and sovereignty of God, and yield ourselves to him to do as he bids us, when he bids us, where he bids us, and in all things to seek to follow his commandments that he may 'preserve us alive, as it is at this day'.

25 And it shall be our righteousness, if we observe to do all these commandments before the LORD our God, as he hath commanded us.

That would have been Israel's righteousness if the people had observed to do all these commandments before the Lord, but it was marred and spoilt by disobedience. We rejoice to know that we who believe in Jesus have a righteousness unto which Israel did not attain, for the Lord Jesus Christ himself is our righteousness.

DEUTERONOMY 8

Deut. 8:1 All the commandments which I command thee this day shall ye observe to do, that ye may live, and multiply, and go in and possess the land which the LORD sware unto your fathers.

Observe, dear friends, that the Lord demands of his people universal obedience to his commands: 'All the commandments which I command thee this day shall ye observe to do.' Christians, although they are not under the law, are under the sweet constraints of love, and that love incites them to complete obedience, so that they desire to leave undone nothing which the Lord commands. And this obedience is to be careful as well as complete: 'All the commandments which I command thee this day shall ye observe to do': not only do them, but do them with care. When the commandment applies to a certain duty, obey it in full, both in the letter and in the spirit, for there are numerous and weighty blessings attached to obedience — not of merit but of grace. If we walk carefully in the fear of God, we shall find that in keeping his commandments there is great reward [Psalm 19:11].

2 And thou shalt remember all the way which the LORD thy God led thee these forty years in the wilderness, to humble thee, and to prove thee, to know what was in thine heart, whether thou wouldest keep his commandments, or no.

It is well to have a good memory, and that is the best memory which remembers what is best worth remembering. There are many things which we would gladly forget, yet we find it hard to forget them; they often rise up at most inappropriate times, and we loathe ourselves to think that we should ever recollect them at all. But, whatever we forget, we ought always to remember what God has done for us. This should excite our gratitude, create deep humility, and foster our faith both for the present and for the future: 'Thou shalt remember all the way which Jehovah thy God led thee these forty years in the wilderness.' If forty years of the Lord's leading should make some of us bless his holy name, what ought you to do, my brethren, who, perhaps, are getting near the fourscore years? What praise and gratitude should be rendered by you to him who has led you all your life long! See what God intends to accomplish by our wilderness experience. It is, first, to 'humble' us. Has it had that effect? Then it is to 'prove' us. Ah, I am afraid it has had that result, and has proved what poor wretched creatures we are! That has been proved in our experience again and again. It is also that it may be known what is in our heart, whether we will keep God's commandments or not.

3 And he humbled thee, and suffered thee to hunger, and fed thee with manna, which thou knewest not, —

What a wonderful sequence there is in these short sentences! 'He humbled thee, and suffered thee to hunger', and one would think that the next sentence would be, 'and allowed thee to starve'. No, it is, 'and fed thee with manna'. They had the better appetite for the manna and were the more ready to see the hand of God in sending the manna, because of that humbling and hunger which God had previously suffered them to endure. 'Fed thee with manna, which thou knewest not.' The very name by which they called it was, 'manna', or, 'What is this?' — 'for they wist not what it was'. 'And fed thee with manna, which thou knewest not.'

3 neither did thy fathers know; that he might make thee know that man doth not live by bread only, but by every word that proceedeth out of the mouth of the LORD doth man live.

God can make us live on bread, if it be sanctified by the Word of God and prayer; he does make our souls to live upon his Word. He could, if so it pleased him, make our bodies live by that Word without any outward sustenance whatever.

4 Thy raiment waxed not old upon thee, neither did thy foot swell, these forty years.

What a wonderful experience the Israelites had in the wilderness! They were always fed, though in a wasted howling wilderness, dry and barren. They always had water following them from that stream which flowed out of the flinty rock, from which you might sooner have expected to strike fire than to obtain water. And as for their garments, they did not wear out. They had no shops to go to, and they were unable to make new clothes in the wilderness, on account of their frequent moving to and fro; yet, were they always clad. Though they were a host of weary pilgrims, marching backwards and forwards for forty years, yet their feet did not swell. Oh, what a mercy that was! 'He keepeth the feet of his saints.' Has it not been so with you also, dear friends? You have said, 'What shall I do if I live so long and if I have to bear so many troubles and make so many marches through the very valley of the shadow of death?' What will you do? Why, you will do as you have done! Trust in God and go on. You shall be fed and you shall be upheld even unto the end.

5   Thou shalt also consider in thine heart, —

Note that we are not only to remember God's dealings with us, but we are to consider them, to ponder them, to weigh them. 'Consider in thine heart.'

5   that, as a man chasteneth his son, so the LORD thy God chasteneth thee.

Do I speak to anyone who is just now under the rod? 'Consider in thine heart' then, that God is dealing with you as a father deals with his sons, 'for what son is he whom the father chasteneth not?' How would you like to be dealt with? Would you rather be without the rod? Then remember that 'if ye be without chastisement, whereof all are partakers, then are ye bastards, and not sons' [Hebrews 12:8]. Do you wish to be treated so? I am sure you do not; you wish to have the children's portion; so you say, 'Deal with me, Lord, as thou art wont to do with those that fear thy name.' We are willing to have the rod of the covenant for the sake of the covenant to which it belongs.

6-8   Therefore thou shalt keep the commandments of the LORD thy God, to walk in his ways, and to fear him. For the LORD thy God bringeth thee into a good land, a land of brooks of water, of fountains and depths that spring out of valleys and hills; A land of wheat, and barley, and vines, and fig trees, and pomegranates; a land of oil olive, and honey;

This also is the experience of the child of God, in one sense, in heaven, but in another, and perhaps a truer sense, even here below. 'We which have believed do enter into rest.' By faith, we take possession of the promised land. When a Christian gets out of the wilderness experience of doubting and fearing and comes into the Canaan experience of a simple faith and a fully assured trust, then he comes 'into a good land, a land of brooks of water, of fountains and depths that spring out of valleys and hills; a land of wheat, and barley, and vines, and fig trees, and pomegranates; a land of oil olive, and honey'; for God gives to his people not only all they need, but something more. He gives them not only necessaries but also luxuries, delights, and joys.

9 A land wherein thou shalt eat bread without scarceness, thou shalt not lack any thing in it; —

When you live in communion with God and he brings you into the full enjoyment of the covenant blessings, then there is no scarceness with you, there is no lack of anything.

9 a land whose stones are iron, and out of whose hills thou mayest dig brass.

Or, copper. Silver and gold they had none; but then the princes of Sheba and Seba were to offer them gifts and bring them their gold and their silver. But, if they had nothing for show, they had plenty for use, for iron is a great deal more useful metal than gold; and the copper, which they hardened into brass, was of much more service to them than silver would have been. God will furnish you, dear brother, with all the weapons you need for the 'Holy War'. There may be no gold and silver ornaments for your pride, but there shall be iron instruments to help you in your conflict with your adversaries.

10 When thou hast eaten and art full, then thou shalt bless the LORD thy God for the good land which he hath given thee.

DEUTERONOMY 8 — Charles Haddon Spurgeon

God permits his people to eat and to be full; but, when they are so, they must take care that they do not become proud and that they do not begin to ascribe their profiting to themselves.

11 Beware that thou forget not the LORD thy God, in not keeping his commandments, and his judgments, and his statutes, which I command thee this day:

Whenever we see the word 'beware' in the Bible, we may be sure that there is something to beware of. The point here to note is that our times of prosperity are times of danger. I remember that Mr Whitefield once asked the prayers of the congregation 'for a young gentleman in very dangerous circumstances', for he had just come into a fortune of £5,000. Then is the time when prayer is needed even more than in seasons of depression and of loss.

12-16 Lest when thou hast eaten and art full, and hast built goodly houses, and dwelt therein; And when thy herds and thy flocks multiply, and thy silver and thy gold is multiplied, and all that thou hast is multiplied; Then thine heart be lifted up, and thou forget the LORD thy God, which brought thee forth out of the land of Egypt, from the house of bondage; Who led thee through that great and terrible wilderness, wherein were fiery serpents, and scorpions, and drought, where there was no water; who brought thee forth water out of the rock of flint; Who fed thee in the wilderness with manna, which thy fathers knew not, that he might humble thee, and that he might prove thee, to do thee good at thy latter end;

Why do we get these passages repeated? Surely it is because we have such slippery memories, and the Lord has to tell his children the same thing over and over again: 'precept upon precept: line upon line, line upon line; here a little, and there a little' [Isaiah 28:10]; because we so soon forget.

17-20 And thou say in thine heart, My power and the might of mine hand hath gotten me this wealth. But thou shalt remember the LORD thy God: for it is he that giveth thee power to get wealth, that he may establish his covenant which he sware unto thy fathers, as it is this day. And it shall be, if thou do at all forget the LORD thy God, and walk after other gods, and serve them, and worship them, I testify against you this day that ye shall surely perish. As the nations which the LORD destroyeth before your face, so shall ye perish; because ye would not be obedient unto the voice of the LORD your God.

'If you sin as they do, you shall fare as they do.'

DEUTERONOMY 8

Deut. 8:1 All the commandments which I command thee this day shall ye observe to do, that ye may live, and multiply, and go in and possess the land which the LORD sware unto your fathers.

Every word here seems emphatic. Like the children of Israel, we are to observe *all* the commandments of the Lord our God; not merely some of them, picking and choosing as we please. It is a very ill conscience which regards some of God's statutes and pays no attention to the others; in fact, the very act of making a selection as to what commands we will observe is gross disobedience. 'All the commandments which I command thee this day shall ye observe to do.'

Notice that we are not only to do as we are bidden but to do it with carefulness: 'ye shall observe to do'. God would not have a thoughtless, careless, blind service, but we must bow our mind and heart as well as our will to his service. Remember also that it is not sufficient to 'observe' the commandments so as to note what they are, but we are to 'observe to do' them. That observation which does not end in right practise is like a promising blossom upon a tree which never knits and which, therefore, produces no fruit.

Further notice that to walk in the ways of God is for our own benefit as well as for his glory: 'That ye may live, and multiply, and go in and possess the land which the Lord sware unto your fathers.' There are, doubtless, many good things which we miss because we are not careful in our walking. I am sure that the happiest life will be found to be that which is most carefully conducted upon the principles of holy obedience to God's commands. There are certain blessings which God will not give to us while we are disobedient to him. Many a father feels that he cannot indulge his child as he would wish to indulge him when he finds the child negligent as to his father's will. So, if we please God, God will please us; but, if we walk contrary to him, he will walk contrary to us. Let me read this most instructive verse again, that it may be further impressed upon your memories and your hearts: 'All the commandments which I command thee this day shall ye observe to do, that ye may live, and multiply, and go in and possess the land which the Lord sware unto your fathers.' To help you in obeying these commands, it is added,

2 And thou shalt remember all the way which the LORD thy God led thee these forty years in the wilderness, to humble thee, and to prove thee, to know what was in thine heart, whether thou wouldest keep his commandments, or no.

Look back, and derive from your past experience a motive for more careful obedience in the future. He does not read his own life aright who does not see in it abundant causes for gratitude; and how can gratitude express itself better than by a cheerful, hearty obedience in the present and the future?

3 And he humbled thee, and suffered thee to hunger, and fed thee with manna, —

These two statements come very closely together: 'Suffered thee to hunger, and fed thee with manna.' I suppose we are not fit to eat heavenly bread till first of all we begin to hunger for it. God loves to give to men who will eat with an appetite: 'He suffered thee to hunger, and fed thee with manna.'

3 which thou knewest not, neither did thy fathers know; —

It was a new kind of food; and even in the day when they ate it, they did not fully know what it was. They saw that it came by a miracle, and it remained a mystery. I think we can say that, though we have fed upon the Bread of heaven — some of us for well-nigh forty years — yet we hardly know, nor dare to think that we know what it is made of, nor can we tell all the sweetness that is in it. We know the love of Christ, but it still passes our knowledge. It is true of us, as of Israel in the wilderness, 'He humbled thee, and suffered thee to hunger, and fed thee with manna, which thou knewest not, neither did thy fathers know.'

3 that he might make thee know that man doth not live by bread only, but by every word that proceedeth out of the mouth of the LORD doth man live.

It is a grand thing to be delivered from materialism, to be freed from the notion that the outward means are absolutely essential for the accomplishment of the divine purpose. If God had so willed it, we could have lived on air, if the air had been sanctified by the Word of God and prayer for such a use. The Lord has, however, chosen to feed us upon bread; yet our highest life, our real life, does not live on bread, but it lives on the Word which proceeds out of the mouth of God. This is one of the passages with which our Lord fought Satan in the desert, and overcame him [Matthew 4]. Happy is that servant of God who will arm himself with this same truth and feel, 'I am not to be provided for merely by money or by anything else that is visible. God will provide for me somehow, and I can leave all care about the means, if the means fail, and get away to the God of the means and lean, not on what I see but on that arm which is invisible.' That which you can see may fail you, for it is, like yourself, a shadow; but he whom you cannot see will never fail you. The strongest sinew in an arm of flesh will crack, but the arm eternal never faileth and never is shortened. Lean on that arm, and you shall never be ashamed nor confounded, world without end. It takes forty years to teach some people that lesson, and some, alas! have not learned it even at the end of eighty years.

4 Thy raiment waxed not old upon thee, neither did thy foot swell, these forty years.

See how God not only cares for his people's food, but for their raiment also. We may, therefore, well take heed to Paul's injunction: 'Having food and raiment let us be therewith content' [1 Timothy 6:8]. Whether it was by a miracle that the Israelites' raiment did not wear out or whether it came to pass, in the order of providence, that they were able to get fresh clothing when it did wear out does not signify at all; it made no difference to them how it was arranged, for it was equal kindness on the part of God who provided for them.

'Neither did thy foot swell.' We call the Arab, sometimes, 'The pilgrim of the weary foot', but the Israelites' feet were not weary. They traversed a stony wilderness, yet God kept them in such health and strength that their feet swelled not even after forty years of journeying. You and I often get worn out in forty hours; forty days are as long as we can hope to go; but God enabled his ancient people to go on for forty years, and still their feet swelled not. Dr Watts sweetly sang,

Mere mortal power shall fade and die,
  And youthful vigour cease;
But we that wait upon the Lord
  Shall feel our strength increase.

The saints shall mount on eagles' wings,
  And taste the promised bliss,
'Till their unwearied feet arrive
  Where perfect pleasure is.

5 Thou shalt also consider in thine heart, that, as a man chasteneth his son, so the LORD thy God chasteneth thee.

We sometimes think that we could do without the Lord's chastening. If he will give us food and raiment and keep our foot from swelling, we will not crave the rod. No, but though we do not ask for it, the rod is one of the choicest blessings of the covenant; and if we are the Lord's children, we shall not go without it. To come under divine discipline, is one of the greatest mercies we can ever have. Many of us, who are now men and women, thank God for earthly parents who have corrected us; we wonder what we should have been if there had been no discipline in our father's house. So, truly, is it with all of us who are God's children; in years to come, we shall prize the chastisement which now makes us grieve. Even now, it is well if, by faith, we can apply to our own heart this text: 'as a man chasteneth his son, so the LORD thy God chasteneth thee'.

6-7 Therefore thou shalt keep the commandments of the LORD thy God, to walk in his ways, and to fear him. For the LORD thy God bringeth thee into a good land, a land of brooks of water, of fountains and depths that spring out of valleys and hills;

There are changes in our condition. Israel was not always in the wilderness; the chosen people were brought into a good land, into a place of rest from their weary wanderings. So it may happen to you and to me that, even in temporal circumstances, God may work a great change for us, and especially will he do this in spiritual matters. After a time of wilderness travelling, we who have believed do enter into rest; we come to understand the gospel, and he who understands the gospel is not any longer in the wilderness. In a certain sense, he has come into the land of promise, where he already enjoys covenant mercies. It is true that the Canaanite is still even in that land, and we have to drive him out; but, it is a good land to which God has brought us, 'a land of brooks of water, of fountains and depths that spring out of valleys and hills'. The Lord makes us drink of the river of his good pleasure; he satisfies us with the cooling streams of his covenant love.

8 A land of wheat, and barley, and vines, and fig trees, and pomegranates; a land of oil olive, and honey;

I will not go into a spiritualizing of all this; but I know that you, who have come to believe in Christ and have entered by faith into his rest, know what sweet things God has provided for you, not merely bare necessaries but choice delights. He gives you to eat of the sweetnesses; he gives you the fatnesses — the wines on the lees, well-refined, and the fat things full of marrow. I trust that there are many here who know the blessed experience of joy and peace in believing. You have entered into a fair region; you have passed through the belt of storms; you have come where the trade winds blow heavenward; your sails are filled; your vessel skips along before the breeze; you are making good way towards the fair havens of eternal felicity.

9 A land wherein thou shalt eat bread without scarceness, thou shalt not lack any thing in it;

a land whose stones are iron, and out of whose hills thou mayest dig brass.

There are deep things hidden away in the gospel treasuries. Silver and gold there may be none; but then, iron and copper are much more useful things, and the most useful things we shall ever want in this life lie hidden beneath the surface of the gospel. If we know how to dig deep, we shall be abundantly rewarded by the treasures which we shall discover. Well now, if your experience has thus changed, if you have left the fiery serpents and the howling wilderness behind you and have come into a place of peace and enjoyment, what follows?

10 When thou hast eaten and art full, then thou shalt bless the LORD thy God for the good land which he hath given thee.

He permits you to eat; not to satiety, but you may eat and be full, only not so full but that you can always bless his name. Do not be afraid of holy joy. Eat and be full of it; only let it never take off your heart from him who gives you the joy. On the contrary, bless thy God for the good land which he has given thee. It is said that, in the olden time, pious Jews always blessed God before they ate and always blessed God after they ate. They blessed God for the fragrance of the flower whenever they smelt it. Whenever they drank a cup of water, they blessed the Lord who gave them drink out of the rock in the desert. Oh, that we were always full of praises of God! Then it would not hurt us to be full of meat; but if we get full of meat and are empty of praises, this is mischievous indeed.

11 Beware that thou forget not the LORD thy God, in not keeping his commandments, and his judgments, and his statutes, which I command thee this day:

That would be practical atheism; not keeping the commandments of God is one of the most vivid ways of forgetting him.

12-14 Lest when thou hast eaten and art full, and hast built goodly houses, and dwelt therein; And when thy herds and thy flocks multiply, and thy silver and thy gold is multiplied, and all that thou hast is multiplied; Then thine heart be lifted up, and thou forget the LORD thy God, which brought thee forth out of the land of Egypt, from the house of bondage;

The other day, a friend asked me this question, 'Whence does God get his princes?' and the answer I gave was, 'He often picks them off dunghills.' Oh, but they sometimes forget the dunghills where they grew and think themselves wonderfully important individuals! Then there is a time of pulling down for them. We cannot eat and be full without having the temptation of getting our heart lifted up. It is a great blessing to have the heart lifted up in one way, that is, in God's ways; but to be lifted up by bread, to be lifted up by silver, to be lifted up by flocks and herds is such a bad way of being lifted up that evil and sorrow must come of it. See, the Lord does not forbid his people to build a house or to eat and to enjoy what he gives them, but he does charge them not to forget the God who gave them these mercies nor to forget where they used to be in slavery: 'Beware that thou forget not the LORD thy God which brought thee forth out of the land of Egypt, from the house of bondage.'

15 Who led thee through that great and terrible wilderness, wherein were fiery serpents, and scorpions, and drought, where there was no water; who brought thee forth water out of the rock of flint;

I cannot but pause as I recollect my own passage through 'that great and terrible wilderness, where there was no water'. When a soul is under conviction of sin, 'fiery serpents, and scorpions, and drought' are very feeble images of the pains and miseries that come of guilt unforgiven. 'Where there was no water.' Oh! what would we not have given then to have understood a little of that gospel which, perhaps, we now despise? Oh! what would we not have given then just to have moistened our burning lips with the living water of the precious Word in which, possibly, now we see no refreshing? May God have mercy upon us for our forgetfulness of his great mercy! Let us, with deep gratitude, think of him again: 'Who led thee through that great and terrible wilderness, wherein were fiery serpents, and scorpions, and drought, where there was no water; who brought thee forth water out of the rock of flint.' 'More likely', says one, 'to bring fire rather than water out of a rock of flint'; and it did seem as if the cross of the curse must have cursed us; yet it blessed us. The Lord brought forth living water out of that Rock which was smitten for guilty man.

16-17 Who fed thee in the wilderness with manna, which thy fathers knew not, that he might humble thee, and that he might prove thee, to do thee good at thy latter end; And thou say in thine heart, My power and the might of mine hand hath gotten me this wealth.

We must not say this about either temporal or spiritual wealth. If we have grown in grace and have become useful and are spiritually a blessing to others, we must not take any credit for it to ourselves, or else down we shall go before long. God did not enrich thee that thou mightest set up for a god in opposition to him. Christ did not love thee that thou mightest make thyself a rival to him. Oh, that must not be! We must never say in our heart, 'My power and the might of mine hand hath gotten me this wealth.'

18-19 But thou shalt remember the LORD thy God: for it is he that giveth thee power to get wealth, that he may establish his covenant which he sware unto thy fathers, as it is this day. And it shall be, if thou do at all forget the LORD thy God, and walk after other gods, and serve them, and worship them, I testify against you this day that ye shall surely perish.

If you live like sinners, you will die like sinners. 'Where, then, is the perseverance of the saints?' asks one. Why, in this, that they shall not live like sinners! God's grace will not let them go wandering after idols, to worship and to serve them. He will keep us faithful to himself; but if we will wander after idol gods, it proves that we are not the Lord's true Israel, and we must expect to be served as others have been who have turned aside to worship idols.

20 As the nations which the LORD destroyeth before your face, so shall ye perish; because ye would not be obedient unto the voice of the LORD your God.

DEUTERONOMY 29:1-21

Deut. 29:1 These are the words of the covenant, which the LORD commanded Moses to make with the children of Israel in the land of Moab, beside the covenant which he made with them in Horeb.

That is the preamble, just as in legal documents there is usually some statement of the purport and intent of the indenture before the matter is proceeded with. These covenants with God are solemn things; and therefore, are they given in a formal manner to strike attention and command our serious thoughts.

2-4 And Moses called unto all Israel, and said unto them, Ye have seen all that the LORD did before your eyes in the land of Egypt unto Pharaoh, and unto all his servants, and unto all his land; The great temptations which thine eyes have seen, the signs, and those great miracles: Yet the LORD hath not given you an heart to perceive, and eyes to see, and ears to hear, unto this day.

'You saw all that, and yet did not see it; you saw the external work, but the internal lesson you did not perceive.' A very mournful statement to make; but God's servants are not sent to flatter man but to speak the truth, however painful the speaking of it may be.

5-6 And I have led you forty years in the wilderness: your clothes are not waxen old upon you, and thy shoe is not waxen old upon thy foot. Ye have not eaten bread, neither have ye drunk wine or strong drink: that ye might know that I am the LORD your God.

Either there had been means of frequent renewal of their garments, or else by a miracle these garments had never worn out; and the very shoes that they put upon their feet on the Passover night were on their feet still; if not the same, yet still they were shod, though they trod the weary wilderness which well might have worn them till they were bare. 'Ye have not eaten bread, neither have ye drunk wine or strong drink' — a nation of total abstainers for forty years. There was no bread in the wilderness for them, and there was no wine. It may have been obtained, as a great luxury, as it probably was; for we have reason to believe that Nadab and Abihu were slain by fire before the Lord because they were drunken when they offered strange fire. But, taking the whole people around, anything like wine had not crossed their lips for forty years, yet there they were, strong and healthy. 'That ye may know that I am Jehovah your God.'

7 And when ye came unto this place, Sihon the king of Heshbon, and Og the king of Bashan, came out against us unto battle, and we smote them:

People not used to war either, and feeble folk, yet they smote the great kings and slew mighty kings, for the Lord was with them.

8-9 And we took their land, and gave it for an inheritance unto the Reubenites, and to the Gadites, and to the half tribe of Manasseh. Keep therefore the words of this covenant, and do them, that ye may prosper in all that ye do.

This, then, was the covenant made with the nation, that God should be their God and he would prosper them: as he had done, so would he do. He would be their protector, defender, strength, and crown and joy.

10-11 Ye stand this day all of you before the LORD your God; your captains of your tribes, your elders, and your officers, with all the men of Israel, Your little ones, your wives, and thy stranger that is in thy camp, from the hewer of thy wood unto the drawer of thy water:

This national covenant embraced all the great men, the captains, the wise men, all that were in authority, 'your elders, and your officers'. It took in all their children, for it was a covenant according to the flesh, and their children according to the flesh are included. 'Your wives', too, for in this matter their was no sex. 'The stranger also'; here we poor Gentiles get a glimpse of comfort, even though from that old covenant we seem to be shut out. 'Thy stranger that is in thy camp' is included. And the poorest and those that performed the most menial service were all to be made partakers of this covenant, 'from the hewer of thy wood unto the drawer of thy water'.

12-15 That thou shouldest enter into covenant with the LORD thy God, and into his oath, which the LORD thy God maketh with thee this day: That he may establish thee to day for a people unto himself, and that he may be unto thee a God, as he hath said unto thee, and as he hath sworn unto thy fathers, to Abraham, to Isaac, and to Jacob. Neither with you only do I make this covenant and this oath; But with him that standeth here with us this day before the LORD our God, and also with him that is not here with us this day:

With the sick that were at home, with the generations that were not yet born, for this was intended to be a national covenant in perpetuity to their children and their children's children to the end of time. Had they kept it, so would it have stood.

16-17 (For ye know how we have dwelt in the land of Egypt; and how we came through the nations which ye passed by; and ye have seen their abominations, and their idols, wood and stone, silver and gold, which were among them:)

Now you have seen how they worshipped idols; you have seen that you may avoid; you have beheld their folly that you may escape from it.

18 Lest there should be among you man, or woman, or family, or tribe, whose heart turneth away this day from the LORD our God, to go and serve the gods of these nations; lest there should be among you a root that beareth gall and wormwood;

For the worship of false gods is the cause of untold mischief and evil: wherever it is found it is a root that beareth gall and wormwood, and God would not have it in a single individual, man nor woman, nay, not in a single family or tribe.

19 And it come to pass, when he heareth the words of this curse, that he bless himself in his heart, saying, I shall have peace, though I walk in the imagination of mine heart, to add drunkenness to thirst:

For there were some who so hardened themselves against God that they said, 'We shall have peace; let us do what we like; let us worship these idol gods more and more and more; let us add drunkenness and idolatry to our thirst.'

20 The LORD will not spare him, but then the anger of the LORD and his jealousy shall smoke against that man, and all the curses that are written in this book shall lie upon him, —

Not light upon him, but lie upon him, rest there and stop there.

20-21 and the LORD shall blot out his name from under heaven. And the LORD shall separate him unto evil out of all the tribes of Israel, according to all the curses of the covenant that are written in this book of the law:

As a huntsman separates a stag from the herd that he may hunt it all the day, so shall God with any idolater that should come amongst his people with whom he made a covenant that day. Oh, how God hates that anything should be worshipped by us but himself; how indignant is he if anywhere anything takes the supreme place in the human heart which ought to be occupied by God alone.

DEUTERONOMY 32:1-39

A very marvelous chapter it is — a song and a prophecy, in which the poet-seer seems to behold the whole future spread before him as in a map, and it is so vivid to him that he describes it rather as a matter present or past, than as a thing which is yet to be. It is the story of God's dealing with his chosen and peculiar people, Israel, from the beginning to the end. The commencement is exceedingly noble.

Deut. 32:1-3 Give ear, O ye heavens, and I will speak; and hear, O earth, the words of my mouth. My doctrine shall drop as the rain, my speech shall distil as the dew, as the small rain upon the tender herb, and as the showers upon the grass: Because I will publish the name of the LORD: ascribe ye greatness unto our God.

All through, the song is for the glorification of God; not a syllable, indeed, in which man is held up to honour, but the Lord alone is exalted in his dealings with his people. He is the rock. All other things are the mere cloud that hovers on the mountain's brow.

4 He is the Rock, —

Immutable, eternal.

4 his work is perfect: —

Sometimes very terrible and very mysterious, but his work is perfect.

4 for all his ways are judgment: a God of truth and without iniquity, just and right is he.

But as for his people, what a contrast between them and their God!

5 They have corrupted themselves, their spot is not the spot of his children: they are a perverse and crooked generation.

What a stoop from the God of truth, without iniquity, to a people full of iniquity — a perverse and crooked generation. We never know so much of our own vileness as when we get a clear view of the excellency of God. What said Job? 'I have heard of thee by the hearing of the ear: but now mine eye seeth thee. Wherefore I abhor myself, and repent in dust and ashes' [Job 42:5-6].

6 Do ye thus requite the LORD, O foolish people and unwise? is not he thy father that hath bought thee? hath he not made thee, and established thee?

Who made the Jews to be a people? Who set Israel apart to be a nation? Who, but God, who bought them with a price when they came out of Egypt and, in his fatherly care, led them through the wilderness?

7-8 Remember the days of old, consider the years of many generations: ask thy father, and he will shew thee; thy elders, and they will tell thee. When the Most High divided to the nations their inheritance, when he separated the sons of Adam, he set the bounds of the people according to the number of the children of Israel.

God's first point in the government of the world was his own people. Everything else was mapped out after he had set apart a place for them — a place sufficient, large, fruitful, and in an admirable position, that there they might multiply and enjoy all the good things which he so freely gave them; and to this day dynasties rise and fall, kings reign or are scattered by defeat, only with this one point in God's eye and purpose in his mind —the upholding of the church in the world — the spread of his glorious truth.

9-12 For the LORD's portion is his people; Jacob is the lot of his inheritance. He found him in a desert land, and in the waste howling wilderness; he led him about, he instructed him, he kept him as the apple of his eye. As an eagle stirreth up her nest, fluttereth over her young, spreadeth abroad her wings, taketh them, beareth them on her wings: So the LORD alone did lead him, and there was no strange god with him.

This is the history of the tutoring of Israel in the wilderness. When they came out of Egypt they were a mere mob of slaves, degenerate by the debasing influence of long bondage. They had to be trained before they were fit to be a nation. Now in all this, let us try to see ourselves. What has God wrought for those of us who are his people in bringing us out from the bondage of sin? And how graciously does he, this day, preserve us as a man guards the apple of his eye! No sooner does anything come near the eye than up goes the hand instinctively to shield the eye; and, let anything happen to the people of God, and the power of God is ready at once for their defence. An eagle has to teach her young eaglets to fly. She will take them on her wings, so they say; cast them off, and let them flutter, and then dash down and come under them and bear them up again till she has taught them to use their wings. And the Lord has been doing this with many here — apparently casting them off, only that, when they fall, underneath them may be the everlasting arms. We have to be trained to faith. It is a difficult exercise for such poor creatures as we are. We are being trained for it at this day. After they had been thus tutored, they were brought into the promised land, which Moses never entered, but yet in his vision of prophecy he sees it all.

13-14 He made him ride on the high places of the earth, that he might eat the increase of the fields; and he made him to suck honey out of the rock, and oil out of the flinty rock; Butter of kine, and milk of sheep, with fat of lambs, and rams of the breed of Bashan, and goats, with the fat of kidneys of wheat; and thou didst drink the pure blood of the grape.

It was a very fruitful land, abounding not merely in necessaries but in luxuries. Palestine bear to its inhabitants all that heart could wish, and for a long time, while they were faithful to God, they lived in the midst of plenty.

15 But Jeshurun waxed fat, and kicked: —

'The little holy nation' — for I suppose that is the meaning of 'Jeshurun'. It is a diminutive word — 'the little religious nation waxed fat. It abounded in prosperity. It grew stout and kicked.'

15 thou art waxen fat, thou art grown thick, thou art covered with fatness; then he forsook God which made him, and lightly esteemed the Rock of his salvation.

Alas! alas! alas! they set up calves in Bethel. They turned aside to Ashtaroth, and worshipped the queen of heaven.

16-17 They provoked him to jealousy with strange gods, with abominations provoked they him to anger. They sacrificed unto devils, —

Demons — not to God.

17 not to God; to gods whom they knew not, to new gods that came newly up, whom your fathers feared not.

There is nothing new in religion that is true. The truth is always old. But only imagine a new God! And verily, we have had lately some new fashions brought up — some new styles of worship. I think they call them mediaeval. They certainly are no older then that — 'new gods that newly came up, whom your fathers feared not'.

18 Of the Rock that begat thee thou art unmindful, and hast forgotten God that formed thee.

Israel was nothing apart from God — a little tribe of people — nothing to be compared with the great nations of the earth. Its only reason for existence was its God. He was its centre, its light, its glory, its power. They had got away from him that formed them.

19-20 And when the LORD saw it, he abhorred them, because of the provoking of his sons, and of his daughters. And he said, I will hide my face from them, I will see what their end shall be: for they are a very froward generation, children in whom is no faith.

There is the mischief — want of faith. Want of faith leads to all manner of sin. Oh! that we had a strong elastic faith to realize the unseen God and keep to purely spiritual worship, not wanting symbols, signs, and outward tokens, all of which are abominable in his sight, but worshipping the unseen in spirit and in truth. But the LORD said:

21 They have moved me to jealousy with that which is not God; they have provoked me to anger with their vanities: and I will move them to jealousy with those which are not a people; I will provoke them to anger with a foolish nation.

And so the idolatrous nations came and conquered Judea. One after another, they trampled down the holy city and let them see that God could use the nations that they despised to be a scourge upon them.

22-25 For a fire is kindled in mine anger, and shall burn unto the lowest hell, and shall consume the earth with her increase, and set on fire the foundations of the mountains. I will heap mischiefs upon them; I will spend mine arrows upon them. They shall be burnt with hunger, and devoured with burning heat, and with bitter destruction: I will also send the teeth of beasts upon them, with the poison of serpents of the dust. The sword without, and terror within, shall destroy both the young man and the virgin, the suckling also with the man of gray hairs.

Now read the story of the destruction of Israel and Judah the overthrow of these two kingdoms — and you will see how, word for word, all this came true.

26-27 I said, I would scatter them into corners, I would make the remembrance of them to cease from among men: Were it not that I feared the wrath of the enemy, lest their adversaries should behave themselves strangely, and lest they should say, Our hand is high, and the LORD hath not done all this.

God always looks out for some reason for mercy when he is dealing with his people, and he found it here — that the heathen nations would not admit that God had thus been chastening his erring people but would begin to ascribe their victories to their own demon gods; therefore, he said he would scatter them.

28-30 For they are a nation void of counsel, neither is there any understanding in them. O that they were wise, that they understood this, that they would consider their latter end! How should one chase a thousand, and two put ten thousand to flight, except their Rock had sold them, and the LORD had shut them up?

That little people would have been victorious over all their enemies if God had still been with them, but they were defeated and scattered because they had grieved the Lord. Oh! what strength believers might have if they would but believe! If we could but cast ourselves upon God in simple, childlike faith, we might play the Samson over again and smite our thousands. But we, too, have little faith in God, even those who have most of it; and when the time of trial comes, we also are a stiff-necked and unbelieving generation, as our fathers were.

31-34 For their rock is not as our Rock, even our enemies themselves being judges. For their vine is of the vine of Sodom, and of the fields of Gomorrah: their grapes are grapes of gall, their clusters are bitter: Their wine is the poison of dragons, and the cruel venom of asps. Is not this laid up in store with me, and sealed up among my treasures?

What an awful text! God lays man's sins by — seals them up amongst their treasures, that they should not be forgotten, and he will bring them to account.

35-36 To me belongeth vengeance and recompence; their foot shall slide in due time: for the day of their calamity is at hand, and the things that shall come upon them make haste. For the LORD shall judge his people, —

He will not always let his enemies triumph over them. He will come back to his people whom he seemed to cast away. 'The LORD shall judge his people.'

36 and repent himself for his servants, when he seeth that their power is gone, and there is none shut up, or left.

He seemed very angry, but how soon he comes back in love and tries his people over again.

37-39 And he shall say, Where are their gods, their rock in whom they trusted, Which did eat the fat of their sacrifices, and drank the wine of their drink offerings? let them rise up and help you, and be your protection. See now that I, even I, am he, and there is no god with me: I kill, and I make alive; I wound, and I heal: neither is there any that can deliver out of my hand.

DEUTERONOMY 32:1-43

Deut. 32:1 Give ear, O ye heavens, and I will speak; and hear, O earth, the words of my mouth.

Because men are so slow of hearing, Moses calls on the heavens and the earth to bear witness against them, and because of the sublimity of his subject, he calls upon the heavens and the earth to pay attention to it.

2 My doctrine shall drop as the rain, my speech shall distil as the dew, as the small rain upon the tender herb, and as the showers upon the grass:

It is good preaching, and good hearing too, when the gospel comes like a gentle shower which saturates and soaks into the soil and refreshes and makes it fruitful; may God the Holy Spirit make it to be so whenever we gather together for worship! The Word of the Lord may be as a driving hail, breaking everything upon which it falls and, so, becoming the savour of death unto death. But may God make it to us as the dew and the small rain from heaven, that it may be a savour of life unto life!

3-5 Because I will publish the name of the LORD: ascribe ye greatness unto our God. He is the Rock, his work is perfect: for all his ways are judgment: a God of truth and without iniquity, just and right is he. They have corrupted themselves, —

What a contrast there is between the incorruptible and immutable God and corruptible man! 'They have corrupted themselves'.

5 their spot is not the spot of his children: they are a perverse and crooked generation.

God's children have spots — the spots caused by sin, which are recognized, mourned over, and struggled against by them; the ungodly have the same sort of spots, but they have no repentance concerning the sin which causes them.

6 Do ye thus requite the LORD, O foolish people and unwise? is not he thy father that hath bought thee? hath he not made thee, and established thee?

Sin is the basest form of ingratitude. We owe everything to God, and we ought therefore to treat him as our Creator and Father should be treated. On the contrary, how often have we requited him evil for good and acted as if we regarded him as our enemy rather than as our best Friend!

7-8 Remember the days of old, consider the years of many generations: ask thy father, and he will shew thee; thy elders, and they will tell thee. When the Most High divided to the nations their inheritance, when he separated the sons of Adam, he set the bounds of the people according to the number of the children of Israel.

His first thought was concerning his own people. He provided Canaan for them. It was just the very land for them, with space enough, and yet with not too much room, so that they might cultivate it all and prove it to be a land flowing with milk and honey. Yet these special thoughts of God, with regard to his own chosen people, did not exclude kind thoughts towards the rest of mankind, for 'he separated the sons of Adam, he set the bounds of the people', that is, the people belonging to other nations; but, still, his deepest and his highest thoughts were concerning the children of Israel.

9-10 For the LORD's portion is his people; Jacob is the lot of his inheritance. He found him in a desert land, and in the waste howling wilderness; he led him about, he instructed him, he kept him as the apple of his eye.

And is not this also a true description of God's love and kindness to you and to me, beloved in the Lord? Did he not find us in the wilderness? Has he not led us about and by our experience instructed us, and has he not guarded us with as much watchful care as a man bestows upon the apple of his eye? Oh, blessed be his holy name, we owe everything to him! He giveth us everything that we have.

11-14 As an eagle stirreth up her nest, fluttereth over her young, spreadeth abroad her wings, taketh them, beareth them on her wings: So the LORD alone did lead him, and there was no strange god with him. He made him ride on the high places of the earth, that he might eat the increase of the fields; and he made him to suck honey out of the rock, and oil out of the flinty rock; Butter of kine, and milk of sheep, with fat of lambs, and rams of the breed of Bashan, and goats, with the fat of kidneys of wheat; and thou didst drink the pure blood of the grape.

God fed his ancient people with the best of the best and gave it to them with no stinted hand; and, oh! when I think of the spiritual food which God has prepared for his people, surely 'butter of kine, and milk of sheep, with fat of lambs', and all such carnal things are but poor in comparison with the provisions of his grace. In a spiritual sense, the Lord hath indeed given to us 'a feast of fat things, a feast of wines on the lees, of fat things full of mallow, of wines on the lees well refined' [Isaiah 25:6]. But now look again at the contrast between the Lord and his ancient people. God's great goodness makes man's sin appear all the blacker:

15 But Jeshurun waxed fat, and kicked: thou art waxen fat, thou art grown thick, thou art covered with fatness; then he forsook God which made him, and lightly esteemed the Rock of his salvation.

Many can endure the trials of adversity who cannot escape the perils of prosperity. Solomon truly said, 'As the fining pot for silver, and the furnace for gold; so is a man to his praise' [Proverbs 27:21]; and many a man has failed in that time of testing. When you come to be wealthy, to be admired, to receive honour among men, then is the time of your severest trial.

16-17 They provoked him to jealousy with strange gods, with abominations provoked they him to anger. They sacrificed unto devils, not to God; to gods whom they knew not, to new gods that came newly up, whom your fathers feared not.

Moses multiplies expressions to show the folly of Israel's idolatry. Only think of 'new gods that came newly up', as if that which is new could be a god! The same thing may be said of the 'new truth' of which we hear so much nowadays. That which is new cannot be true. Certainly, there is nothing new in theology but that which is utterly false. The idols, which the Israelites worshipped, were not only new gods, but they were strange gods, which their fathers feared not. Worse than that, they were demons: 'they sacrificed unto devils not to God'. How low had even the chosen people sunk!

18-27 Of the Rock that begat thee thou art unmindful, and hast forgotten God that formed thee. And when the LORD saw it, he abhorred them, because of the provoking of his sons, and of his daughters. And he said, I will hide my face from them, I will see what their end shall be: for they are a very froward generation, children in whom is no faith. They have moved me to jealousy with that which is not God; they have provoked me to anger with their vanities: and I will move them to jealousy with those which are not a people; I will provoke them to anger with a foolish nation. For a fire is kindled in mine anger, and shall burn unto the lowest hell, and shall consume the earth with her increase, and set on fire the foundations of the mountains. I will heap mischiefs upon them; I will spend mine arrows upon them. They shall be burnt with hunger, and devoured with burning heat, and with bitter destruction: I will also send the teeth of beasts upon them, with the poison of serpents of the dust. The sword without, and terror within, shall destroy both the young man and the virgin, the suckling also with the man of gray hairs. I said, I would scatter them into corners, I would make the remembrance of them to cease from among men: Were it not —

Here is a sweet word of grace amid the just judgements of Jehovah: 'Were it not'.

27 that I feared the wrath of the enemy, lest their adversaries should behave themselves strangely, and lest they should say, Our hand is high, and the LORD hath not done all this.

So he spared them for his own name's sake; and, to this day, when God can find no other reason for showing mercy to the guilty, he does it for his name's sake; and this is a blessed plea, to be urged by a man who can see no reason why God should have mercy upon him. He may say, 'Lord, do it for thy name's sake, to make thy grace and thy mercy illustrious in the salvation of such a poor, hopeless wretch as I am.'

28-32 For they are a nation void of counsel, neither is there any understanding in them. O that they were wise, that they understood this, that they would consider their latter end! How should one chase a thousand, and two put ten thousand to flight, except their Rock had sold them, and the LORD had shut them up? For their rock is not as our Rock, even our enemies themselves being judges. For their vine —

That is, the vine of God's enemies.

32-34 is of the vine of Sodom, and of the fields of Gomorrah: their grapes are grapes of gall, their clusters are bitter: Their wine is the poison of dragons, and the cruel venom of asps. Is not this laid up in store with me, and sealed up among my treasures?

What a striking and startling question that is, as though God laid up the memory of man's sin, sealed it up, and kept it in a secret place against the day when he shall call sinners to account, and visit them for their iniquities! What an awful thing it is to have the sins of one's youth laid up, sealed up, and put away in God's treasury, and the sins of middle life and perhaps the sins of old age, too, to be brought out, by and by, and laid to our charge! Who shall be able to stand in that great day? Only those who are washed in the blood and robed in the righteousness of Christ Jesus our Lord.

35-38 To me belongeth vengeance and recompence; their foot shall slide in due time: for the day of their calamity is at hand, and the things that shall come upon them make haste. For the LORD shall judge his people, and repent himself for his servants, when he seeth that their power is gone, and there is none shut up, or left. And he shall say, Where are their gods, their rock in whom they trusted, which did eat the fat of their sacrifices, and drank the wine of their drink offerings? let them rise up and help you, and be your protection.

To you who trust in anything except God, the day will come when you will hear such terrible words as these — 'Now let your riches save you; let your pleasures and your vices cheer you; go ye now in your own wicked ways, and see if you can find any comfort in them!' What holy sarcasm there is in these words, which will cut to the quick the conscience when it is once fairly aroused!

39-43 See now that I, even I, am he, and there is no god with me: I kill, and I make alive; I wound, and I heal: neither is there any that can deliver out of my hand. For I lift up my hand to heaven, and say, I live for ever. If I whet my glittering sword, and mine hand take hold on judgment; I will render vengeance to mine enemies, and will reward them that hate me. I will make mine arrows drunk with blood, and my sword shall devour flesh; and that with the blood of the slain and of the captives, from the beginning of revenges upon the enemy. Rejoice, O ye nations, with his people: for he will avenge the blood of his servants, and will render vengeance to his adversaries, and will be merciful unto his land, and to his people.

It is only in mercy, you see, that the Lord deals with his people; they cannot stand before him on the ground of justice, but in his mercy is their place of refuge. May we all find that mercy by fleeing for refuge to lay hold upon the hope set before us in Christ Jesus and his glorious gospel! Amen.

DEUTERONOMY 33

Deut. 33:1 And this is the blessing, wherewith Moses the man of God blessed the children of Israel before his death.

A very beautiful thought, that he should conclude his life with a blessing. Though they had greatly grieved and provoked his spirit, he was always meek and tender, but he had very much to bear from them, and this is the end of it all, that he will dismiss them with his blessing.

2-3 And he said, The LORD came from Sinai, and rose up from Seir unto them; he shined forth from mount Paran, and he came with ten thousands of saints: from his right hand went a fiery law for them. Yea, he loved the people; all his saints are in thy hand: and they sat down at thy feet; every one shall receive of thy words.

'Yea, he loved the people.' God's appearance on Sinai was a token of his love to them, even though it amazed them and distressed many of them. Yet still, it was a great thing that God should come so near to these people and should reveal his will to them. Dear friends, if God should come to you with his fiery law, if he should humble you, and make you 'exceeding fear and quake', it would be a token of love. The ungodly are left to go in their sin, but as for you, if you are one whom he loves, he will rebuke you, and he will bring his law to do its work upon your heart and conscience. It seems strange to you, but so it is. 'From his right hand went a fiery law for them. Yea, he loved the people.' Oh! it is so, because he loves them he reveals to them his fiery law. 'All his saints are in thy hand.' A place of safety, a place of privilege, where they learn how precious they are to him, for he holds them so dear that he keeps them always in his hand. 'All his saints are in thy hand, and they sat down at thy feet.' Another place for saints; they are always learning; they are disciples; they sit with meek humility at their Master's feet and drink in his words: 'Everyone shall receive of thy words.' Those who know not God's love trifle with God's words and reject them; those whom he loves receive his words and feed upon them.

4-6 Moses commanded us a law, even the inheritance of the congregation of Jacob. And he was king in Jeshurun, when the heads of the people and the tribes of Israel were gathered together. Let Reuben live, and not die; and let not his men be few.

Here is his blessing, 'Let Reuben live.' Reuben's great sin had lost him his birthright, yet Moses gives him as much of his blessing as he can. If we are not allowed to draw the largest blessing, let us go as far as we can.

7-10 And this is the blessing of Judah: and he said, Hear, LORD, the voice of Judah, and bring him unto his people: let his hands be sufficient for him; and be thou an help to him from his enemies. And of Levi he said, Let thy Thummim and thy Urim be with thy holy one, whom thou didst prove at Massah, and with whom thou didst strive at the waters of Meribah; who said unto his father and to his mother, I have not seen him; neither did he acknowledge his brethren, nor knew his own children: for they have observed thy word, and kept thy covenant. They shall teach Jacob thy judgments, and Israel thy law: they shall put incense before thee, and whole burnt sacrifice upon thine altar.

Judah was the royal tribe and had to do much with warfare. 'Lord give him power in prayer!' This is the peculiar benediction of those who have to lead the way in the battles of God. In the service of God, Levi was impartial; he did not wink at sin in his dearest relatives. You remember how they took the sword and went through the camp and slew their own brothers when they found them guilty of idolatry, and because of this faithfulness we read, 'They shall teach Jacob thy judgments, and Israel thy law.' Above all things, a teacher of the truth of God must be fearless and impartial in the delivery of God's Word; then God will bless him, and it shall be said of such, 'They shall teach Jacob,' etc.

11 Bless, LORD, his substance, and accept the work of his hands; smite through the loins of them that rise against him, and of them that hate him, that they rise not again.

True hearts alone can be God's priests; he will not accept sacrifices from those who will dally with his truth and trifle with his Word.

12 And of Benjamin he said, The beloved of the LORD shall dwell in safety by him; and the Lord shall cover him all the day long, and he shall dwell between his shoulders.

They that have God near them are safe indeed. There is no protection in such a world as this like constant communion with God. We have to go out into a world full of all manner of evil. Go not out into the world without thy God. Let him dwell with thee and cover thee all the day long, and so shalt thou be safe.

13 And of Joseph he said, Blessed of the LORD be his land, for the precious things of heaven, —

Oh! in a spiritual sense, what a rich blessing this is! And remember it came upon that tribe whose father was the most afflicted of all Jacob's sons. If thou art an afflicted Joseph, rejoice, for one of these days thou shall have the capacity for receiving great blessings.

13 for the dew, —

The Lord send us that dew tonight to rest upon our branch.

13 and for the deep that coucheth beneath,

These deep eternal springs out of which we drink the divine water springs.

14 And for the precious fruits brought forth by the sun, and for the precious things put forth by the moon,

They shall have blessings both ways, in the day and in the night. Those whom God blesses, the sun doth not smite by day nor the moon by night, but on the contrary, they are blessed both in the one and in the other.

15-16 And for the chief things of the ancient mountains, and for the precious things of the lasting hills, and for the precious things of the earth and fulness thereof, and for the good will of him that dwelt in the bush: —

Oh! that we may enjoy ever the good will of God, who wills good to us, who in all his dealings with us has a good will towards us. Oh! that we may have the good will of him that dwelt in the bush!

16-18 let the blessing come upon the head of Joseph, and upon the top of the head of him that was separated from his brethren. His glory is like the firstling of his bullock, and his horns are like the horns of unicorns: with them he shall push the people together to the ends of the earth: and they are the ten thousands of Ephraim, and they are the thousands of Manasseh. And of Zebulun he said, Rejoice, Zebulun, in thy going out; and, Issachar, in thy tents.

You that go much abroad in the world, God give you to rejoice in your opportunities of doing good. You that never go abroad, but live at home in the kitchen and the parlour, learn to rejoice in your tents, for there, too, you have a sphere of holy service.

19-22 They shall call the people unto the mountain; there they shall offer sacrifices of righteousness: for they shall suck of the abundance of the seas, and of treasures hid in the sand. And of Gad he said, Blessed be he that enlargeth Gad: he dwelleth as a lion, and teareth the arm with the crown of the head. And he provided the first part for himself, because there, in a portion of the lawgiver, was he seated; and he came with the heads of the people, he executed the justice of the LORD, and his judgments with Israel. And of Dan he said, Dan is a lion's whelp: he shall leap from Bashan.

'And of Gad, he said, Blessed be he that enlargeth Gad.' God knows how to enlarge his people, give them more grace, more gifts, more opportunities of usefulness. Which he did. His tribes enlarged their boundaries by a sudden leap. God gives his people sometimes their leaping times; they leap from Bashan: some great purpose is accomplished, some great feat is done.

23 And of Naphtali he said, O Naphtali, satisfied with favour, and full with the blessing of the LORD: possess thou the west and the south.

What a condition of heart to be in! 'Satisfied with favour, and full with the blessing of the Lord.' Beloved, may you enjoy that tonight!

24 And of Asher he said, Let Asher be blessed with children; let him be acceptable to his brethren, and let him dip his foot in oil.

Then will he leave a mark wherever he goes of holy unction. He possesses it himself, and he will impart it to others.

25 Thy shoes shall be iron and brass; and as thy days, so shall thy strength be.

Will not some believer grip that promise tonight and find it true?

26-28 There is none like unto the God of Jeshurun, who rideth upon the heaven in thy help, and in his excellency on the sky. The eternal God is thy refuge, and underneath are the everlasting arms: and he shall thrust out the enemy from before thee; and shall say, Destroy them. Israel then shall dwell in safety alone: the fountain of Jacob shall be upon a land of corn and wine; also his heavens shall drop down dew.

'Israel then shall dwell in safety alone.' There is no place for God's people like a separated place; they must get without the camp; they must not be numbered among the people. Notice, there is none like unto the God of Israel, and there is none like unto Israel.

29 Happy art thou, O Israel: who is like unto thee, O people saved by the LORD, the shield of thy help, and who is the sword of thy excellency! and thine enemies shall be found liars unto thee; and thou shalt tread upon their high places.

As God is by himself, so all his people are favoured beyond all others.

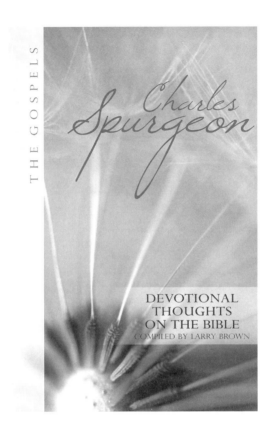

The book you have just read, Devotional thoughts on the Bible – The Pentateuch *is the first of a multi-volume collection that will be published over the coming years building up to a complete library of Spurgeon's exposition from the Bible. The next volume to be published in 2007 is* Devotional thoughts on the Bible – The Gospels (ISBN 978 085234 6631).

www.evangelicalpress.org

A wide range of excellent books on spiritual subjects is available from Evangelical Press. Please write to us for your free catalogue or contact us by e-mail.

Evangelical Press
Faverdale North, Darlington, DL3 0PH England
Evangelical Press USA
P. O. Box 825, Webster, NY 14580 USA
email: sales@evangelicalpress.org

www.evangelicalpress.org